The Edinburgh Companion to Robert Burns

Edited by Gerard Carruthers

Edinburgh University Press

© in this edition Edinburgh University Press, 2009
© in the individual contributions is retained by the contributors

Edinburgh University Press Ltd
22 George Square, Edinburgh

www.euppublishing.com

Typeset in 10.5 on 12.5pt Goudy
by Servis Filmsetting Limited, Stockport, Cheshire

A CIP record for this book is available from the British Library

ISBN 978 0 7486 3648 8 (hardback)
ISBN 978 0 7486 3649 5 (paperback)

The right of the contributors
to be identified as authors of this work
has been asserted in accordance with
the Copyright, Designs and Patents Act 1988.

Contents

Editions and Abbreviations		vi
Series Editors' Preface		vii
Brief Biography of Robert Burns		viii
	Introduction	1
	Gerard Carruthers	
1	Burns and Publishing	6
	Gerard Carruthers	
2	Burns and Women	20
	Sarah Dunnigan	
3	Burns and the Rhetoric of Narrative	34
	Kenneth Simpson	
4	Burns and the Poetics of Abolition	47
	Nigel Leask	
5	Burns and Politics	61
	Colin Kidd	
6	Burns's Songs and Poetic Craft	74
	Kirsteen McCue	
7	Burns and Robert Fergusson	86
	Rhona Brown	
8	Burns and Romantic Writing	97
	Fiona Stafford	
9	Burns the Critic	110
	Corey E. Andrews	
10	Burns, Scott and Intertextuality	125
	Alison Lumsden	
11	Burns and Virgil	137
	Steven R. McKenna	
12	Burns and Transnational Culture	150
	Leith Davis	

Endnotes	164
Further Reading	186
Notes on Contributors	192
Index	194

This collection is dedicated to four inspirational
Burns scholars: Norrie Paton, G. Ross Roy,
Ken Simpson; and in memory of
Donald Low.

Editions and Abbreviations

Unless otherwise stated the editions of Burns, and their abbreviations, used in the Companion are as follows:

L: The Letters of Robert Burns, ed. J. De Lancey Ferguson and G. Ross Roy, 2 vols (Oxford University Press: Oxford, revised edition, 1985).

K: The Poems and Songs of Robert Burns, ed. James Kinsley, 3 vols (Clarendon Press: Oxford, 1968). Abbreviated K. References are to Kinsley's text number, rather than to page number unless otherwise stated. Line numbers are also provided. Titles do not necessarily follow those provided by Kinsley but accord sometimes with common usage and where this makes the discussion easier to follow. For instance, Kinsley's 'A Fragment' is referred to as 'When Guilford Good'.

Series Editors' Preface

In 1919, T. S. Eliot (or perhaps a sub-editor) posed the provocative query, 'Was there a Scottish Literature?' and critical angst on this subject has ensued over the ninety years since. The view of the editors of this series – and a prime motivation for its production – is that however valid the question within one concept of literary tradition, it does not make sufficient room for the nature of literatures produced by multilingual and multivalent cultures. The question was always more complex than Eliot seemed to allow. Further, by their nature, certain Scottish literary works have also been subsumed into the corpora of other literary traditions – for instance, medieval Irish, Latin, or modern English. Such intercultural richness and hybridity, we argue, is not a weakness in a literature's history, but a token of international openness and cosmopolitan potential.

Study and research, not to mention creative writing, since 1919 and perhaps especially of the last twenty years, make Eliot's still historically interesting query redundant as a serious contemporary enquiry. To be fair, the political and educational structures are still in place that at times separated Scottish literature in Gaelic from that in English or Scots – and led sometimes to amnesia regarding that in other languages like Latin. But that Scottish literature was, and is, is clearly recognised. It glories in the resources of historic canons in at least four languages that each stand as internationally important, worthy of careful study and richly enjoyable, and it is now absorbing work in, or influenced by, languages from Scotland's newer vibrant language cultures.

Much new scholarship supports the authoritative, accessible, succinct and up-to-date studies comprising the various volumes of the *Edinburgh Companion to Scottish Literature*. These recognise that worldwide interest in Scottish literature, both in universities and among the reading public, calls for fresh insight into key authors, periods and topics within the corpus. Each of these three categories of *Companion* is represented in the 2009 publications. This first tranche of our new series marks the vigour and rigour of the study of Scottish literature and its enjoyment. It sets aside old questions, and gets on with the acts of studying and enjoying.

Ian Brown
Thomas Owen Clancy

A Brief Biography of Robert Burns

Robert Burns was born on 25 January 1759 at Alloway in Ayrshire, the eldest child of William Burnes and Agnes Broun. Burns's father was a seven-acre tenant who, along with his neighbours, employed for a time a tutor, John Murdoch, to teach their sons. William himself tutored Robert and his brother, Gilbert, in geography, letters and in Presbyterian theology. After farming for eleven years at Mount Oliphant, William Burnes took the lease of the 130-acre Lochlea farm in 1777, which was to bring him finanical difficulties and near bankruptcy in 1784, the year of his death. William's problems arguably stand behind Burns's poem, 'To a Mouse', and the figure of his hard-working, pious father stands behind 'The Cotter's Saturday Night'. Burns's first composition, however, was the song, 'O Once I Lov'd' written for Nellie Kilpatrick, his companion in the autumn harvest during 1774.

In 1780, with himself as president, Robert formed, with Gilbert and five friends, the Tarbolton Bachelors' Club, a kind of debating society. In 1781 Burns also became a Freemason at Tarbolton, the same year in which he was apprenticed as a flax dresser at Irvine. In April 1783 Burns began his *Commonplace Book* in which he writes until 1785 a variety of poetry and prose. Following William's death the Burnes family moved to another farm at Mossgiel, where the poor harvests brought them struggle for the next four years. In 1785, Burns wrote his first poem in Scots, 'The Death and Dying Words of Poor Mailie'. In the same year, Burns's first child, Elizabeth (the first of at least thirteen pregnancies in at least five women), was born to Elizabeth Paton, a servant at Lochlea. Sometime not long after he met the woman who was eventually to become his wife, Jean Armour. During 1785–6, Burns's 'kirk satires', circulated in manuscript form and satirising elements of the local Presbyterian church, brought the poet both censure and acclaim. In a letter of 3 April 1786, the poet signed his name 'Burnes' for the last time, thereafter changing to 'Burns'. Rejection from the Armour family as a suitable husband for Jean (who had fallen pregnant in early 1786), apparently caused Burns to consider emigrating to the slave plantations of Jamaica with Mary Campbell ('Highland Mary'). However, the death of Mary, probably in

October, and the publication of Burns's *Poems, Chiefly in the Scottish Dialect* (published in Kilmarnock on 31 July) which became ever more successful as the winter of 1786–7 wore on caused Burns to change his plans. Reconciled with Jean, he set off, alone, to take up residence in Edinburgh with a plan successfully realised in April of 1787 of publishing an expanded edition of his book in the Scottish capital. This duly appeared on 17 April 1787. In May–June 1787 Burns toured the Borders and kept a journal of his travels; in late June he kept another journal of a tour of the Highlands and Stirlingshire. Both of these periods of travel provided Burns with much food for historical and cultural thought for poems and songs. In this year also, Burns began his relationship with the song editor, James Johnson, by contributing several songs to the first volume of Johnson's *Scots Musical Museum*; and many more of the poet's songs appeared in Johnson's subsequent publications.

By 1788 Burns was perhaps less enamoured of his fame and his experiences in Edinburgh and he took the lease of a farm at Ellisland in Dumfriesshire. In the same year he was trained in the excise (or tax) service, becoming an excise officer in September 1789. In 1790, Burns wrote his longest poem, arguably his greatest, *Tam o' Shanter*. In 1791 Burns gave up his farm and he and Jean moved their family to a house in the centre of Dumfries. In December of the same year, Burns took his leave of Agnes McLehose, with whom he had enjoyed an embroilment in the Scottish capital, as Agnes was about to emigrate to Jamaica. As well as the 'Slyvander' and 'Clarinda' correspondence, this relationship produced one of Burns's most famous songs, 'Ae Fond Kiss, and Then We Sever'. The year 1793 saw an enlarged edition of Burns's *Poems, Chiefly in the Scottish Dialect* and the publication of some songs by George Thomson. Many of Burns's songs appeared in Thomson's volumes of the *Select Collection* until the early decades of the nineteenth century, and forged his reputation with European classical composers as they made use of this material.

Burns had been enthusiastic in greeting the French Revolution in 1789, but with the threat of French invasion, he joined the Dumfries Volunteers on 31 January 1795, a local militia formed as a home guard. By December of that year Burns was seriously ill and he died on 21 July 1796 with Jean unable to attend his funeral four days later as she gave birth to a son on that same day. Burns's death was due, possibly, to rheumatic fever or brucellosis. His death, as with many areas of his life (personal behaviour, in religion and in politics), remains hotly debated in the early twenty-first century.

Edinburgh Companions to Scottish Literature

Series Editors: Ian Brown and Thomas Owen Clancy

Titles in the series include:

The Edinburgh Companion to Robert Burns
Edited by Gerard Carruthers
978 0 7486 3648 8 (hardback)
978 0 7486 3649 5 (paperback)

The Edinburgh Companion to Twentieth-Century Scottish Literature
Edited by Ian Brown and Alan Riach
978 0 7486 3693 8 (hardback)
978 0 7486 3694 5 (paperback)

The Edinburgh Companion to Contemporary Scottish Poetry
Edited by Matt McGuire and Colin Nicholson
978 0 7486 3625 9 (hardback)
978 0 7486 3626 6 (paperback)

Forthcoming titles include:

The Edinburgh Companion to Muriel Spark
Edited by Michael Gardiner and Willy Maley
978 0 7486 3768 3 (hardback)
978 0 7486 3769 0 (paperback)

The Edinburgh Companion to Robert Louis Stevenson
Edited by Penny Fielding
978 0 7486 3554 2 (hardback)
978 0 7486 3555 9 (paperback)

The Edinburgh Companion to Irvine Welsh
Edited by Berthold Schoene
978 0 7486 3917 5 (hardback)
978 0 7486 3918 2 (paperback)

The Edinburgh Companion to Scottish Romanticism
Edited by Murray Pittock
978 0 7486 3845 1 (hardback)
978 0 7486 3846 8 (paperback)

Introduction

Gerard Carruthers

On 25 of January 2009 the 250th anniversary of the birth of Robert Burns (1759–96) was commemorated. According to one calculation, somewhere in the order of 900,000 Burns Suppers celebrate 'Burns Night' around the world in the early twenty-first century. Another marker of Burns's global identity is that along with 'Happy Birthday' his 'Auld Lang Syne' is the most sung song in the world. Burns has also enjoyed a particularly strong reception in both the USA and in the old Soviet Russia. His work has been translated into upwards of forty languages, including Esperanto, Faroese and Latin, with a Bengali version currently being prepared to attest to Burns's reach beyond the West.[1] He is a poet with a huge popular following as is demonstrated by the World Burns Federation, comprising of some 400 Burns Clubs in five or six continents (depending on how these are counted). Between 1786, the first year of Burns's publication, and 1986, it is calculated that there were 2,000 different editions of his poems.[2] Increasingly, Burns is returning as a serious subject for study on university courses and by academics specialising in the eighteenth century and Romantic periods (though if there has long been a dearth in this respect, roughly from the late nineteenth century, Burns has remained a consistently, continuously included poet in comprehensive anthologies of 'English Poetry' throughout the nineteenth and twentieth centuries).[3] Burns might be argued to be an even greater song-writer than a poet. He is certainly Scotland's greatest song-writer even if, for what this is worth, he is challenged for the title of best Scottish poet by those who would champion instead William Dunbar, Robert Henryson or Hugh MacDiarmid. In his musical significance, Burns is also a figure of remarkably broad reach, with many of his songs staples not only of the Scottish but of a much wider folk canon. His songs are admired by everyone from such famous 'traditional' performers as Sheena Wellington and Jean Redpath through The Dubliners, Eddi Reader and Paolo Nuttini to Bob Dylan.[4] Not only this, but Burns's profile in classical music, where his work has been set for performance by Beethoven, Haydn, Vaughan Williams, Shostakovich and James MacMillan, to name only a few, is an important facet of European culture.

The notable universalism of Burns's reception is mirrored in his particularly national context. When at the opening of the Scottish parliament on 1 July 1999 Sheena Wellington sang, 'Is there for honest poverty . . .' ('A Man's a Man for a' That') she was performing in front of, and with the approval of, nearly the whole political spectrum from left to right.[5] What this tells us about is the power of myth, a pervasive Scottish mythology of the demotic national character of which the ploughman poet seems to be both its best exemplar and most erudite expresser. Burns's use in a Scottish parliament of wide ideological hue might actually provide a hint as to how politically malleable the poet's legacy has been. Work remains to be done on the conservative consumption of Burns, but it is interesting that in the immediate decades following his death Burns Clubs were allowed to flourish (perhaps even from 1801 if Greenock Burns Club's year of origin is accepted). And this at a time following a revolutionary decade and in ensuing years perfervid as the period of Chartist agitation, when the British government was extremely nervous of any organisations of popular 'association'. More certainly 'loyalist' is the Orange Order imported into Scotland towards the end of the eighteenth century, which to some extent appropriated Burns as part of its culture. Given the 'Britishness' and 'Unionism' of this organisation, a considerable impediment to their appreciation of Burns, one might think, ought to be the poet's Scottish national patriotism (in songs like 'Robert Bruce's March to Bannockburn' ['Scots Wha Hae']). Prominent Orangeman William Motherwell (1797–1835) co-edited *The Works of Robert Burns* (Glasgow, 1834–6), as he proselytised generally for a depoliticised culture of the common folk, and as his Tory political concern through the 1820s and 1830s was to keep the unwashed masses within the bounds of limited political participation (the less enfranchised the better, so far as he was concerned).[6] One might also point out that the Scottish collaboration in the nineteenth-century British Empire was often through officials and settlers carrying with them, among other things, editions of Burns. Whatever else the Scottish poet represented here, it was certainly not those principles so beloved by, and associated with Burns by many in the late nineteenth and twentieth century Labour movement including the Communist Party. The 'Kailyard' movement of fiction in Scotland during the 1880s and 1890s, supposedly wilfully escapist of the modern world in its retreat into Arcadia, is derogatorily named via a Burns intertext. Ian Maclaren's *Beside the Bonnie Brier Bush* (1894) took its title from a line of Burns, 'There grows a bonie brier-bush in our kailyard' (*K* 587, l. 1). In Maclarens's text, if the Kailyard detractors are correct, the poet had become, then, part of a distinctive Scottish literary world of mawkish sentiment and trivial parish affairs.[7] Precisely as a result of such associations, for the Scottish literary revival of the early twentieth century, especially its chief spokesmen, Hugh MacDiarmid and Edwin Muir, Burns had become essentially an unusable part of the Scottish past.

Burns, like many writers, can be used and abused for different ideological purposes. If J. De Lancey Ferguson could rightly complain in 1955 that previously 'They Censored Burns' in the interests of a conservative world outlook, what are we to make of the practices of a recent edition of Burns determined to present the poet as an impeccably leftist radical in the 1790s?[8] Among other manipulations of texts in a bid to attribute previously 'lost poems' of a radical nature, the editors of that edition silently remove the locus of 'Airdrie' from below one poem which points in fact to an altogether different writer. Equally in another instance they excise the initial 'F' (an inconvenient pointer to the name, presumably, of the actual poet). They also slyly plant the initials 'R.B.' à propos another poem in an attempt to make the case that a text sent to the *Gentleman's Magazine* of 1794 is by Burns rather than, as is more likely, a bowdlerised text sent to the periodical by another hand.[9] In Burns's own lifetime, how are we to read politically Burns the writer of Jacobite songs such as 'Awa Whigs Awa', though himself avowedly a supporter of the Whigs in the 1790s? What about the Burns of 'A Man's a Man for a' That' and his intentions, apparently, to work on the slave plantations of Jamaica? For that matter, what about his treatment of women? Burns expresses sincere support for the American and French Revolutions, while in the 'Heron Ballads' of 1795 he writes broadside poetry on behalf of a parliamentary candidate who was to vote against the abolition of slavery once elected and who was favoured by Henry Dundas, arch-opponent of the French Revolution. What about Burns the member of the Royal Dumfries Volunteers, formed in 1795 as a home guard against potential French invasion (though is it easy for anyone to contemplate the occupation of one's homeland by a foreign power no matter the political principles they avow)? Many of these puzzles and paradoxes, controversies and canards, are dealt with more particularly in the essays that follow in this volume, but in the twenty-first century, arguably, we are on the verge of a new and exciting phase of Burns criticism and scholarship. The intense renewed interest in Burns's work and also in his whole cultural afterlife and hinterland during 2009 suggests that this is the case.[10]

Burns's own biography and his poetic output have often been manipulated, as all famous lives are to some extent, through the generations for their own uses. Burns himself, though, arguably led the way here in creatively assembling elements for self-definition. In the preface to his first book of poems published at Kilmarnock, *Poems, Chiefly in the Scottish Dialect* (1786) Burns presented himself as nervous of his awaiting public and his work as garbed in 'rustic [. . .] native language'.[11] In the Edinburgh edition of the same book in 1787, while maintaining his 'honest Rusticity', he describes himself as 'A Scottish Bard, proud of the name, and whose highest ambition is to sing in his country's service'.[12] Quite legitimately we see Burns here expanding his regional poetic identity to that of a national one. If the *literati* of the late Scottish Enlightenment had fixed on this local prodigy, perhaps as a kind of noble savage, then why should he not occupy the national space they were proffering to him as they lionised him in the Scottish capital in early 1787? No matter, that he was not really a 'bard' with all its connotations of minstrelsy, but was actually steeped in the eighteenth-century poetry of the British Isles, especially Alexander Pope, James Thomson, Allan Ramsay, Thomas Gray and Robert Fergusson, to say nothing of his immersion in earlier writers such as Milton and Shakespeare. Burns had discovered the Scots poetry of Robert Fergusson (1750–74) in 1784 or 1785, in a way that sharply energised his own practices. Fergusson, with Ramsay and others, represented a literary tradition as sophisticated as anything in eighteenth-century England. However, in one of his poems written for Fergusson in 1787 he addresses his poetic predecessor as, 'Ill-fated Genius! Heaven-taught Fergusson' (*K* 144, l. 1). Here Burns recycles the epithet which he had had bestowed on him by Henry McKenzies's review published in *The Lounger* on 9 December 1786.[13] Neither Burns nor Fergusson was 'heaven-taught' but Burns is willing to play along, even as his transference onto Fergusson of the idea applied to Burns of appearing 'out of nowhere', points up the fact that, to some extent, Burns had come out of Fergusson. According to a whole line of criticism, tradition and belonging were not easy for Burns, especially because of a fractured national culture in which political and linguistic identities were trammelled by competing British and Scottish priorities. We might today question whether this was such a handicap as has sometimes been claimed. Burns was a Scots language poet utilising what he had initially learned from Ramsay and Fergusson. He was also a 'mainstream' satirical and didactic poet of the eighteenth century (as the opening poem, 'The Twa Dogs', in both 'Kilmarnock' and 'Edinburgh' editions of his *Poems* amply demonstrates with its usage of the rhyming couplet as accomplished as any in the late eighteenth century). Burns was also a figure of the Scottish (and wider) Enlightenment empathising promiscuously in his life and work with Covenanters, Jacobites, Lowlanders, Highlanders, highborn and lowborn, men and women, with Britons and with foreigners. With its interests in psychology, sociology and history, the Enlightenment had taught Burns that human identity was multifarious, and that many different kinds of identities might be sympathised with. In creatively projecting numerous identities Burns shows himself, perhaps, to be a modern writer, though have not the best writers, in fact, always inhabited various characters and personae? In 'To A Louse' (*K* 83), Burns's poem that combines traditional elements of eighteenth- century Scots poetry with a psychology derived from Adam Smith, the narrator pleads: 'O wad some Pow'r the giftie gie us / *To see ourselves as others see us!*' (ll. 43–4). Burns had the gift, certainly, to see others clearly, while also in complex cultural detail. He might be any of perplexed, horrified, or even amused at the perspectives of others as they have attempted to view him down the centuries, with huge cultural baggage (the perceiver's as much as the poet's) but not always clearly.

The chapters of this volume cover much of the crucial terrain in Burns's work and life. Featured are his key influences from Scottish sources such as Robert Fergusson and in the song tradition (especially Allan Ramsay). Reconsidered are Burns's relations with women, religion and politics, both with regard to the constitutional variety and also one of the hottest issues of the late eighteenth century, slavery. New readings of all of the foregoing are joined by sharply focused chapters on Burns as a critic, as a writer of 'national narrative' and as a user of 'rhetoric' (in all of these essays Burns's debt to classical traditions emerges as never before). Dealt with are Burns's ongoing and outgoing literary relations, with Walter Scott (along with Burns the writer who has done most to broadcast to the modern world the cultural image of Scotland), with writers of the Romantic period and in the poet's international, indeed, 'transnational' writing and significance. All of these areas reveal a Scottish writer and also a world writer.

CHAPTER ONE

Burns and Publishing

Gerard Carruthers

As with many writers, much of the work of Robert Burns was not widely known until some time after his death. The poet himself was often careful in publishing his writings not to court too much controversy, most especially in matters of religion, sexual behaviour and politics. Elsewhere I have suggested that we might, to some extent, usefully think of Burns's 'official' canon, what he and sometimes others thought it wise for him to publish, and his 'reserved' oeuvre, work that had a very much more limited circulation in the poet's lifetime and even beyond.[1] The present essay explores 'official' and 'reserved' categories, examining something of both the print and manuscript circumstances surrounding the canonicity of Burns's oeuvre, and it reflects from this 'textual availability' on the shaping of Burns's reputation during and after his lifetime.

The earliest gathering up of Burns's work is found in *The First Commonplace Book*, which the poet compiled from April 1783 to October 1785.[2] This private journal tells us about Burns's early self-conception and sensibility as a writer. It speaks of a sometimes pietistic young man as he includes 'A Penitential Thought, in the Hour of Remorse – Intended for a Tragedy', 'A Prayer in the Prospect of Death', 'Stanzas on the Same Occasion', 'A Prayer, under the Pressure of Violent Anguish' and 'Remorse'. A similarly pensive sensibility is viewed in the inclusion of world-as-cruel-place texts, 'Winter, A Dirge', 'O Raging Fortune's Withering Blast' and 'Epitaph on My Own Friend, and My Father's Friend, Wm Muir in Tarbolton Miln'. Burns's earliest song, 'O Once I Lov'd' appears, as do others including: 'Song, Composed in August', 'My Father was a Farmer upon the Carrick Border' and what was to become the official version of 'Green Grow the Rashes'. It might be suggested that these songs are all about 'respectable' peasant experience, 'O Once I Lov'd' (*K* 1) hymning 'handsome Nell' (l. 4) thus:

> She dresses ay [always] sae clean and neat,
>   Both decent and genteel;
> And then there's something in her gait
>   Gars [makes] ony dress look weel. (ll. 17–20)

In the songs, and in the pensive and religious pieces just mentioned, we find a serious young man of sentimental sensibility, a dominant cultural and literary mode in late eighteenth-century Britain. There are, however, some minor notes in *The First Commonplace Book*, which later become more pronounced in Burns's poetic oeuvre. There is the mildly scurrilous epitaph, 'On a Celebrated Ruling Elder', suggesting that Satan might find this individual useful in helping keep Hell in order. We also find a 'Song' (K 46) celebrating 'my girl' (l. 1) and:

> Her hair well buckl'd, her stays well lac'd,
> Her taper white leg with an et, and a, c,
> For her a, b, e, d, and her c, u, n, t,
>   And Oh, for the joys of a long winter night!!! (ll. 8–11)

Clearly, this 'Song', written during Burns's affair with his family's servant, Elizabeth Paton (d. 1817) during 1784, represents something that goes much deeper than 'O Once I Lov'd'. It marks the start, in fact, of Burn's most 'reserved' corpus of work delighting in explicit sexuality. He enjoys such bawdry particularly in the context of male cronyism, as he shows in the case of his 'Song' by quoting it around three years later as a suitable accompaniment in a letter to Robert Ainslie (1766–1838) congratulating his friend on his virility after the birth of his first child (*L* I, pp. 130–1).

The First Commonplace Book also sees Burns's opening attempts as a poet in Scots. His 'The Death and Dying Words of Poor Mailie' looks back to Robert Fergusson's 'The Sow of Feeling', where Fergusson satirises the age of sentiment through the figure of a female pig lamenting that she has lost both her husband and her brother (since these are one and the same thing) taken away to be eaten by humans. Burns has his ewe, Mailie, enjoining her son with her dying breath not to go on the randan and to be mannerly and neat in appearance. Here we find a theme that is developed further through Burns's oeuvre (for example, in 'To a Louse'): the stupidity of the human conceit of imposing its own standards upon nature. Burns, in contrast to the more melodramatic and rather po-faced notes of his poetic and song sensibility earlier in *The First Commonplace Book*, displays in 'Poor Mailie' a more hard-headed, sardonic realism, the keynote in some of his best work. Two other poems in Scots are found in this source, verse-epistles to John Lapraik (1727–1807), described by Burns in the first of these as an 'An Old Scotch Bard'. These, in a quite obvious way, exemplify a young poet who is now reaching out from his private work-book actually to make contact with a neighbouring Ayrshire writer. Burns is here in search of a local, poetic community; it might even be argued he succeeds in *creating* this in an official, published sense since Lapraik's *Poems on Several Occasions* only appears in 1788 two years in the wake of the path-breaking publication of Burns himself. In the first epistle (K 57) we see Burns defining himself not only against the present (Lapraik) but also with regard to the eighteenth-century history of poetry in Scots:

> O for a spunk [spark] o' ALLAN's glee,
> Or FERGUSSON's, the bauld an' slee [clever]
> Or bright LAPRAIK's, my friend to be,
>   If I can hit it!
> That would be *lear* [learning] enough for me,
>   If I could get it. (ll. 79–84)

Among Burns's earliest work in the 'Habbie Simson' or 'Standard Habbie'[3] stanza, Burns's epistle to Lapraik is inspired by the historic usage of the form by Allan Ramsay (1684–1758) and Robert Fergusson (1750–74). For these poets it had been a cultural signature, deriving from a mentality that disliked the supposed puritanism of Whig, Presbyterian, Calvinist Scotland. The 'Habbie' stanza carried with it connotations of Jacobitism and was for most of the eighteenth century especially associated with an East-Coast locus (Ramsay and Fergusson being based in Edinburgh). Burns brings about something of a cultural transposition in writing in the stanza so extensively from a south-west, predominantly Presbyterian locus, so that in time the form becomes known to many as the 'Burns stanza'. In this instance we see that with Burns the idea of the Scots language poet is on its way to becoming universalised as something more generally Scottish than it had been. It becomes less party political, not so sectarian even, than it was down to the time of Fergusson in being associated with a Jacobite, Tory, Episcopalian and even sometimes Catholic inclined cultural predisposition, exclusive, contemptuous very often of Whiggish, Presbyterian sensibilities.

If Burns's literary identity as a Scots poet was that which has historically won out over others, and even if we can see Burns himself beginning to mint this identity in *The First Commonplace Book*, this was something that involved struggle, opposition and rather gradual success in fully coming to the fore. We find evidence of this mixed set of circumstance in 'Holy Willie's Prayer' (K 53), among Burns's absolutely greatest work but remaining for long part of the poet's reserved oeuvre. If, in *The First Commonplace Book* and in his work to Lapraik, we see Burns's writing for himself and then for another poet, 'Holy Willie's Prayer' marks the beginning of a wider public fame for Burns. If the poet himself is to be believed, in his famous autobiographical letter to Dr John Moore (1729–1802) of August 1787, his poem so 'alarmed the kirk-Session [. . .] that they held three several meetings to look over their holy artillery, if any of it was pointed against profane Rhymers' (L I, p.144). The implication would seem to be that, as with 'The Holy Fair' a text from around the same time, 'Holy Willie's Prayer' was passed around his local neighbourhood in one or more manuscript forms. Like 'The Holy Fair', as described in Burns's words, we might assume of 'Holy Willie's Prayer' that 'With a certain side of both clergy and laity it met with a roar of applause' (*L* I, p.144). If there were those in the Kirk who were alarmed by 'Holy Willie's Prayer', there were others who were amenable to enjoying the poem, such as the Rev. John McMath (1755–1825) to whom Burns sent a copy in September 1785. Burns's poem stands in a long tradition of identifying the character of the hypocritical puritan. Going back at least as far as the early seventeenth century in the dramas of Ben Jonson, in the Scottish context the mode includes the play *The Assembly* (1692) by Archibald Pitcairne (1652–1713) and Allan Ramsay's poem 'Elegy on John Cowper, Kirk-Treasurer's Man' (1718). Burns's protagonist is an antinomian, convinced of his salvation through faith alone. Predestined for paradise as part of the faithful elect at the beginning of time by God, Willie is free from the constraints of the moral law in his earthly life. Indeed, even his supposed 'sins' of fornication and drunkenness are co-opted so as to be part of God's plan for someone who can do no wrong:

> Maybe thou lets this fleshly thorn
> Buffet thy servant e'en and morn,
> Lest he o'er proud and high should turn,
>   That he's sae gifted;
> If sae, thy hand maun e'en be borne
>   Untill thou lift it.— (ll. 55–60)

Willie's smug faith (in himself) and his carnality, to say nothing of his scatological unattractiveness where he can remember previously pissing himself 'wi dread' (l. 88) in the face of a contretemps with an enemy, made him the least flattering imagined portrait of a Calvinist, yet by a Scottish writer. Burns's poem confirmed the longstanding Pitcairne–Ramsay stereotype of the canting, egotistical and selfish parameters of the character. However, its author emerging himself from the Presbyterian–Calvinist heartland of Ayrshire, Burns's poem is never seen as motivated, unlike these earlier writers, by confessional and ideological hostility as such. Indeed, Burns's success in internalising to the 'moderate' Scottish Presbyterian community the critique of the Scottish antinomian fanatic is confirmed by 'Holy Willie's Prayer', inspiring the work of another Presbyterian writer, James Hogg (1770–1835), in his novel *Private Memoirs and Confessions of a Justified Sinner* (1824).[4]

'Holy Willie's Prayer' emerges out of local church and cultural politics. Burns's Willie is a composite figure, a poetic revenge on a number of individuals of the Presbytery of Ayr who had attempted to discipline Burns's friend

Gavin Hamilton (1751–1805) for his slack attitude to the Sabbath. Called to account by the Kirk authorities, and in large measure due to the eloquence of defending lawyer, Robert Aiken (1739–1807) (in response to whose forceful counter-arguments, Burns's Willie urinates on himself), the charges against Hamilton were dismissed.[5] The episode also reveals the important patronage Burns at this time was deriving from the Ayrshire Enlightenment, and the favour through his poem that Burns is returning. Hamilton and Aiken are important in the production of Burns's book, *Poems, Chiefly in the Scottish Dialect* published at Kilmarnock on 31 July 1786. Burns described Aiken as his 'first poetic patron' (*L* I, p. 66), and for the very good reason that of the 612 subscriptions to the 'Kilmarnock' volume, the lawyer took out 145 of these for himself and on behalf of many like-minded professional individuals in Ayr and its environs. Gavin Hamilton was also a lawyer as well as a land-owner, Robert and his brother Gilbert becoming his tenants when they rented from him Mossgiel Farm. Burns dedicated the 'Kilmarnock' edition to Hamilton, acknowledging a professional relationship and a warm friendship (Hamilton apparently encouraged Burns as a farmer as well as a poet); and also to the Ayrshire Enlightenment in general, which, unlike Scottish Calvinism, with its traditional hostile approach, most certainly saw worth in creative literature. For Hamilton, 'Holy Willie's Prayer' was, of course, not only a worthy but also a useful poem, trumpeting the triumph of a new kind of cultural leader in Ayrshire and in Scotland.

However, if in one sense 'Holy Willie's Prayer' marked a certain confidence in Burns's public profile as a poet, in another it registered the opposite. 'Holy Willie's Prayer' is absent from the 'Kilmarnock' edition and, indeed, is never officially published in Burns's life. While he is alive, the text appears in 1789 in chapbook form (cheaply produced pamphlets that were often sold door to door by itinerant salesmen, or 'chapmen'). It is also absent from the first collected edition of Burns's work edited by James Currie in 1800, and its appearance in the essentially pirated book edited by Thomas Stewart, *Poems Ascribed to Robert Burns, the Ayrshire Bard* (1801) is silently ignored in the numerous editions of Burns (among which reprintings of Currie were dominant) over the next decade and a half. David Irving in his *The Lives of the Scottish Poets* (1804) is amongst the earliest critics to notice 'Holy Willie's Prayer', which, in rather contradictory terms, he calls a 'wholesome satire on hypocrisy' while at the same time declaiming that it is 'reprehensible for the extreme indecency which it occasionally exhibits'.[6] In 1808 Robert Cromek's volume *Reliques of Robert Burns* appeared. This was a volume that made much of exposing hitherto hidden aspects of Burns's life (most famously identifying 'Highland Mary' for the first time). However, it elicited surprise from Walter Scott when he reviewed it in the *Quarterly Review* in February 1809. Why, he wondered, had Cromek failed to include either 'Love and Liberty, A Cantata' or 'Holy Willie's Prayer' given that Stewart had printed both? The time was clearly right according to Scott for the mainstream publishing of Burns items such as these that had previously been deemed 'contraband'.[7] In fact, it is only with the extended 1818 Edinburgh edition of Currie (who had died in 1805) that 'Holy Willie's Prayer' begins to be incorporated as part of the official Burns canon.

Burns himself, of course, had been shy of publishing 'Holy Willie's Prayer', keeping it for a rather select, even upper-class, private audience. With a letter of February 1788, Burns enclosed the poem for James Cunningham, fourteenth Earl of Glencairn (1749–91) and the poet's patron, who had much to do with arranging the large subscribers' list, this time over 1,300 individuals, for the Burns's 'Edinburgh' edition, as well as later being the sponsor of his career in the excise service. 'Holy Willie's Prayer' is also to be found in the Glenriddell manuscript that the poet compiled for Captain Robert Riddell (1755–94), one of the most cultured men in Dumfries, and Burns sent it too to Mrs Dunlop's son Anthony Dunlop (1775–1828), but dared not show it to the mother. If Mrs Frances Dunlop (1730–1815) represented a confidante, and something of a patron, through much of Burns's career, she had certain limits beyond which Burns could not tax her in terms of exposure to his work. A very different kind of woman, clearly, was Lady Don (1752–1801), sister of Glencairn. Among a special manuscript collection Burns prepared for her are to be found both 'Holy Willie's Prayer' and 'Love and Liberty'.

It is interesting to compare Burns's religious poetry which was officially published in his lifetime. 'The Holy Fair' (K 70) was included in the 'Kilmarnock' and the subsequent 'Edinburgh' editions of *Poems, Chiefly in the Scottish Dialect*, published in 1787 and 1793–4. This poem in the 'Christ's Kirk' stanza, the second of the eighteenth-century Scots poetry cultural signatures associated with Ramsay and Fergusson, offers similar psychological terrain to that of 'Holy Willie's Prayer'. It concerns an Ayrshire field preaching, at which people would gather in the eighteenth century to hear sermons from various ministers of religion. In Burns's poem the supposed religious *raison d'être* of the occasion represents actually a sublimation of other urges. One of the most remarkable moments in the poem concerns a particular preacher:

> Hear how he clears the points o' Faith
>   Wi' rattlin an' thumpin!
> Now meekly calm, now wild in wrath,
>   He's stampan, an' he's jumpan!
> His lengthen'd chin, his turn'd up snout,
>   His eldritch [unearthly] squeal an' gestures,
> O how they fire the heart devout,
>   Like cantharidian plaisters
>   On sic a day! (ll. 109–17)

Like Holy Willie, this preacher has something of the night about him and is rendered as Willie is in somewhat animalistic terms. With his 'snout' the preacher is porcine, and we should be aware of received scriptural parlance where the Devil is associated with pigs. The sermoniser's excited delivery, dwelling implicitly on sinfulness, is having the effect of an aphrodisiac (of which plaster of cantharides was a type) on some of his listeners. Throughout 'The Holy Fair' Burns sees religious fervour as really rather kinky, as actually counter-productive to the supposed moral message it purports to have, and he drives his point home in the final stanza, as he sums up the event:

> How many hearts this day converts,
>   O' Sinners and o' Lasses!
> Their hearts o' stane, gin night are gane
>   As saft as ony flesh is.
> There's some are fou o' *love divine*;
>   There's some are fou o' *brandy*;
> An' monie jobs that day begin,
>   May end in *Houghmagandie* [sexual intercourse]
>   Some ither day. (ll. 235–43)

'The Holy Fair' is not as graphically specific in terms of bodily functions as 'Holy Willie's Prayer', and it does not feature any Calvinist protagonist so explicitly, nefariously hypocritical. Presbyterian minister of the 'moderate' Church Party and Professor of Rhetoric and Belles Lettres at Edinburgh University, Hugh Blair (1718–1800) had reservations, but these were far from entirely proscriptive. Blair objected, for instance, to Burns's use in the 'Kilmarnock' edition of 'salvation' with such levity at the end of the lines 'For Sawney speels [climbs] the holy door, / Wi tidings o' salvation' (ll. 102–3).[8] Consequently for the 'Edinburgh' edition, Burns changed the word to 'damnation', which one might not think to be much of a concession towards maintaining Christian decorum. Largely, the religious disapproval of Burns was generally confined to traditional Presbyterians from humble backgrounds. One such was the Paisley poet, James Maxwell (1720–1800) who condemned Burns both for 'The Holy Fair' and 'The Ordination'. In its rather precise English diction and couplets, Maxwell's 'On the Ayr-shire Ploughman Poet, or Poetaster, R.B.' perhaps implicitly also registers distaste for Burns's Scots language mode. Even as Maxwell protests, however, what he reveals for us is the extent to which the tastes of Presbyterians were changing:

> Tho' some take his part, who make preaching their trade.
> For some of our clergy his Poems esteem,
> And some of our elders think no man like him.
> But let them esteem him, and value his lies,

By consequence then they the scriptures despise.
Tho' some of that function he favours indeed,
Who seem true adherents to his hellish creed.⁹

Assured that the tide was in his favour, that his kirk satires were enjoyed both by the great and the good and by a more general Presbyterian audience, Burns beefed up his quantity of these for the 1787 'Edinburgh' edition of *Poems, Chiefly in the Scottish Dialect*. In this book 'The Ordination', 'The Calf' and 'Address to the Unco Guid, or the Rigidly Righteous' all appear, the first and third of these having been available to Burns for publication in the 'Kilmarnock' edition had he so chosen.

If Burns derived, certainly, some praise and notoriety during his lifetime for his kirk satires, another very different kind of work dealing with Scottish religion, 'The Cotter's Saturday Night' (*K* 72) was for long his most celebrated and most 'canonised' poem, perhaps the most frequently quoted and individually reprinted of Burns's texts prior to his death. In it Burns praises the simple virtue of Presbyterian worship, especially amidst the hard-working country folk. Written in the Spenserian stanza (which ought to be seen, generally, along with the 'Habbie Simson' and 'Christ's Kirk' stanzas as representing part of the antiquarian mode of eighteenth-century poetry in Scots, with its connotations of cultural wholesomeness), it recalls Robert Fergusson's 'The Farmer's Ingle' (1773) on a similar theme of virtuous, hardy, non-luxurious country living. Burns's added component, however, is religion:

> The chearfu' Supper done, wi' serious face,
>   They, round the ingle, form a circle wide;
> The Sire turns o'er, with patriarchal grace,
>   The big *ha'-Bible*, ance his Father's pride:
> His bonnet rev'rently is laid aside,
>   His *lyart* [grizzled] *haffets* [locks on the temples] wearing thin and bare;
> Those strains that once did sweet in Zion glide,
>   He wales a portion with judicious care;
> '*And let us worship God!*' he says with solemn air. (ll. 100–8)

Here, when first published, was something entirely unexpected for any readers who might have been aficionados of the Scots poetry tradition that Burns was ostensibly following. Praising the Presbyterian or Whiggish character was something that would have been entirely alien to Burns's predecessors, Ramsay and Fegusson. In his infamous review in *The Lounger* (9 December 1786), Henry Mackenzie (1745–1831) admiringly noticed the poem while failing to mention 'The Holy Fair' (even when turning his attention to Burns's 'more humorous poems').[10] Reviewing the 'Kilmarnock' edition, John Logan (1748–88), a former Presbyterian minister now the editor of the London-based periodical the *English Review*, and most certainly an admirer also of 'The Holy Fair', called 'The Cotter's Saturday Night' 'without exception, the best poem in the collection'.[11] If Burns's poem was continuously admired while he was living, Maria Riddell (1772–1808) writing as 'Candidior' for her memoir of the poet, within a month of his death, highlighted it particularly, along with 'Tam o' Shanter' and 'To a Daisy', as a production exemplifying 'the maturity of his genius'.[12] And Francis Jeffrey, William Hazlitt and Lord Byron all conspired as the most discerning critical opinion to make 'The Cotter's Saturday Night' the most acutely lauded of all Burns's works in the two decades following the poet's death.[13] Not only this, but there are clear signs that posthumously, Burns's kirk satires were slipping back in appeal (either because the immediacy of the real events that these often documented was being lost, or, more likely, because of a refining of taste in early nineteenth-century Britain). John Gibson Lockhart, who in 1828 wrote what proved to be the most influential life of Burns until the twentieth century, opined in his biography, 'That the same man should have produced the "Cottar's [sic] Saturday Night" and "The Holy Fair" about the same time–will ever continue to move wonder and regret.'[14] If with Lockhart and others in the nineteenth century we see a disjunctive approach where Burns is berated for supposed scurrility in the kirk satires, this was reversed during much of the twentieth century by those who saw 'The Cotter's Saturday Night' as unpalatable in its veneration of Presbyterianism. Tom Crawford, suggesting a review of this more recent situation, summed up in 1960 that, 'Chiefly because of its sentimental rhetoric and English diction, it has long been fashionable to despise "The Cotter's Saturday Night".'[15] The twentieth century saw a nationalist roughening in taste for 'Scottish literature' that effectively decanonised the centrality of 'The Cotter's Saturday Night' in Burns's oeuvre. It is a poem, however, as 'genuinely' Burns as 'The Holy Fair'. 'The Cotter's Saturday Night' is a text signalling the emergence of one of a number of dissenting Protestant writers in the latter eighteenth century (Blake and Coleridge being two others) whose distance from metropolitan cultural assumptions becomes a powerful motor in Romanticism. Sublime nature (including human nature) was to be found in unexpected, off-centre places including the humble Ayrshire Presbyterian cottage. The over-insistence on the 'raucle [rough]-tongued' Burns (*K* 81, 'The Author's Earnest Cry and Prayer', l. 127), however, of say 'Holy Willie's Prayer' rather decanonised 'The Cotter's Saturday Night'. Indeed, there was for long an assumption (not entirely dispelled today) that the latter text represented an all too 'official' Burns, where the poet paid pious lip-service to something he little believed in. In fact in its own way, with the rehabilitation of the Scottish Presbyterian figure from its previous canting, extremist character, it springs from an impetus in the poet equally as iconoclastic as is to be found in 'Holy Willie's

Prayer'. It is perhaps even more innovative given that the that text comes out of such a well-trod tradition.

If Burns's kirk satires caused nervousness in their publication, even more controversial was Burns's writing on sexual activities. Here most starkly we see the poet's reserved oeuvre. 'Libel Summons' (sometimes also called 'The Court of Equity' or 'The Fornicators' Court') was privately printed in 1810 and 1823, with Walter Scott (1771–1832) being a connoisseur owner of one of only ten copies of the latter edition. In the first part of the twentieth century, it was published as an antiquarian curiosity in 1913, for the enjoyment of responsible scholars, by Hans Hecht and as an appendix to her biography of 1930 by Catherine Carswell as evidence (accurately) of a hidden side of Burns's culture.[16] It was not, however, included in a major edition of Burns's works until James Kinsley did so in 1968 (K 109). The poem represents an imaginary mock court, mimicking the set-up of Scottish ecclesiastical courts (at Presbytery level) to punish sexual malefactors and the subsequent public haranguing of these at church services. Scurrilously describing the styles of sexual intercourse of a number of individuals according to their professions, the poem moves towards its end as it humorously sentences a supposedly stubborn denier of his fornication to a very public punishment:

> You MONSIEUR BROWN, as it is proven,
> JEAN MITCHEL's wame by you was hoven;
> Without you by a quick repentance
> Acknowledge Jean's an' your acquaintance,
> Depend on't, this shall be your sentence. –
> Our beadles to the Cross shall take you,
> And there shall mither naked make you;
> Some canie grip near by your middle,
> They shall bind as tight's a fiddle;
> The raep they round the PUMP shall tak
> An' tye your han's behint your back;
> Wi' just an ell o' string allow'd
> To jink an' hide you frae the croud. (ll. 136–48)

While these lines might be dismissed as schoolboy humour, there is something more serious going on. We have to remember Burns being frowned upon by the Kirk for fathering an illegitimate daughter in 1785. Not long after he produced his poem, Burns was publicly rebuked in the kirk with his future wife, Jean Armour (now pregnant), on three successive Sundays in July and August of 1786 for the sin of fornication. If Burns was to be treated like a miscreant schoolboy, then why not respond with schoolboy humour? Also, the imaginary humiliation laughed at in the lines just quoted might be seen to be a humorous transferral of the very real humiliation that Burns felt around this time, not only for his disapproval in the community but for the view adopted by the Armours that Burns was someone not worthy of their daughter. It is in this period that Burns contemplates (whether seriously or not) a retreat into an obscure and ignominious career in the slave plantations of the West Indies. It is at this time, too, that Burns is working hard on projecting his official poetic self through the preparation of the 'Kilmarnock' volume. We see, then, an interesting moment in 1786 when Burns is juggling his official and reserved poetic sides, as the roads to fame and obscurity seemed equally to be beckoning him.

For Hugh Blair writing notes for Burns in 1787, as Burns prepared to compile the 'Edinburgh' edition of his poems, 'Love and Liberty, A Cantata' (K 84) as it is now known was a set of texts 'altogether unfit [. . .] for publication. They are by much too licentious.'[17] Amidst the drunken, sexual revelry of a group of tramps and chapmen, however, serious sociological points are registered about the dispossession of women, old soldiers and Highlanders. If the behaviour of the underclass depicted is somewhat rebarbative, their status it is suggested like other layers of society is rather locked in, predetermined even. This is a society of the haves and have-nots, and fair, moral dealing is somewhat beside the point:

> Here's to BUDGETS [leather bags], BAGS and WALLETS!
>   Here's to all the wandering train!
> Here's our ragged BRATS and CALLETTS [wenches]!
>   One and all cry out, AMEN!
> A fig for those by LAW protected,
>   LIBERTY's a glorious feast!
> Courts for Cowards were erected,
>   CHURCHES built to please the Priest. (ll. 274–81)

It was first published in chapbook form in Glasgow 1799 by Stewart and Meikle, with a slightly fuller version appearing in Thomas Duncan's *Poem's Chiefly in the Scottish Dialect* (Glasgow, 1801). With Duncan's volume, with chapbooks and with Stewart's *Poems Ascribed to Robert Burns, the Ayrshire Bard*, we see something of an 'unofficial', mass market for new Burns work in the several years following the poet's death, standing somewhat in distinction to the much more conservative reprintings and expansions of Currie's 'official' edition. In some ways the most notorious exemplar here is the volume, *Letters Addressed to Clarinda* (Glasgow, 1802) produced by Thomas Stewart. This published twenty-five letters from Burns in the guise of 'Sylvander' to Agnes McLehose ('Clarinda') (1758–1841), so exposing properly for the first time the seemingly dubious relationship between the poet and a married woman. A rapt public and attempted legal action from Caddell and Davies the publishers of the Currie edition, with the support of Mrs McLehose, ensued. This attempt to have the volume suppressed was dismissed since the letters were deemed to be the property of the Burns estate. On this basis, however, Burns's brother, Gilbert, successfully won a 'bill of suspension' against the volume which, in the end, did little good since reprintings followed in Ireland and America, where Scotland's legal writ, of course, did not apply; and it remained as popular as ever.[18]

Burns's most fugitive work is to be found in the context of *The Merry Muses of Caledonia*. This collection of bawdy songs was first printed in 1799, in one tradition produced in Dumfries though more likely to have been printed in Edinburgh since this was where the Crochallan Fencibles met. According to the title page of *The Merry Muses*, the book was produced 'for the use' of this drinking club. Although Burns's precise hand in many of the songs is difficult to determine, we find a bawdy variant of Burns's classic 'Comin Thro' the Rye', that seems likely to belong to the poet. The version found in *The Merry Muses* features the following closing stanza:

Mony a body meets a body,
   They dare na weel avow;
Mony a body fucks a body,
   Ye wad na think it true.[19]

What we have here is a typical Burnsian moment of satire on human hypocrisy: '[I]f you knew who was doing what to whom in secret you would not believe it, or maybe you would.' Sidney Goodsir Smith, on the basis of no very tangible evidence, claims that the bawdy variant of 'Comin' Thro' the Rye' is, in fact, the original text.[20] Although probably indeterminable, the best logic from what we know of Burns's career is that Burns (possibly) writes the bawdy version later on, around the time when he is drinking in Daniel Douglas's tavern where the Fencibles met. Two bawdy versions of 'Green Grow the Rashes' probably also show Burns again parodying his own 'official' respectable folk-song idiom. If these represent largely drunken release, other items among *The Merry Muses* have a serious political edge, most especially 'Why Shouldna Poor Folk Mowe [fuck]' which surveys the European political scene and lampoons, among others, Catherine II of Russia. who had placed her lover, Stanislaus Poniatowski, on the Polish throne. Polish resistance to Russian control in 1792–3 was quashed, and at a time of much perturbation across Europe. 'Why Shouldna Poor Folk Mowe' implicitly proposes that so much are the little people merely discounted canon-fodder in the games of the great and powerful that they should make love, not war. Sex, the only pleasure vouchsafed to the lowly, is also used in the song as imagined revengeful pain on the powerful:

When Kate laid claws,
   On poor Stanislaus,
An' Poland was bent like a bow, a bow;
   May the diel in her arse,
   Ram a huge prick o' brass,
An' damn her to hell wi' a mow.

In the nineteenth century *The Merry Muses* went through a series of 'privately' printed editions in Glasgow, Dublin and London (in the case of one of the last of these the '1827' being produced almost certainly in 1872, masked in this way so as to escape potential censure under indecency laws). In a rather bizarre republication, Duncan McNaught on behalf of the Burns Federation and editing it under the pen-name of 'Vindex' in 1911, sought to clear Burns of having written most of the material and, of course, since Burns had died in 1796 pointed out that the 1799 publication had nothing to do with the poet. Privately produced earlier, but officially enabled after the trial of the British publishers of *Lady Chatterley's Lover* in 1960 under the obscenity laws, the edition by Sydney Goodsir Smith and James Barke was legally published in 1965 (having been privately published in 1959), going to paperback in 1966 with strong international sales.

The slowest set of Burns's work to emerge fully into the light is that pertaining to politics. Works that appeared in the 'Kilmarnock' volume, such as 'The Twa Dogs', 'The Author's Earnest Cry and Prayer' and 'A Dream' were certainly outspoken. The first of these depicted an often dissolute political class in contradistinction to a humble, poor but literate peasantry. As Liam McIlvanney has suggested, '[C]oming immediately after a preface which craves the indulgence of "the Learned and Polite", there is a bracing frankness in a poem which exposes the shameful condition of Scotland's rural poor, and points an admonitory finger at the Scottish ruling class.'[21] Pointing to another perceived imbalance in the political state of things, 'The Author's Earnest Cry and Prayer' complains that economic conditions were being rigged under parliamentary regulation to the advantage of English gin distillers and the disadvantage of Scottish whisky distillers. 'A Dream' is in many ways the most scathing of these texts, as it mentions the playboy lifestyle of the Prince of Wales, crippling taxation and a corruptly unrepresentative parliament that King George III was resolutely set against reforming. The 1787 'Edinburgh' edition expanded this canon of political pieces only slightly with the inclusion of 'When Guilford Good', a piece satirising Britain's mismanagement of its elections as well as its loss of the American colonies, probably written in 1784. Burns had thought of including it in the 'Kilmarnock' edition but John Ballantine (1743–1812), possibly, or one of several individuals who were advising Burns in the lead-up to publication seem to have cautioned against printing the piece (L I, p. 31). It was only with the approval of the Earl of Glencairn and Henry Erskine (1746–1817) that Burns went ahead and published. For many liberal-minded men of politics, such as these, loss of America was beside the point in terms of diagnosing British political incompetence since the colonies had been unjustly treated (L I, p. 77). Burns himself clearly came to realise this, and this is why he took their advice. However, they clearly thought the general sweep of the poem in criticising the controlling British political élite good enough to be published.

The 1793 'Edinburgh' edition published nothing more in terms of large-scale political productions by Burns, and Currie's edition was conservative politically in what it chose to include. Burns's 'Address of Beelzebub', written in 1786, was not published until it appeared in *The Scots Magazine* in February 1818. This ferocious satire sees a prince of Hell egging on the powerful Earl of Breadalbane (1762–1834) to treat his Highland tenants even more savagely inconsiderately than he has done already, and to prostitute their women in Drury Lane and put their children to hard labour. (In these pre-Clearance times, Breadalbane had intervened to prevent some of his impoverished tenants seeking a better life in emigrating to Canada.). 'Ode [for General Washington's Birthday]' from 1794 was only partially printed in Cromek's *Reliques* in 1808 and was not fully published until it appeared in *Notes & Queries* in 1874. The 1874 version brought into the light potentially treasonable sentiments celebrating the 1770s revolution in America and contemplating the fact that British tyranny still pertained within its own borders in the 1790s. The 'Fête Champêtre' was belatedly published in the eighth edition of Currie (updated by Gilbert Burns (1760–1827)) in 1820. Not all that consequentially, it gently mocks the British parliament. The piece had been sent to John Ballantine (1743–1812) in 1788, and demonstrates not so much political sensitivity but merely the often slow process of Burns's editors tracking and publishing his manuscript work (L I, p. 300). Other political work such as 'Ode to the Departed Regency Bill', which appeared in the London *Star* in 1789 and 'The Heron Ballads' of 1795 which appeared in broadside form, Burns regarded as 'political Squib[s]' as he expressed it in the case of the 'Ode' in a letter to Mrs Dunlop (L I, p. 392). He regarded these works, accurately, as occasional poetry perhaps not canonically central in his published output. The idea of Burns having to be careful about the appearance of the political poetry that he wrote can be seen to be partially confirmed, however, even though some of his best and most trenchant political work did appear 'officially'. With his 'Address of Beelzebub' and the 'Ode [for General Washington's Birthday]', Burns was clearly more careful. Burns's official canon and his reserved oeuvre tell us much about a writer who enjoyed great creative and cultural freedom but who had sometimes to watch his step.

CHAPTER TWO

Burns and Women

Sarah Dunnigan

There's ae wee faut they whiles lay to me,
I like the lasses – Gude forgie me! (*K* 57, 'Epistle to John Lapraik', ll. 97–8)

Burns's 'confession' in the epigraph above perhaps 'explains' why his life was filled with women (Wilhelmina Alexander (1756–1843), Elizabeth Paton (d. 1817), Alison Begbie, Jean Armour (1767–1834), Frances Anna Wallace Dunlop (1730–1815), Agnes McLehose (1758–1841), Anna Park, Maria Riddell (1772–1808), to name only a few), and his art replete with lasses (those of 'Tarbolton'; the carnivalesque celebrants of 'The Holy Fair'; the 'lasses feat' of 'Halloween', not to mention 'Mary Morison', the 'Highland Lassie', and numerous other 'bonnie lasses' who are the subjects and dedicatees, both known and unknown, of Burns's songs and lyrics). In 'To William Simson' (*K* 59) 'Lasses gie [his] heart a screed' (l. 26) but poetry is a catharsis for any pain they cause: 'I kittle up my rustic reed; / It gies me ease' (ll. 29–30). The apparent inextricability of the poet's life and art from each other has generated a mythical Burns whose relationships with women comprise a fable of heroic, heterosexual masculinity; uber-machismo has been a celebrated part of 'the Caledonian Bard''s literary and literal procreation: 'Where women were concerned, it was always too easy for him to drop the thin cloak of acquired culture and revert to his peasant hood';[1] 'The love of women was necessary to him but equally necessary his absolute domination as the male';[2] 'Burns could have been in love with a woman and in love with every woman'.[3] There is, to be sure, evidence, in Donny O' Rourke's words, of Burns at 'his shitty chauvinist worst'.[4] But the cherished myth of 'the priapic drunk'[5] belongs to a larger culture – of Burns Clubs, Burns Nights, and Burnsian lionisation – which has sometimes marginalised women, though a woman, Maria Riddell, wrote the first life of Burns.[6] Well might Ian McIntyre caution that 'Burnsians have had to brace themselves against the impact of feminism.'[7] Yet in terms of approaches to, and readings of, Burns's poetry, there is surprisingly little proof of such 'impact'.

This essay seeks to disentangle the subject of 'Burns and women' from its mythical web, exploring what such 'mythologisation' reveals about culturally pervasive ideas of femininity. The letters of Agnes McLehose, the famous 'Clarinda', permit some visibility or agency to be restored to one of Burns's most controversial female acquaintances. More broadly, the question of women in Burns's poetry entails exploration of ideas about desire, sexuality, and morality, and about how society and culture both foster and inhibit identity. The chapter is arranged thematically, discussing some familiar work (for example, 'The Cotter's Saturday Night') as well as lesser known material (for example, *The Merry Muses*). Burns's poetic representation of women is complex because they are both real and imagined: 'Highland Mary', for example, was one Mary Campbell (?1766–86) who posthumously survives in both hagiographical and salacious histories about Burns. She, like other women, has her own 'lived' particularity in Burns's work but is also his 'literary' invention and a composite of the period's aesthetic, social and sexual ideals of femininity. Burns's literary self-presentation is also artful: his confession, 'I like the lasses', shows a wry collision between the supposedly revelatory mode of the 'Epistle' form and an awareness of his own public fashioning. His poem on a 'love-begotten daughter' (K 60) illustrates this perfectly: it both enacts the choric voice of disapproval ('Tho' now they ca' me, Fornicator' (l. 7)) and is a tender, fatherly benediction for his child born out 'o' Wedlock's bed' (l. 34). Burns's attitudes to women and sex are assumed to be transparent but, like all representations of sexuality in the eighteenth century, they are still historically and culturally shaped. It is too easy to be glib about Burns and his attitudes towards female and male sexuality, or to assume that Burns is either a defender or defamer of women. Burns's poetry does not deal in such simplistic polarities. His lyrics present him as the admirer, lover, confidant, satirist, trickster and abject subject of women but this does not suggest a lack of psychological coherence on Burns's part, or that an 'either/or', feminist or antifeminist, approach is best. Sensitivity to the cultural movements out of which Burns wrote, the literary influences which shaped his art, and the social and intellectual roles of women in the period fosters fairer and more nuanced understandings.

Lastly, any account of Burns and women should note that Burns's (naturally) female muse takes multifarious form: in the second verse-epistle to Lapraik (K 58) she is persistent and cajoling, a 'tapetless, ramfeezl'd hizzie' (l. 13); in 'The Vision' (K 62), she is 'Coila', mother to her rustic bard. Wearing '[g]reen, slender, leaf-clad Holly-boughs' (l. 49) and showing a glimpse of flesh (ll. 62–6), her dress is emblazoned with a familiar landscape topography and images of 'Heroes' such as Wallace. This is a characteristically eclectic yoking of Scottish martial heroism, medieval visionary tropes and conventional ideas of the maternal feminine. In 'reading' the cloak of his poetic godmother, Burns reads both his nation and vocation. But there were other muses too. Both Burns's mother and wife were gifted song performers. His first song, written when he was fifteen, was for Nelly Kilpatrick who inspired Burns by singing 'a song [. . .] composed by a small country laird's son [about] one of his father's maids'.[8] So many threads in Burns's creative life wind back to women.

Myths of Femininity:
'Highland Mary', Mary, Queen of Scots and 'Clarinda'

Virtually all of the women who impinged on Burns's life have garnered their own mythology: Wilhelmina Alexander ignored Burns's courtship, died unmarried, but treasured a poem that he wrote for her ('The Lass o' Ballochmyle'); Frances Dunlop was consoled in bereavement for her husband by the 'Kilmarnock' edition;[9] whilst Jean Armour is forever Burns's long-suffering, dutiful, unbeautiful wife. The Burnsian narrative constructed by biographers and critics has imposed particular roles on these and other women. De Lancey Ferguson, for example, defines three categories of Burns's women: 'The foremost group consists of women who profoundly stirred him, and on whom for a time at least he concentrated his intellect and his affections as well as his desires [. . .] Next come the women who engaged his passing fancy, and for whom he felt some tenderness, but who did not influence him deeply or long . . . below these was a third group . . . who were mistresses and nothing more.'[10] There are shards of truth here but it renders these women little more than alternate muses and mistresses.

The example of 'Highland Mary' best exemplifies how the Burnsian cult has spawned its own feminine myths. Margaret Campbell was born at Auchamore in Argyllshire on 18 March 1766, and worked as a dairymaid in Greenock before dying at the age of twenty-three; Burns probably planned to elope with her, and she 'survives' in a handful of popular lyrics. In Burns's nineteenth-century reception history, Campbell is reincarnated as a pure and innocent virgin. Victorian artists such as Thomas Faed imagine 'Highland Mary' in a pre-Raphaelite fusion of earthiness and purity, frozen in the eternal posture of the farewell to which Burns alludes in his songs. Campbell posthumously inspired her own cult of Mariology: in a rather odd inversion of the religious sensibilities associated with Burnsian culture, a contributor to the *Burns Chronicle* in 1921 writes 'At Mary's Shrine': 'When olden faiths depart / Thy love, a constant power, prevails / And stays the troubled heart',[11] as if to conflate the Virgin Mary and Highland Mary in their salvific powers. Burns's Victorian romantic biographers created an appetite for Marian relics (such as the bibles supposedly exchanged between Campbell and Burns) but also fuelled reaction against the 'Mariolaters'. In the winter of 1920 the exhumation of Campbell's grave in Greenock yielded a child's coffin. The implication that she died in childbirth sealed earlier efforts to suggest that she was not the hagiographers' virginal maiden. Ironically, it was Catherine

Carswell's biography that offered such a 'conversion' from the innocent 'child' into a woman 'heav[y] with the weight of Robert's child'.[12] Burns sups wine with his Edinburgh patron while mother and child are interred in earth; her death, and his apparent estrangement from Armour, sets his creativity free. Perhaps Carswell wanted her Campbell to be other than a virginal icon but she only perpetuates the obsession with her sexuality.

Burns, however, made his own Marian icon for posterity, sculpting a poetry of deliberate pathos round Campbell. One song (K 389) is devoted to the creation – or consecration – of her delicate, deathly beauty: 'Now green's the sod, and cauld's the clay, / That wraps my Highland Mary!'(ll. 23–4). Burns's awareness of the power of cultural images, and female icons especially, is also seen in his fascination for another Mary – Mary Stuart, Queen of Scots. By Burns's period, the Stuart queen had undergone many cultural and political metamorphoses through the forces of Jacobitism, sentimentalism, antiquarianism and Romantic nationalism. Burns's 'Lament for Mary Queen of Scots' (K 316) blends elegiac pastoral and ballad language with political point. The poem imagines Mary's rhetorical encounter with Elizabeth, the English queen who ordered her execution, permitting her to chastise the latter as 'thou false woman' (l. 33). There is retribution too: '[g]rim vengeance' (l. 35) wields a sword of justice to inflict a gaping wound in Elizabeth: 'weeping blood' (l. 37) is proof of the feminine compassion 'never known' (l. 38) to her, as if the stigmata of her guilt. Burns's Marian poem is full of romantic pathos but is also politically charged; when he sent William Tytler (1711–93) the lyric, he wrote: 'Burn the above verses when you read them, as any little sense that is in them is rather heretical' (L I, p. 112).

In the case of 'Clarinda', there is more historical information to attest that she, or rather Agnes McLehose, was more than the 'eminently poetic reality'[13] of 'Highland Mary'. Declared by Burns in 'Clarinda' (K 217) as 'fair Sun of all her sex' (l. 13), McLehose is the subject of 'Ae Fond Kiss'. The episode of 'Sylvander and Clarinda', the self-styled 'Arcadian names'[14] which Burns and McLehose devised for their correspondence, has been seen as the paradigm of Burns's supposed liaisons with socially upper-class women, a rhetorically overblown 'delicious passion' (and adulterous for she was married to James McLehose, a nefarious lawyer). Their correspondence was first published in 1843, after McLehose's death, by her grandson. Carswell portrays McLehose as 'bird-like [...] feathery crest, pretty bosom pushed to pigeon height by her stays'.[15] Carswell's novelistic portrait exemplifies a McLehose who is alternately arch seductress and anxious Calvinist, seeking 'to bring her Ploughman Poet to Jesus'.[16] Frustrated biographers have long strived to discover, in their terms, 'A Glimpse of Clarinda' or 'The Real Clarinda'[17]

Yet the 'truth' of the relationship cannot be gleaned from such 'epistolary dressing up'.[18] Fictionality is woven into the fabric of these letters.

'Friendship' is the desired nomenclature but a contested term; as 'Clarinda' reflects: 'Love and Friendship are names in everyone's mouth; but few, extremely few, understand their meaning' (p. 11). The letters question what 'authenticity' is, invoking and parodying Neoplatonic discourse and fashionable texts such as Goethe's *Werther*. Their verbal and emotional intricacies recall the erotic epistolary fiction so popular in the period (a genre in which women could possess both writerly and sexual agency). The hyperbole and playfulness of Burns's 'Sylvander' letters have frequently been observed but McLehose's exchanges are also wry, ironic and artful. Narrating herself, or her alternate 'Clarinda' self, she explores ideas about perception and spectatorship. Sylvander constructs her (as 'an Eloisa, a Sappho') but she also enacts a series of roles. She declares 'had I been a man, I should have been you' (p. 11) – flattery, of course, but a speculative gender shape-shifting prompting a defence of her own imaginative and emotional capacities. Also claiming to be born in 1759 ('Madam Nature has some merit by her work that year') she declares they share 'the same mould': 'I am not vain enough to think myself equal in abilities; but I am formed with a liveliness of fancy, and a strength of passion little inferior.' (pp. 11–12). Sylvander might portray her as his muse but he is hers too: 'I believe you (being a genius) have inspired me; for I never wrote so well before.' (p. 13). In a letter of 3 January 1788, Clarinda rescinds her efforts ('I can't but laugh at my presumption') but in 'rhyming humour' encloses some quatrains (p. 13) which parody the Habbie Simson stanza whilst satirising 'the first fruits of my muse' in the voice of eighteenth-century criticism: 'It has no poetic merit; but it bespeaks a sweet feminine mind' (p. 55).

McLehose's letters both fear and covet transparency: 'I wish you to know me, as "I really am"' (p. 55). She writes that 'I want no controversy – I hate it' (p. 57), though it defined their affair, even in its afterlife. McLehose should be remembered, not as the married woman who may or may not have slept with Burns, but as an epistolary writer of crisp elegance and ludic grace who crafted an erotic and intellectual dialogue with him.

Beauty, Sensibility and 'Women of Feeling'

Burns's love poetry is tender, bawdy, beautiful and comic by turns. As those lyrics associated with 'Highland Mary', 'Clarinda' and other women suggest, they often possess their own private history or stories of desire. Though it seems an unlikely comparison, his love poetry resembles Renaissance erotic verse in being both an abstract expression of desire and a social 'token' or exchange. Echoes of earlier amatory traditions are found elsewhere in Burns's lyrical eroticism. Female beauty is a persistent subject. Songs such as 'On Cessnock Banks a Lassie Dwells' (*K* 11) evoke the conventionalised blazon of medieval and Renaissance poetry, the device by which the desired woman is conjured up through the rhetorical anatomising of her beauty: 'her teeth are like the nightly snow (l. 33) and 'Her lips are like yon cherries ripe' (l. 37). Burns subverts this litany by finally celebrating her 'mind' (l. 51) as the superlative beauty, evoking the witty volte-face of those Renaissance love lyrics that play with Neoplatonism.

Burns's love lyrics also forge associations between desire, women and nature as in 'The Posie' (K 372):

> The primrose I will pu', the firstling o' the year;
> And I will pu' the pink, the emblem o' my Dear,
> For she is the pink o' womankind, and blooms without a peer;
>   And a' to be a posie to my ain dear May – (ll. 5–8)

The language of nature here is metonymic (the flower is his beloved but also her virginity). The lyric's coupling of nature with women reflects enduring metaphorical associations between nature and the feminine – beauty but also nurturing fecundity. Often reflecting folk song and medieval pastoral, Burns's love lyrics place women, and courtship, in and against nature. This endorses Burns's role as the poet of 'the rustic reed' but also mirrors contemporary cultural portrayals of nature's restorative simplicity and harmony where, as the fiction of Rousseau and Goethe shows, women play an organic role in fostering such 'natural' innocence. This Romantic 'redemption' of woman and nature – which classical and medieval misogyny viewed negatively – is knowingly alluded to by Burns. In 'Song. On Miss W. A.' (K 89), the following verse

> But Woman, Nature's darling child,
>   There all her charms she does compile,
> And all her other works are foil'd
>   By th' bony Lass o' Ballochmyle. (ll. 21–4)

expresses love but wittily gestures to the shift in Enlightenment and Romantic philosophy whereby the identification between woman and nature no longer represents the irrational materiality of the feminine but, in Kant's words, 'the more refined sentiments that belong to the domain of culture [. . .] she [nature] gave the female sex mastery over men'.[19]

Not only is Enlightenment moral philosophy refracted through Burns's lyric portraits of women but also the cult of sensibility. This was a popular literary and cultural movement which extolled, in Burns's own words, 'the feeling heart': the emotionally exquisite sensibilities of literary protagonists opened up experience in new moral and conceptual ways. 'Men of feeling' popularly dominated fiction but women of feeling, equally melancholic and suffering, populate Burns's poetry. 'Ca the Yowes' (K 185), in which a girl sings to her 'Shepherd-lad' of a love 'Till clay-cauld Death sall blin' my e'e' (l. 27), crystallises how song 'speaks feelingly to the heart'.[20] Placing these Burnsian female voices – lamenting lovers and bereaved women – in the culture of sensibility makes them more than exercises in conventional feminine pathos. That Burns should 'ventriloquise' the female voice is also interesting. What has been termed 'cross-gendered writing' is a phenomenon of long-standing precedent: Burns's abandoned female speakers – the woman of 'I Look to the North' or 'Willie's Bride' whose new husband fights in a war orchestrated by 'men o' State' – can trace a lineage back to Ovid's *Heroides*. Such ventriloquism is sometimes seen as a negative act of appropriation. Though Burns might be said to 'possess' the female voice (and 'female experience' by proxy), such lyrics still articulate women's experience of social and sexual marginality. Many, such as 'The Bonie Lad that's Far Awa', present the voice of the pregnant young woman spurned by society: 'My father pat me frae his door, / My friends they hae disown'd me a' (ll. 9–10). McGuirk argues that such lyrics typify a 'complacent attitude toward unwanted or unwed pregnancy [. . .] more to do with the wishes of Burns than with the psychology of women'[21] but it might also be claimed that such 'dispossessed women' give powerful voice to moral and social hypocrisies. Other female-voiced lyrics ironically expose how marriage gives women market value: in 'My Tochers the Jewel', the female speaker rejects an acquisitive lover so that her true value can be appreciated. In another, 'What Can a Young Lassie Do wi' an Auld Man' (K 347) the girl laments how her mother sold her 'Jenny, for "siller and lan"'! (l. 4); married to an old lover, her aunt advises her to 'heartbreak' (l. 15) him until he dies in order to get his 'brass' (l. 16). Though this speaker conjures up the rapacious women of medieval fabliau, the persistent complaints of 'ill-married' women in Burns suggest they are more than conceit or jest but bind sympathy and sensibility with political force.

Where, however, sentiment dominates in the portrayal of women – in the roles of daughter, mother, (potential) wife – is in 'The Cotter's Saturday Night' (K 72). This 'simple Scottish lay' (l. 5) resembles an allegorical vignette, the poetic equivalent of the popular eighteenth-century rural painting: Jenny personifies the dutiful daughter (stanza 4); maternal and paternal roles are fixed ('The Mother wi' her needle and shears [. . .] / Father mixes a', wi' admonition due', ll. 43; 45), sanctioned by an authoritatively patriarchal religion (stanza 14). Courted by a 'neebor lad', Jenny and her virginity occupy five stanzas. Fearful that 'Jenny's unsuspecting youth' might be 'betray[ed]' (l. 85), the narrator censoriously intervenes to eulogise female chastity and the tragic archetype of 'the ruin'd Maid' (stanza 10). The supper ceremony intervenes, foreclosing the threat of the daughter's lapse from her prescribed role, and restoring order to the microcosmic scene of 'old Scotia's grandeur' (l. 163). This seems the poetic equivalent of the popular conduct books for women written by John Gregory or James Fordyce. Yet the Jenny-vignette may also ironically invoke fashionable literary notions of femininity and, in particular, the sentimental novel. If the Clarinda–Sylvander correspondence resembles Laclos's *Les Liaisons dangereuses*, then fear of the 'wild, worthless Rake' (l. 63, couched in English rather than Scots) hyperbolically evokes the distresses of Richardson's Clarissa. Literary satire, rather than reactionary ideology, might be the poem's chief impulse after all.

The Merry Muses: Cultures of Desire

The Merry Muses, the notorious collection of songs and lyrics published after the poet's death,[22] occupies an uneasy, marginal place in the Burns canon. Seen either as virtuosic proof of Burns's sexual appetites (as in the infamous 'Nine Inch will Please a Lady') or as a text whose flagrant carnality needs censoring, it has mostly been avoided by critics.[23] Response to the work's portrayal of women might be equally polarised. The Besses and Megs whose bodies and desires are laid bare might be celebrated as voluptuaries challenging eighteenth-century ideologies of chaste womanhood or condemned as the sexually base creatures of a misogynistic imagination. In fact, both responses, each with a grain of plausibility, suggest again the importance of cultural context. The *Muses*' women might be seen as less aberrant if understood within the broader contexts of eighteenth-century libertinism and a popular, often radical, culture of pornography.

'Libertinism' in Burns's period usually refers to an élite, usually aristocratic, male coterie whose sexual practices and cultural sensibility might be characterised as decadent and excessive, ironic and contemptuous of contemporary mores. The lyric 'I am a Fornicator' exemplifies Burns's libertine pose – except that it, and the collection as a whole, transgresses libertinism's conventional social class. Named protagonists ('Muirland Meg') and a local rural topography of sexual encounters give the *Muses*' erotica a peculiarly 'homely' quality; its bucolic, folk pastoral, with allusions to 'country cunts' and affinities with bawdy broadside ballad traditions, is perhaps Burns's knowing subversion of aristocratic libertinism. Yet what it shares with libertine culture is being the product of an exclusively male coterie. Its full title is *A Collection of Favourite Scots Songs, Ancient and Modern; Selected for Use of the Crochallan Fencibles*, an Edinburgh 'drinking club whose title parodied the idea of a civil militia' and 'celebrated not simply conviviality but also maleness and masculinity'.[24] This homosocial context may have fostered a culture in which women were the sexual objects of cultural exchange and commodification. Yet the *Muses*' portrayal of female sexuality arguably complicates this assumption.

Although the word, 'pornography', does not appear in English until 1857, it is a helpful term (along with the categories of 'erotica' and 'obscenity') by which to characterise the *Muses*' mode and intent in presenting the 'explicit depiction of sexual organs and sexual practices with the aim of arousing sexual pleasure'.[25] In terms of narration and voice, the lyrics borrow the staple dramatic devices of pornography (the 'instructional' dialogue between women, and cautionary exchanges between men). The collection partly depends on shock value, consisting of deliberately comic affronts to decency and it anatomises (indeed fetishises) both female and male genitalia (for example, the paired lyrics 'There's nae Hair on' t / There's Hair on't'; 'Put Butter in my Donald's Broose') in a way which evokes the visual print culture of eighteenth-century erotica. Inflected with comic grotesquery, such lyrics present a carnivalesque democracy of the appetite.

Approaching the *Muses* from the perspective of early modern pornographical traditions is also interesting because of their recognised anti-establishment nature, especially in the Enlightenment period: 'a vehicle for using the shock of sex to criticise religious and political authorities', pornography was 'linked to free thinking and heresy, to science and natural philosophy, and to attacks on absolutist political authority'.[26] Its anti-authoritarianism might especially have interested Burns. This does not mean that the collection is not about sex, and sexuality, but it thereby mirrors Burns's general political sensibilities and imbues his representation of explicitly desiring women and men with a political contemporaneity and satirical wit. 'Comin over the hills ...' takes pleasure in maligning the moral and spiritual authority of David and Solomon, and 'The Patriarch' mocks the fleshliness of the Old Testament biblical narrative of Rachel; other lyrics mock the tyranny of legality ('The Law Act Sederunt') whilst 'Errock Brae', where a Cameronian soldier's sexual prowess is praised more than a bishop's or a priest's ('But the solemn league and covenant / He laid below my arse ...'), manages to be both a religious and political joke. 'I'll Tell You a Tale o' a Wife' presents the female counterpart of Holy Willie, instructing how sexual hypocrisy might be practised – 'the fauts o your cunt' – with a clear conscience.

So too more broadly might the *Muses*' depictions of female sexuality counter prescriptive ideologies of proper female conduct in granting woman the autonomy of sexual pleasure and power ('When on my back I work like steel / An bar the door wi my left heel / The mair you fuck the less I feel ...' ('The Reels o Bogie'), or 'Cuddy the Cooper' where a woman pays for gratification). However, there is often an aggression and violence to the sexual encounters which euphemistic discourse fails to disguise: 'Donald in a sudden wrath / he ran his Hieland dirk into her ...' ('Comin ower the Hills o Coupar'). This is certainly part of the collection's viscerality (for example, 'Again he wan atweesh my thies, / An, splash! Gaed oot his gravy': 'Denty

Davie'). Its somewhat mechanistic philosophy may approach reductive degradation (for example, 'Ye'se Get a Hole to Hie it in'; though the most bizarre lyric is probably 'Jenny Macraw': 'She cut off her cunt an she hang't on a thorn'). Women offer up their bodies but are also offered up for violation: 'but cowp her owere among the creels, / An bar the door wi baith your heels / the mair she bangs the less she sueels / An hey for houghmagandie': 'Gie the Lass her Fairin'). Such graphically voyeuristic violence is found with lyrics interestingly related to the conventional female lament which elegises the loss of virginity: 'How can I keep my maidenhead . . .' becomes a poem about vaginal pain ('The stretching o' t, the strivin o't' . . .); another pointedly depicts the social and moral hypocrisy of women who sneer at a young girl made pregnant by a 'sodger lown' ('Wha'll Mow Me Now?'). *The Merry Muses* is therefore an uneven compendium of violent male desires as well as social sympathy for women; a collection which purveys the material reality of sex along with its hyperbolic, comic distortions; the product of a homosocial and Enlightenment culture which may objectify women, both culturally and sexually, but portrays sexual desire, both female and male, as wholly natural, morally unjudged, and as part of the formative, creative passions which shape human identity.

Enlightenment Women

Burns's correspondence with Agnes McLehose showed how 'an epistolary relationship' fostered an exchange of ideas as well as attitudes popularised by the cult of sensibility. It also points to the broader and important role which women played in Burns's intellectual and creative life. Carol McGuirk writes perceptively that

> Women were the only admirers whose notice Burns could comfortably accept. It is well known that Burns liked women generally, but such literary friends as Maria Riddell became especially important in his later years, when his residence at Dumfries removed him from the 'patrons' who had begun his vogue at Edinburgh'.[27]

Such friendships were not without complications (as those with Riddell and Frances Dunlop attest)[28] but the epistolary network of female correspondents surrounding Burns points to a coterie of intellectual, literary women in whom Burns found sympathy and affinity, contradicting the assumption that Burns's 'muses' were always sexual in inspiration. Amongst the creative women with whom Burns corresponded were the poets Janet Little (1759–1813) and Anna Laetitia Barbauld (1743–1825).) A congruence between the cultures of Enlightenment and sensibility may have nurtured such communication, as 'the man of feeling' rendered himself open to the 'civilising' and 'delicate' influences of women.[29] How, then, might Burns's poetry be considered in relation to Enlightenment attitudes towards women – when the figure of the learned woman was frequently derided – and its nascent feminist debates?[30]

The exemplary poem in this instance is 'The Rights of Women', written for Louisa Fontenelle (1773–99), an actress of numerous 'beauties' (L II, p.160) who had performed in London and Edinburgh; and whose very title seems an unquestionable allusion to Mary Wollstonecraft's A *Vindication of the Rights of Women* (1795), which had demanded social, political and economic equality for women. Seldom, however, is it considered equal in political power to Burns's song 'For A' That. . .', a lyric indebted to Thomas Paine's 'Rights of Man'; against that song, Crawford considers it 'artificial, contorted and unconvincing'.[31] Certainly, the poem dilutes the revolutionary spirit of Wollstonecraft's feminist vision. Presenting the 'rights of man' as an accepted orthodoxy which 'even children lisp', the narrator is the self-appointed spokesman for 'The Rights of Woman' (K 390). Such rights include protection (woman is a 'tender flower', l. 9). Revealingly, '[t]o keep that Right inviolate's the *fashion*' (l. 14, my emphasis): what must a 'man of sense' (l. 15) do but defend women now that 'these Gothic times are fled' (l. 21)? The poem concludes on a seemingly parodic note with the 'revolutionary' call: 'Ah, ça ira! The majesty of woman!!!' (l. 38). Carruthers observes how this poem demonstrates the impossibility of seamlessly categorising Burns, whether as sentimental poet, 'licentious libertarian', political revolutionary or political cynic.[32] It is also worth noting that the poem's effort to galvanise men's chivalric protection and admiration of women goes right against the grain of Wollstonecraft's repudiation of philosophers' 'old-world attitudes to women [. . .] "If women be ever allowed to walk without leading-strings, why must they be cajoled into virtue by artful flattery and sexual compliments?"'[33]

There are, however, other instances in which Burns displays more tolerance, or sympathy, for changing Enlightenment thought about women. 'Green Grow the Rashes, O' (K 45) is celebrated for its portrayal of love's complete occlusion of the world, and may not seem the place for a protofeminist defence. Yet the stanza,

Auld Nature swears, the lovely Dears
    Her noblest work she classes, O:
Her prentice han' she try'd on man,
    An' then she made the lasses, O. (ll. 17–20)

presents an argument used in defence of female equality, if not superiority, which has an intellectual and theological lineage winding back to the medieval period; Eve was made last (after Adam) and therefore God had time to make her more perfect.[34] Another well-known lyric, 'To a Louse', makes its female protagonist the subject of philosophical reflection. In church the narrator contemplates the creature's vigorous ascent of the finely clothed Jenny who knowingly 'displays' herself but unknowingly becomes subject to a broader, imperious social gaze. Is this an anti-feminist piece in which the young woman's beauty symbolises female artifice and vanity more monstrous than the rapacious louse? Or does it evoke sympathy for Jenny, naïve and impercipient, as she is watched by the douce congregation? Such 'sympathy', as Carruthers has argued, is also of the Enlightenment kind, developing Adam Smith's theory of moral identification: 'we are to imagine ourselves in place of another but looking back at our original self . . . We would be stripped of our pride . . . even to the extent of losing self-love.'[35] Rather than being a poem about female vanity, then, it has greater poignancy as a meditation on the brittleness of the public image or 'selfhood' which the individual constructs against the world. Jenny is more an emblem of the fragile human ego than of the deceitful womanly artifice feared by misogyny.

Tam o' Shanter: Fear of the Feminine?

'Tam o' Shanter' (K 321), that ribald, comic, devilish tale beloved by Burns Night celebrants, is a vernacular visit to the Underworld – but an infernal realm that is largely feminine in its forms and powers. Burns's anti-hero embarks on a journey, fuelled by drunken rashness, which unleashes a vision of Satanic carnivalesque horror but also promises deliverance from the 'wrath' of his wife, Kate, in Nannie: 'ae winsome wench and wawlie' [ample] (l. 164) whose 'cutty sark' raises not just Tam's desire but an entire 'hellish region' of uncanny merrymakers who set off in pursuit of the trespasser. This is a traditional tale in many senses. Rich in traditional folkloric material, it is also most often celebrated and critiqued for its traditional constructions of gender: the drunken, lascivious husband ('sweet' with the landlady); the put-upon, resentful wife; the fleshly young temptress; even Kirkton Jean's role as prophetess. Well might A. L. Kennedy suggest that it is a 'wishful middle-aged male fantasy . . .'.[36] A cautionary tale of the perils of wine and women, it has been judged 'a poem which plays a game involving a female challenge to the male, but makes it clear that [. . .] it's the male who wins. That male is a boozing, fraternal male of the sort that Burns knew and liked from his masculine clubs.'[37] As Christopher Whyte has shown, the poem's language is obviously gendered: in terms of authorial self-characterisation and narratorial address, this is a man speaking to other men (with the exception of the rueful apostrophe to 'Ah gentle dames!', it addresses 'ilk man and mother's son').[38] And yet 'this tale o' truth' is far from clear, though its 'truths' about women and men have been taken for granted – such as 'This truth fand honest Tam' that wives resent the temporary escape of husbands to the convivial brotherhood of the tavern; or that woman, whether in her incarnations as wife or temptress, is punitive: Kate's 'wisdom' suppresses Tam's instinctive spirit and Nannie seeks revenge for his sexual appetite. Emasculation is the consequence for both instances of female suppression. What literally drives Tam to flee on 'noble Maggie', and is the poem's principal symbolic drive, seems to be fear of the feminine: women, both human and supernatural, remind Tam and his male readers of their 'own carnal contingence'.[39]

This, however, is not a new story. Tam's narrative is replete with allusions to other 'queer stories': to the biblical tale of Susannah and the Elders, and the mythical fate of Actaeon, torn apart by his own hounds after Diana changed him into a stag; both illustrate the perils of male voyeurism. The prefatory allusion to Gavin Douglas's *Eneados* invokes a medieval context, perhaps especially the worlds of medieval dream vision poetry where sensory and strange elements often have allegorical meaning (the word 'reason' is repeated in the poem, casting it as a fable of reason versus desire). Tam's story also evokes traditional tales of the abduction and punishment of mortals by resentful otherworldly beings where frequently, though not exclusively, the 'victim' is male. Nannie is therefore a particularly robust version of the traditional fay (though her 'sark' seems less than otherworldly since got by her 'grannie' for 'twa pund'?). Her beauty is juxtaposed with the ugliness of her troupe of hags or witches, a vision of simultaneous desirability and repulsion. Significantly, the narrator acknowledges that her beauty defeats his poetic powers, yoking the feminine to ideas of excess and unrepresentability. It is unsurprising but still interesting that Tam should see witches. Since the late medieval period, the figure of the witch has embodied specific cultural fears about women. This particular demonisation of the feminine, as is well known, led to the violent persecutions of innocent women (especially prevalent in Scotland in the early modern period). This may seem far flung from the poem's comically demonic revelry presided over by Auld Nick himself. Yet perhaps the poem suggests that the real forces of demonisation are neither feminine nor occult but 'man-made': Tam also notices 'upon the haly table [. . .] A garter, which a babe had strangled; / A knife, a father's throat had mangled, / Whom his ain son o' life bereft' (cf. ll. 130–9), having ridden through a landscape engraved with their memory ('And near the thorn, aboon the well, / Whare Mungo's mither hang'd hersel'', ll. 95–6). If the real horror is ordinary humanity, then fears about witches, and the demonic feminine, are folly; after all, Tam rides blithely into a night so haunted 'a child might understand' (l. 77).

For this reason, it is difficult to accept entirely the premise that 'it's the male who wins'. 'Drink' and 'cutty-sarks' warn men of the fate of 'Tam o' Shanter's mare' who ends up tail-less; a symbolic castration if ever there was one (except that Maggie is, self-evidently, a female horse). Burns's poem, then, opens up a Pandora's box of gendered readings. Moralistic readings are subverted by the fact that its overt 'morals' (e.g. ll. 59–67) are in English and arguably parodic. The 'cut off' tail conceivably cautions against 'cutting off' the tale by meanings too circumscribed or narrow – of which one, perhaps, is that it is a joke got only by men.

This essay has suggested that the complexity of Burns's representation of women shows how distorted and simplifying the myth of the 'priapic drunk' has been. 'Burns's women' are a fusion of archetype and psychological complexity; they are imagined out of contemporary cultural contexts such as the Enlightenment and Romanticism, and are entangled in fashionable and controversial movements such as the cult of sensibility and the vogue for pornographic literature. We cannot 'know' women, such as Mary Campbell or Agnes McLehose, beyond what Burns's poetry and their own words, where they survive, tell us; but alertness both to the mythologies which shroud them, and their textual voices, helps to accord them the visibility and seriousness which they deserve. In that way, too, critical approaches to women and gender in Burns might be renewed. Perhaps one of the least desirable consequences of Burnsian culture and criticism is that Burns is perpetually appropriated. Often such forms of 'ownership' have excluded women, deliberately or not, as his readers and interpreters. An interesting illustration of this exists in the form of a work published in 1886 called *Robert Burns: An Inquiry into Certain Aspects of his Life and Character and the Moral Influence of his Poetry*. Its Victorian writer is deeply in sympathy with Burns, both emotionally and socially; but, as if to acknowledge its transgressive subject matter, and her transgression in writing about it, she identifies herself only as 'a Scotchwoman'.

CHAPTER THREE

Burns and the Rhetoric of Narrative

Kenneth Simpson

The annotated edition of the letters of Burns makes no mention of Aristotle, Cicero, Horace or Quintilian. Common to each of these classical rhetoricians is the recognition that the essence of rhetoric is the ability to persuade. Aristotle, for instance, observed of rhetoric, 'The modes of persuasion are the only constituents of the art: every thing else is merely accessory'.[1] Judged on these terms, many of Burns's poems and letters are masterpieces of rhetoric, the artifice that conceals artificiality, the subtly disguised means of fashioning reader response. Terming Burns 'an unrepentant rhetorician', R. D. S. Jack notes that Burns's rhetoric 'is seldom of the overtly virtuosic sort anticipated by the Castalians. His is the classical aim of using art to conceal art (*ars est celare artem*).'[2]

Burns learned of the art of rhetoric from his schooling by John Murdoch (1747–1824) whose principal text-book was Arthur Masson's *Collection of English Prose and Verse* (2nd edn, 1767), which included extracts from Mrs Elizabeth Rowe's *Letters Moral and Entertaining*. His skills in oratory were honed in the school-boy debates at Kirkoswald with fellow-pupils such as William Niven (1759–1844) and Thomas Orr (d. 1785). When the master, Hugh Rodger (1726–97), scoffed at the topic of one debate, 'Whether is a great general or a respectable merchant the most valuable member of society?', Burns challenged Rodger, giving him the choice as to which side he would represent. Rodger opting for the general, Burns counter-argued the case for the merchant. It was the pupil who triumphed, the effect on the teacher being that Rodger's 'hand was observed to shake; then his voice trembled; and he dissolved the school in a state of vexation pitiable to behold'.[3] The skills of the self-acknowledged 'excellent English scholar' (*L* I, p. 135) allied with the combativeness of youth ('a stubborn, sturdy something in my disposition', he called it (*L* I, p. 135)) would produce the 'satirical seasoning' to which David Sillar (1760–1830) testified with the caveat, 'while it set the rustic circle in a roar, [it] was not unaccompanied by its kindred attendant – suspicious fear'.[4] Rhetorical prowess can enchant and unnerve in equal measure.

In his *Poetics* Aristotle stresses the role of imitation in the learning process. It was certainly so with Burns's acquisition of the arts of rhetoric. Whatever formal training he may have had from Murdoch was far exceeded in importance by the example of his reading. Burns was, as he informed Dr Moore (1729–1802), 'a good deal noted for a retentive memory' (*L* I, p. 135), and the extent of his adolescent reading he listed as follows:

> Pope's works, some plays of Shakespear, Tull and Dickson on Agriculture, The Pantheon, Locke's Essay on the human understanding, Stackhouse's history of the Bible, Justice's British Gardiner's directory, Boyle's lectures, Allan Ramsay's works, Taylor's scripture doctrine of original sin, a select Collection of English songs, and Hervey's meditations. (*L* I, p. 138)

Catholic in range, these texts would vary in their significance as models of rhetoric, but Burns prefaces the catalogue with this forthright acknowledgement of a major formative influence on both his writing and his conduct: '[M]y knowledge of modern manners, and of literature and criticism, I got from the Spectator.' Therein lay a wealth of examples of neoclassical rhetoric. By the age of twenty-three Burns was writing to Murdoch, doubtless to impress his old tutor but also with substance as the evidence of the poems and letters confirms: 'My favourite authors are of the sentiml kind, such as Shenstone, particularly his Elegies, Thomson, Man of feeling, a book I prize next to the Bible, Man of the World, Sterne, especially his Sentimental journey, Mcpherson's Ossian, & c.' (*L* I, p. 17). That the influence of such texts extends beyond literary composition is confirmed by his rider, '[T]hese are the glorious models after which I endeavour to form my conduct.' There is a striking paradox here in that Burns absorbs the rhetoric of sensibility, the artifice essential to present oneself as naturally and openly emotional; and hence artless. To this end, Burns read voraciously. David Sillar recalled:

> Some book (especially those mentioned in his letter to Mr Murdoch) he always carried, and read when not otherwise employed. It was likewise his custom to read at the table. In one of my visits to Lochlea, in time of a sowen supper, he was so intent on reading, I think *Tristram Shandy*, that his spoon falling out of his hand, made him exclaim, in a tone scarcely imitable, 'Alas, poor Yorick!'[5]

Burns read, absorbed, and – as he acknowledged – used to further effect. 'I like to have quotations ready for every occasion,' he wrote to Mrs McLehose (1758–1841), adding tactlessly, 'They give one's ideas so pat, and save one the trouble of finding expression adequate to one's feelings' (*L* I, p. 207). In a later letter to Mrs Dunlop (1730–1815) he adds a further function, tantamount to recognition that literature provides both a shield and a ready weapon, 'I pick up favorite quotations, & store them in my mind as ready armour, offensive or defensive, amid the struggle of this turbulent existence' (L II, p. 165). For Burns literature is a constant, a bulwark in the flux of life.

His letters testify in terms of both reference and practice to his familiarity with rhetoric. Here he ruefully admits a failure:

> I used all my eloquence, all the persuasive flourishes of the hand, and heart-melting modulation of periods in my power, to urge her [Miss Erskine Nimmo] out to Herveistoun, but all in vain. My rhetoric seems quite to have lost its effect on the lovely half of mankind. (L I, p. 165)

Many of the letters are works of consummate artistry, unsettling those commentators who, seduced by the 'Heav'n-taught ploughman'[6] myth, 'sought [. . .] a rural naivete', as J. De Lancey Ferguson astutely pointed out (L I, p. xliv). In fact, Burns's letters and poems abound in rhetorical topoi. Especially in letters to women, ranging from Alison Begbie to Agnes McLehose, he delights in using the modesty topos which, as R. D. S. Jack has suggested, he had 'seen practised by Dunbar and Henryson'.[7]

The narrative skill of the poems and letters bespeaks the novelist manqué. Plainly influenced by Sterne's *Tristram Shandy*, and perhaps also by Rousseau's *Confessions*, the autobiographical letter to Dr Moore is introduced as the outcome of 'a whim to give you a history of MYSELF' (L I, p. 133). Despite the assurance, 'I will give you an honest narrative' (L I, p. 133), it is in fact a subtle exercise in the projection of self-images, with affinities to Sterne's masterpiece and the Modernist and Postmodernist self-begetting fictions of which it was the progenitor. Two letters may be briefly cited as exemplars of Burns's narrative expertise. The account of Mrs Carfrae, his Edinburgh landlady, 'a staid, sober, piously-disposed, sculdudery-abhoring Widow [. . .] in sore tribulation respecting some "Daughters of Belial" who are on the floor immediately above' (L I, p. 83) is a cameo worthy of Smollett; and the letter (L I, p. 125) recording the horse-race with the Highlander down Loch Lomondside shows the ability to modulate narrative pace to mimic meaning in a way that anticipates the perfection of this technique in the verse-narrative of 'Tam o' Shanter'. Such evidence prompts regret that his circumstances prevented Burns from trying his hand at fiction; and from proceeding with 'some kind of criticisms on novel-writing' (L I, p. 440) which his reading of Moore's *Zeluco* had suggested. This was a project he was loath to relinquish: almost a year later (14 July 1790) Burns was informing Moore, 'I have gravely planned a Comparative view of You, Fielding, Richardson & Smollet [sic], in your different qualities & merits as Novel-Writers' (L II, p. 37). It didn't happen (as he acknowledged would probably be the case), but his readiness to contemplate it testifies to his responsiveness to the subtleties of fictional narrative. And for Burns, crucially, 'Fiction [. . .] is the native region of Poetry' (*L* I, p. 181). Far from rural life being merely reflected by his muse, it is transformed by his imaginative power, of which rhetoric is the main implement. Voltaire shrewdly described Quintilian's *Institutio Oratoria* as 'Lying as a Fine Art'.[8] For Burns as much as the classical rhetoricians the essence of the art of rhetoric is pretence.

Classical rhetoric foregrounds oratorical skill and engages with the modulations of the speaking voice. Burns is expert in the creation of personae that plead a case or manipulate a debate. 'The Twa Dogs' (*K*: 71) offers a canine dialogue about the life-styles of their respective masters, and it is Luath, the farm-dog, that proves to be the master tactician. When Caesar, the laird's dog, holds forth on the hardships suffered by the peasantry Luath responds, not with the expected endorsement, but the claim that their life of honest toil has compensations that family and fellowship provide. Having heard Caesar out, Luath then concedes one point to him:

> There's monie a creditable *stock*
> O' decent, honest, fawsont folk,
> Are riven out baith root an' branch,
> Some rascal's pridefu' greed to quench. (ll. 141–4)

This is a masterstroke in that, unknown to Caesar, it enables Luath to control the direction of their exchanges. His mention of one type of injustice to the peasantry prompts Caesar to enlarge on the debauched life-style of the gentry. With *faux-naïveté* Luath asks, 'But will ye tell me, master *Cesar*, / Sure *great folk's* life's a life o' pleasure?' (ll. 185–6). This serves to trigger a more vehement denunciation of the inertia-bred neurosis and decadence of the upper classes which Caesar, the aristocrat's dog, then contrasts with the honest endeavours and natural life-style of the peasantry.

If Luath is a master of ironic strategies, the dying ewe who is the principal narrator of 'The Death and Dying Words of Poor Mailie, the Author's only Pet Yowe, An Unco Mournfu' Tale' (*K* 24) is a victim. Burns probably found his inspiration in 'Lucky Spence's Last Advice' where Allan Ramsay fuses classical valediction, the Scottish animal-poetry tradition, and the example of the fables of Aesop and Henryson, to serve the interests of social satire. Equally cleverly, Burns offers through his dying sheep keen insights into human nature. Mailie's worthy aim is to offer from her death-bed useful guidance to her offspring; but in so doing she reveals a measure of self-interest in that she takes pride in her example, as is evident from her counsel, 'An' when ye think upo' your Mither, / Mind to be kind to ane anither' (ll. 59–60). Unwittingly, however, she has contradicted herself spectacularly: her advice to her master, Burns, is never again to tether a sheep (thus avoiding her fate being repeated), but when she turns to concern herself with her offspring such Rousseauistic endorsement of liberal and natural rearing is undermined by her insistence that they remain in the parish and avoid bad company. The narrating persona has been subject to the ironic observation – in this case benign – of the poet.

The same technique, that of ironic self-revelation, is employed in 'Holy Willie's Prayer', though here the authorial irony is altogether more hostile. Holy Willie prays to his omniscient deity using the language of his rural community and the rhetoric of his creed. Addressing his God as an intimate he congratulates him on choosing him as one of the Elect, and he indicates that if it is God's will that he stray into illicit fornication then he will endure it. As his religion stresses predetermination and allegedly guarantees his election, the prayer should be unnecessary and the outcome inevitable. Yet both his admission of his tremulous response to the new religious liberalism and the vehemence of his plea for vengeance bespeak the underlying insecurity of a creed and its adherent under threat. Holy Willie has revealed this unknowingly. Equally typical of Burns's oblique strategies and informed by an even subtler irony is 'To a Louse' (*K* 83). In church, the narrator has studied an attractive young fellow-worshipper so minutely as to detect the louse that is attempting to ascend her elaborate bonnet. The poem offers various exemplars of the vanity of aspiration – the louse itself, the aerialist Lunardi, and Jenny, on whom the narrator has feasted his eyes. The encounter elicits this wish from him:

> O wad some Pow'r the giftie gie us
> *To see oursels as others see us!*
> It wad frae monie a blunder free us
>   An' foolish notion:
> What airs in dress an' gait wad lea'e us,
>   And ev'n Devotion! (ll. 43–8)

True to the use of realistic detail and exempla in the rhetoric of preaching, the narrator has produced his own alternative sermon, thereby unwittingly adding himself to the exemplars of 'airs [in] Devotion'.

Burns wrote from Edinburgh in January 1787 to Dr Moore, 'For my part, my first ambition was, and still my strongest wish is, to please my Compeers, the rustic Inmates of the Hamlet, while ever-changing language and manners will allow me to be relished and understood' (*L* I, p. 88). In itself, this represents a striking bifurcation of style and substance. It finds a parallel in the extent to which many of the poems (including those discussed thus far) support dual, or even multiple, perspectives. Each might be said, on the 'Heav'n-taught Ploughman' thesis, to reflect rural incidents; equally, each is a subtly nuanced piece of rhetoric in which the poet offers profound insights into human nature. These poems play to a wide range of levels of reader responsiveness, from the naïvely literalist to a sophisticated alertness to levels of irony.

While Burns may have had no knowledge of Quintilian, his two long narrative poems exemplify the recurring concern of the classical rhetorician – the inter-relationship of narration and argumentation.[9] Five years apart in composition, 'Death and Doctor Hornbook' and 'Tam o' Shanter' each relate a human being's encounter with the supernatural. In each, the creation of an unnamed but personalised narrator enables the poet to engage with issues of truth and fiction and their relationships.

The sub-title of 'Death and Doctor Hornbook', 'A True Story' (K 55), immediately raises the question of the veracity and objectivity of something which is so personally related; it may even give rise to the suggestion that the conjunction of the two words is oxymoronic. 'SOME books are lies frae end to end' (l. 1) according to the narrator at the outset, and even the clergy are guilty, having used 'holy rapture' (l. 4) to sell lies and nonsense by citing scriptural authority. His tale, in contrast, is true, 'just as true's the Deil's in hell, / Or Dublin city' (ll. 9–10). By positing alternatives here, the narrator qualifies the authority of his assertion; and, since a surprise encounter with Death awaits him, can he be so certain of the whereabouts of the Devil?

The narrator's account of his journey is notable for the way in which the rhythms and rhymes so mimic the sense as to suggest he is reliving the experience in the telling:

The Clachan yill had made me canty,
I was na fou, but just had plenty;
I stacher'd whyles, but yet took tent ay [always]
    To free the ditches;
An' hillocks, stanes, an' bushes kenn'd ay [knew]
    Frae ghaists an' witches. (ll. 13–18)

It is a highly paradoxical situation: the narrator's tale involves the reader in the immediacy of the situation, while his attempts to prove that he was not inebriated reveal just how far his perception was compromised by alcohol. What is 'true' about his tale is that he could not distinguish whether the rising moon had three or four horns; that – by his own admission – he had difficulty maintaining a straight course; and that he encountered 'Something' which induced a fear of the other-worldly. Our narrator is being affectionately ironised: his tale is 'true' to his intentions, but it reveals more than he realises – the profounder truth that Burns is communicating, namely that 'truth' is subjective, relative to the individual's perceptions. Thus the narrator tries to come to terms with the unknown by means of the known: the creature's 'stature seem'd lang Scotch ells twa' (l. 37) and its shanks 'were as thin, as sharp an' sma'/ As cheeks o' branks' [bridles] (ll. 41–2). Again assessing purely in terms of his own experience, the sociable peasant-farmer, seeing Death's scythe, asks why he has been mowing in the sowing season. Through the use of the narrator's perspective Death is familiarised. Rendered redundant by the incompetent amateur apothecary, Hornbook, Death needs a sympathetic ear which, in the bargain struck between them, the narrator provides. In the ensuing dialogue the predominant voice, as vernacular and colloquial as the narrator's, is that of Death, who thereafter serves as Burns's agent. The irony of Death serving the needs of the poet is a most telling one. His catalogue of Hornbook's remedies – close to mock-heroic – enables Burns in Sternean fashion to target the pretensions of supposedly learned professions. Now leading the narrative on Burns's behalf, Death cites examples of those who have met their deaths at the hands of Hornbook who has been enlisted by their devious relatives for that very purpose. The point of demystifying Death now becomes fully apparent: for Burns what truly warrants fear is not the allegedly supernatural but the incompetence and malice of human beings.

Themes broached in 'Death and Doctor Hornbook' are subject to more searching investigation by the mature poetic intelligence that created 'Tam o' Shanter' (K 321). The poem's sub-title, 'A Tale', is deceptively simple, and deliberately so. The narrator tells his tale of Tam; sublimely detached, Burns thereby tells a subtle tale of the relationships between truth and fiction. No mean rhetorician himself, the narrator and his tale are subsumed within the larger rhetorical schema of the poet.

Title, sub-title and epigraph indicate the presence of the poet prior to his narrator's account, rooted as it is in traditions oral and oratorical; in effect, the written word is prelude to the allegedly spoken. The epigraph, 'Of Brownyis and of Bogillis full is this buke', line 18 of the 'Proloug' to Book 6 of Gavin Douglas, *Eneados*, immediately raises the issue of the relationships between epigraph and tale and serves at the outset to differentiate naïve and sophisticated readers. Burns had already experimented with such framing devices in 'The Holy Fair' and 'Hallowe'en'.

That Burns turns to Gavin Douglas for his epigraph is no accident. Plainly he is paying homage to the great makar as a major source of inspiration; but he is also locating himself and his poem within the rhetorical tradition of poetry that Douglas so brilliantly exemplified. 'Tam o' Shanter' can be seen as the product of a series of creative conversations among poets that transcend nationalities and centuries and have their common roots in rhetoric. In responding to the request from Augustus Caesar for a national epic, Virgil offered in the *Aeneid* what was equally a response to Homer. *Eneados* reveals Douglas in a highly productive dialogue with Virgil; and in reading it Burns is prompted to enter the debate with his three great predecessors.[10]

As Theo van Heijnsbergen has observed: '[A]uthors write new stories by finding gaps and openings in the "authorities",'[11] a point well substantiated by Henryson's 'The Testament of Cresseid' and his challenge, 'Quha wait gif all that Chaucer wrait wes trew?' Burns's attitude to literary authority is comparably ambivalent: reverence still permits of innovation. As Burns fills gaps in the inherited story of the human's encounter with the other-worldly, so too, because of Burns's choice of narrator, the reader becomes involved in speculating about amplification of the narrator's account. In effect, we now have three narratives: the narrator's, Burns's, and the reader's; all of which resonate with the poem's recurrent motif of perspective.

With his remarkable capacity for absorption, Burns learnt much from Douglas. *Eneados* demonstrated how the expressive resources of vernacular Scots might be exploited for maximum effect. The greatest Scottish writers are never happy to leave things alone, to defer absolutely to the conventions of the material they inherit; of this *Eneados* offered a formidable example. Douglas is much more than a translator of Virgil: with the addition of a prologue to each book *Eneados* invites the reader to see patterns of comparison and contrast between prologue and book, and prologue and prologue. The effect is to highlight the importance of perspective and the fluctuations thereof. Ian S. Ross has argued convincingly for 'the aesthetic principle that prologues and translated books are part of a unified long poem',[12] and he draws analogies with the work of Ezra Pound (who so admired *Eneados*) and other Modernist masters of the long narrative poem. It is a similar coherent unity of the poem's diverse constituent parts that Burns achieves in 'Tam o' Shanter'.

In *Eneados* Burns encountered abundant evidence of the rhetorical subtlety, the craftiness of the craft of poetry. In lines 11–12 of the 'Proloug' to Book 1, he would read this tribute to Virgil: 'I meyn thy crafty warkis curyus, / Sa quyk, lusty, and maist sentencyus.' In the lines that follow (ll. 19–36) Douglas demonstrates his skill in rhetoric by apparently demeaning it; that is, he makes extended use of the modesty topos. Reverting to praise of Virgil, he describes him as 'So inventive of rethorik flowris sweit' (l. 70). When he turns to address the reader Douglas's narrator subtly implies that his work is subtle with the injunction, 'Consider it warly, reid oftar than anys; / Weill at a blenk sle poetry nocht tayn is' (ll. 107–8). It is in precisely this tradition of 'sle poetry' that Burns wishes 'Tam o' Shanter' to be located.

Nothing substantiates this claim better than Burns's use of his narrator. Conveniently for the poet, his narrator likes the sound of his own voice and relishes having an audience; and he proves to be a skilled raconteur, a pub-philosopher confident of his understanding of human nature. Enjoying post-market conviviality, he assures us, 'We think na on the lang Scots miles' (l. 7) and equally ignore the reckoning to be paid, the return to

> our sulky sullen dame,
> Gathering her brows like gathering storm,
> Nursing her wrath to keep it warm. (ll. 10–12)

Adept in the use of simile and metaphor (as in the course of the poem he will demonstrate familiarity with apostrophe, periphrasis, digression, opposition, amplification and abbreviation), he also offers echoes of Odysseus's wanderings and his eventual return to Penelope. This is an educated narrator very much in control of his material: from the general 'truth' he moves to the specific example of Tam, thereby establishing a pattern that recurs throughout the poem – the alternation between incident and commentary, between specific example and generalised observation.

The narrator also proves an accomplished ironist: his tongue is firmly in his cheek as he expresses concern for Tam: 'O Tam! hadst thou but been sae wise, / As ta'en thy ain wife *Kate's* advice!' (ll. 17–18). If Tam had, the narrator would have had no tale to tell. After reproducing Kate's reproaches with the cumulatively expressive interplay of the lines beginning 'That [. . .] That [. . .] Thou [. . .]', he then reverts to feigned concern, this time for the female sex in general:

> Ah, gentle dames! it gars me greet,
> To think how mony counsels sweet,
> How mony lengthen'd sage advices,
> The husband frae the wife despises. (ll. 33–6)

Since this is so obviously at odds with his boozy fraternising the reader is increasingly alerted to the fact that our pub-philosopher may not mean everything he says; 'sweet' and 'sage' are somewhat qualified by the term 'lengthen'd'. As well as playing to his listeners, the narrator plays with them, drawing them within the compass of his irony. In a version of the rhetorical device of *correctio* he exclaims, 'But to our tale' (l. 37),[13] thereby implicating the listener in the delay in getting started, when in reality his lengthy scene-setting has been invaluable to him in rooting in the real world his subsequent tale of the encounter with the supernatural. But it is also 'our' tale in that growing suspicion of the narrator's reliability involves the reader in interrogation of what he says, and, hence, dialogue with the text.

The narrator proves expert at the structuring of his material and the modulation of language, syntax and tone (*divisio* in classical rhetoric). 'Tam o' Shanter' is a poem of various movements, the first of which culminates in personified Care, a would-be intruder from the realms of neoclassicism, acknowledging his failure to spoil the conviviality so vividly conveyed by drowning himself 'amang the nappy' [ale] (l. 54). This section ends with the narrator rendering Tam's experience and perspective: with enough ale and good company he is 'glorious, / O'er a' the ills o' life victorious!' (ll. 57–8).

In an echo of the fluctuation in language levels in both the *Aeneid* and *Eneados*, language, pace and tone then change dramatically with the series of images of transience, commencing 'But pleasures are like poppies spread' (l. 59). The shift to middle high style conveys a stark reminder of the essential flux of all created life, and the reader is thereby advised against over-indulgence (as typified by Tam) or fixity of perspective; even truth itself is subject to flux and relative to the moment. Gerard Carruthers has rightly observed, 'The fragility of the moment or the basic unit of truth is precisely what is at issue throughout Burns's poem'.[14] From the generalisation, 'Nae man can tether time or tide' (l. 67), the narrator turns to focus once again on Tam who must set his journey in motion on a tempestuous night, redolent of the storms in both the *Odyssey* and the *Aeneid*, on which 'ne'er poor sinner was abroad in' (l. 72). Narrative tension is created subtly by the claim that even 'a child might understand, / The Deil had business on his hand' (ll. 77–8). Appropriately, in yet another change of focus, the narrative homes in on Tam, singing to keep his spirits up but aware of the risk of being caught by 'bogles' (l. 86).

The verve of the language and the momentum of the syntax carry the reader along with Tam on his journey, with the narrator acting as guide to the local landmarks, detailed in the lines 'By this time he was cross the ford ... Whare *Mungo's* mither hang'd hersel' (ll. 89 and 96). After this litany of horrors and another reminder of the violence of nature as backcloth ('Before him *Doon* pours all his floods ... Near and more near the thunders roll' (ll. 97 and 100)), all of which is tension-raising, the narrative takes yet another unexpected turn: outdoing nature's 'lightnings' (l. 99) is the radiance emanating from the allegedly haunted Kirk-Alloway which resounds with 'mirth and dancing' (l. 104). Having skilfully created a level of expectation, the narrator pauses to share once again his worldly wisdom in an apostrophe to whisky on account of its fortifying effects. Again there is a strong pause after 'And, wow! *Tam* saw an unco sight!' (l. 114), giving the reader time to speculate as to what it was, before the narrator describes the second of the evening's parties, that of the Devil and his witches who are celebrating their triumphs and displaying their trophies, these being rendered in a mock-epic catalogue.

Exemplifying the refusal topos, the narrator then declines to do what he then proceeds to do: unlawful though it would be to name the ultimate in atrocities, he then lists them:

Three lawyers' tongues, turned inside out,
Wi' lies seamed like a beggar's clout;

Three Priests' hearts, rotten, black as muck,
Lay stinking, vile, in every neuk. [additional lines in the manuscript printed in
    K after l. 142]

The corruption of these professions far exceeds the enormity of the achievements of the Devil and his cohorts. Responsive to the comment of Alexander Fraser Tytler (1747–1813) that these lines 'derive all their merit from the satire they contain, [hence] are here rather misplaced among the circumstances of pure horror',[15] Burns omitted them from the edition of 1793. Objection to a shift of perspective from Tam's viewpoint to the narrator's at this point is without substance: the whole narrative has been characterised by just such fluctuation; and, from his compliment to the town of Ayr onwards, the narrator has never been slow to interpose his own views into the narrative. Tytler's criticism would only hold good if the narrator and the poet are one and the same, an identification which I would refute.

Yet another change of focus, pace and tone directs the reader firstly to Tam, the fascinated voyeur, and then to the dance of the witches with the Devil providing the music. The momentum of these lines creates a measure of suspense: how, one wonders, will Tam respond? True to form, the narrator halts his account to boast to Tam, man to man, of what his reaction would have been had the witches been 'queans, / A' plump and strapping in their teens' (ll. 151–2). By pausing to flaunt both his machismo and his authority over his narrative, however, he has tripped himself up, revealing his fallibility. In an ironic juxtaposition of perspectives it is Tam who proves to be more observant than our narrator, as the latter, to his credit, acknowledges: 'But *Tam* kend what was what fu' brawlie, / There was ae winsome wench and wawlie [ample]' (ll. 163–4). In yet another delaying tactic the narrator, having cited her attractiveness, delays elaborating until he has given details of her subsequent career. With such whimsicality the narrator deliberately tries the patience of his audience. Then, with the narrative focus restored to the immediate present, he observes the shortness of the young witch's smock and her pride in flaunting her physique. This prompts him to pause yet again, this time to address Cutty Sark herself. Virtually reliving the episode, the narrator has once more to change tack (another instance of the *correctio* topos): 'But here my Muse her wing maun cour; / Sic flights are far beyond her pow'r' (ll. 179–80). Once again the joke is on him, however, as he has already conveyed the sexual excitement which the young witch's dance has prompted. Unwittingly he has thereby aligned himself with Tam. In what is the real climax of the tale Tam, so aroused by Cutty Sark, allows natural instinct to triumph over reason, thereby alerting the witches to his presence and threatening his survival. Ironically, however, his excited cry directs the ongoing course of the narrative. Undaunted by this qualification of his authority, the narrator chooses to preface his account of the outcome with a multiple, or epic, simile commencing 'As bees bizz out wi' angry fyke' [fuss] (l. 193). The situation is acutely paradoxical: the momentum of the narrative is checked and, courtesy of the analogies which the narrator is intent on drawing (they reflect his learning), the reader confronts extreme velocity in slow motion.

Every time the narrator exerts his authority over his tale Burns ensures that it is undermined with subversive details or circumstances. The irrepressible puppet-master is blissfully unaware of his subjection to the supreme authority of his creator. His apostrophe to Tam, 'Ah, *Tam*! Ah, *Tam*! Thou'll get thy fairin! [present from a fair] / In hell they'll roast thee like a herrin!' (ll. 201–2), suggests that, engaging with the immediate present of his account, he has so empathised with Tam as to suggest an alternative outcome to the one which he then proceeds to record. Truth is, in effect, sacrificed in the interests of the raconteur's creation of the illusion of spontaneity: witness his exhorting Meg, 'do thy speedy utmost' (l. 205), apparently raising the possibility that a horse may shape the conclusion of his tale. With women (Kate, Kirkton Jean, Cutty Sark) so central to Tam's experience, it is supremely ironic that his fate should reside in the haunches of a mare. True to the 'wild ride' encounter with the supernatural, there is visible proof in the severed tail of Maggie.

Given that the poem concerns a journey and that its telling is characterised by fluctuations in pace and perspective, what are we to make of the concluding six lines, exuding fixity and finality and advising moderation? It may be that our narrator, as widely read as he is worldly wise, concludes with a *moralitas* in order to give his tale authoritative status by adhering to convention. While the Christian *moralitas* authorises and brings closure, Henryson's fables are characterised by a *moralitas* in which the narrator offers analysis of what precedes. As Robert L. Kindrick has noted, 'Henryson found the *moralitas* to be a valuable rhetorical tool and wrestled with concerns about apparent discrepancies between the story and the moral interpretation'.[16] Indeed, in Henryson's *Morall Fabillis* the *moralitas* is sometimes manifestly at odds with what the narrative has been saying.

In 'Tam o' Shanter' Burns complicates this relationship further. In telling his tale the narrator has aligned himself with Tam on the side of natural instinct, while his conclusion stresses the moral and practical value of self-restraint; there is manifestly a discrepancy between the logic that the poem constructs and the import of the *moralitas*. This is quite deliberate on Burns's part. The *moralitas* provides the ultimate demonstration of the fact that the narrator's tale is in dialogic relationship with Burns's poem; that is, the poet's implicit *moralitas* differs markedly from that of his narrator. From a poem pervaded by motion and temporality the inevitable outcome is confrontation of the impossibility of fixing Truth. Thus the effect of the narrator's *moralitas* is, ironically, to ensure that the poem is open-ended; Maggie's tail may be cut short, not so Burns's tale. The ultimate irony is that, with his attempt to bring closure, the narrator finally and unwittingly liberates the reader from the authority he has so exploited. While the narrator has employed rhetoric to foster belief, the poet's rhetoric has quite the opposite effect, encouraging possible ways of seeing rather than certainties. Since the motif of looking pervades the poem it is both logical and highly appropriate that the reader is left celebrating and exemplifying the essential relativity and subjectivity of perspective.

This emphasis on subjectivity supports a case for locating Burns in the vibrant cultural climate of Scotland in the second half of the eighteenth century. The investigation of identity is integral to the work of the Scottish philosophers; simultaneously novelists such as Smollett, principally in *Humphry Clinker* (1771), and Mackenzie in *The Man of Feeling* (1771) and *Julia de Roubigné* (1777) (and followed later by Galt, Hogg and the Scott of *Redgauntlet*), forge narrative forms expressive of the subjectivity of perspective; and, concurrently, the great Scottish portraitists such as Raeburn and Allan Ramsay the younger, achieve the objectifying of their subjects on canvas. That said, Burns must not be severed from the tradition handed down from the makars who, argues van Heijnsbergen, 'pave the way for empiricist notions of perception in poetry'.[17] They require that the reader experience, not merely read, the text. Lurking spectre-like behind Burns's most subtle of 'sle' poems are Douglas and Henryson, whose 'Proloug' to his *Morall Fabillis* reminds the reader that 'feinyeit fabils of ald poetre / Be not al grunded vpon truth'.

CHAPTER FOUR

Burns and the Poetics of Abolition
Nigel Leask

The bicentenary of the abolition of the Atlantic slave trade in 2007 rekindled interest in Burns's personal involvements in and attitude to slavery, a question which has been long smothered by what Murray Pittock has termed the 'celebratory anaphora' marking Scottish attitudes to the national poet and his works.[1] There is always a danger, however, given the scanty evidence available concerning Burns and slavery, of resorting either to postcolonial blame, or else special pleading, based largely on speculation as to 'what would have happened' had Burns travelled to Jamaica in 1786 to work as 'a Negro Driver' as he planned.[2] This chapter discusses Burns's poetic use of the discourse of slavery in the historical context of the abolition movement, before scrutinising one of the few instances in the poet's correspondence that explicitly discusses slavery, with a view to casting some more light on the question.

If one might admire the stirring internationalism of Burns's democratic hymn 'Is There for Honest Poverty' (K 482), the sentiments of the opening stanza present, perhaps, something of a problem. Here is the opening stanza, based on the text as it appeared in a letter from Burns to George Thomson (1757–1851) dated January 1795:

> Is there, for honest Poverty
> That hings his head, and a' that;
> The coward-slave, we pass him by,
> We dare be poor for a' that!
> For a' that, and a' that,
> Our toils obscure and a' that,
> The rank is but the guinea's stamp,
> The Man's the gowd for a' that. (ll. 1–8)

Despite the odd syntax of the opening line, Burns's song begins in a spirit of proud defiance, distinguishing (a personified) 'honest poverty' that 'dares be poor' from the obsequious 'coward-slave' who 'hings his head' in silent acceptance of oppression. To contrast the 'free-born Briton's' independent rights with the 'slave' of French or Spanish absolutism was of course a commonplace of eighteenth-century patriot discourse, most famously in Thomson and Mallett's stirring anthem from *Alfred*, 'Rule Britannia, Britannia rules the waves, Britons never will be slaves.' Burns's 'Honest Poverty' redeploys a rhetoric of servitude evident elsewhere in his writings. He most often uses the term 'slave' to describe a negative relationship of feudal dependence, as in lines 65–8 of 'Man was Made to Mourn, A Dirge' (*K* 64):

> If I'm design'd yon lordling's slave,
> By Nature's law design'd,
> Why was an independent wish
> E'er planted in my mind?

The existence of reason ('an independent wish') in the human mind differentiates man from the bestial condition, in this case providing an irrefutable proof that slavery is contrary to 'Nature's law'. Burns's development of this idea a decade later in 'Honest Poverty' is to suggest that those who accept their subordination to 'yon lordling' without 'daring to be poor' somehow deserve their fate, in contrast to the poor 'man of independent mind, / [Who] looks and laughs at a' that' (ll. 23–4).[3] Similarly, the use of the word 'coward' in 'coward slave' resonates with other usages in the Burns corpus: the 'coward few' who have sold their country's liberty for 'hireling traitor's wages' (l. 12) in signing the 1707 Treaty of Union in 'Such a Parcel of Rogues' (*K* 375), or 'May coward shame distain his name, / The wretch that dares not die' (ll. 23–4) in 'McPherson's Farewell' (*K* 196). Notably none of these usages have any reference to West Indian chattel slavery as it was being debated in the final decades of the eighteenth century: whatever Burns's own view of the matter, it is certainly not the case that the epithet 'coward slave' was applicable to Caribbean chattel slaves, whose brave and unremitting resistance to their European masters eventually contributed in large part to their emancipation, albeit at a most appalling cost of human suffering.

Although 'For a' That' was originally a bawdy song, the most direct source of Burns's 'Honest Poverty' is a Jacobite parody 'Tho' Geordie reigns in Jamie's Stead', described by Tom Crawford as 'one of the best of all Scottish political songs':[4]

> Tho' Geordie reigns in Jamie's Stead,
> I'm grieved yet scorn to shaw that,
> I'll ne'er look down nor hang my Head
> On rebel Whig for a' that;
>
> For still I trust that Providence
> Will us relieve from a' that,

Our Royal Prince is weal in Health,
And will be here for a' that.

As Murray Pittock notes, the '"He's coming yet for a' that" in Burns's reworking becomes an "*Its* coming yet", promising universal brotherhood rather than the restoration of kingly justice [. . .] Jacobite language is made a contemporary vehicle for radical value.'[5]

These examples suffice to show that the use of the term 'slave' in what I'll call a 'transferential' sense (that is, not literally denoting African chattel slavery)[6] is commonplace in eighteenth-century political discourse, providing an obvious rhetorical resource for Burns's political song. I want to propose here that the phrase had assumed a more literal and problematic significance in late 1794–5 when Burns wrote 'Honest Poverty'; following closely in the wake of the Scottish sedition trials, certainly, but also the first, abortive wave of the movement for the abolition of the slave trade.[7] One support for this hypothesis lies in the fact that the anonymous version of Burns's song published in the periodical and newspaper press (starting with the radical *Glasgow Magazine* in August 1795) omitted the first stanza beginning 'Is there for honest Poverty', opening instead with the lines 'What tho' on hamely fare we dine, / Wear hodden grey, and a' that'.[8] The seditious nature of Burns's song in the political climate of 1795 was camouflaged by nearly everything else published in the *Glasgow Magazine*; a serialised biography of Thomas Muir of Huntershill, recently transported to Botany Bay for sedition; anti-monarchical selections from George Buchanan's *Dialogue on the Constitution of Scotland* translated by 'Agrestis' (probably James Thomson Callander); and poetry of a distinctively republican stamp by Sir William Jones, Edward Williams and Dr John Aikin. The short-lived magazine was also committed to the cause of abolishing slavery, as is evident in articles in the August and September issues, and this may well have led the editors to omit the first stanza of Burns's 'Honest Poverty'. Did newspaper editors with an abolitionist agenda (self-exempted from copyright laws, they frequently took considerable licences with the texts they reprinted) deliberately omit the 'coward slave' stanza because it was offensive to the humanitarian sensibilities of their readers in 1795–6?

Scotland and Abolition

Although much has been written about the Jacobinism of 'Honest Poverty', it is perhaps not surprising that it has never been connected with abolitionism, the other popular humanitarian movement of the revolutionary decade. The long silence surrounding Scottish attitudes to both slavery and abolition has been broken by the work of historian C. Duncan Rice, and more recently, Iain Whyte and Colin Kidd, so that we are now in a better position to understand the movement's importance, both in its early abolitionist (1787–1807), and later emancipationist (1807–38) phases.[9] Despite Scotland's disproportionate role in the Atlantic slave economy, and the wealth which flooded into Glasgow and the country as a whole from the Virginia and Caribbean trade,[10] her civil and ecclesiastical institutions nobly rallied to the cause. Many of Burns's associates and patrons were keen abolitionists; Rev. William Greenfield (d. 1827) of Edinburgh was one of Scotland's leading petitioners, and William Creech (1745–1815), Hugh Blair (1718–1800), Henry Mackenzie (1745–1831), and Dr Blacklock (1721–91) were all active in the cause. The involvement of both the evangelical Rev. John Russell (1740–1817) and the moderate Rev. William Dalrymple (1723–1814) of Ayr (both mentioned in the 'Kirk Satires') reveals the extent to which abolitionism bridged the theological gulf dividing the Church of Scotland in the later decades of the eighteenth century. In Scotland, as in the rest of Britain, the mass petitioning movement enjoyed considerable success: in 1788 Wilberforce and Pitt instigated a Commons inquiry into the slave trade, and Sir William Dolben, MP for Oxford, brought in a bill to regulate conditions on slave ships, which became law in 1791.[11]

The abolitionists mobilised the full rhetoric of sensibility to encourage sympathy with the African victims of oppression. In October 1787 the society adopted a seal designed by Wedgwood showing 'An African [. . .] in chains in a supplicating position, kneeling with one knee upon the ground, and with both hands lifted up to Heaven, and round the seal [. . .] the following motto [. . .] "Am I not a Man and a Brother?". Wedgwood turned off these seals by the thousands, and it became fashionable to wear them as pins in the hair or clothing.'[12] Women were particularly well represented at national level; in 1787 at least eighty-five women subscribed to the Abolition Society.[13] Women novelists, poets and hymn-writers dedicated the superior sensibility and benevolence conventionally associated with the 'gentle sex' to the cause of abolition. Hannah More's *Slavery, a Poem*, Helen Maria Williams's *Poem on the Bill Lately Passed for Regulating the Slave Trade*, and the 'Bristol Milkmaid', Ann Yearsley's *Poem on the Inhumanity of the Slave Trade*, all three long verse diatribes against the trade, were published in 1788, in support of Dolben's Bill.[14]

In many cases, enthusiasm for abolition was combined with a more radical demand for the emancipation of African slaves. This proved a hostage to fortune after the outbreak of the French Revolution, and especially the St Domingue revolt in 1791. The association between anti-slavery activism, revolution politics and violent insurrection severely compromised the success of Wilberforce's parliamentary motion for abolition in 1792. It was 'severely trimmed through an amendment from Government's leading Scottish member, Henry Dundas, who proposed simply that "the slave trade ought to be gradually abolished"'.[15] In the 1790s Tory abolitionists had to work hard

Robert Burns, Helen Maria Williams and Slavery

Robert Burns's attitude to slavery is compromised by the fact that in 1786, having failed economically as an Ayrshire tenant farmer, and legally pursued by the father of Jean Armour (whom he had recently made pregnant), he sought employment as a 'book keeper' or 'Negro driver' on the plantation of Dr Patrick Douglas at Port Antonio in north-east Jamaica. Burns stated in his autobiographical letter of 2 August 1787 to Dr John Moore that publication of his 'Kilmarnock' poems raised the 'nine guineas' fare necessary to pay his passage to Jamaica, thereby saving him from the fate of being obliged to indenture himself to the plantation owner. ''Twas a delicious idea that I would be called a clever fellow' on account of the volume of poems, he wrote, 'even though it should never reach my ears a poor Negro-driver, or perhaps a victim to that inhospitable clime gone to the world of Spirits' (*L* I, p. 144). But an admiring letter from the blind poet Dr Blacklock encouraged him to publish a second edition of his poems and, 'rousing [his] poetic ambition', led to the abandonment of the Jamaica scheme in favour of a trip to Edinburgh (*L* I, p. 145). Notable here is the fact that the sympathy solicited by Burns is for the health-risk run by the 'poor Negro driver' rather than for his slaves. By the same token, we look in vain for any glimmer of ethical doubt concerning slavery in Burns's valedictory poem 'On a Scotch Bard Gone to the West Indies' (*K* 100) published in 1786 in the 'Kilmarnock' volume.

Like many other Scots of his station, Burns might have protested that he 'couldn't afford to keep a conscience' regarding slavery. The standard get-out clause for Burns as aspiring 'Negro driver' is the beautiful song 'The Slave's Lament' (*K* 378) published in the *Scots Musical Museum* in 1792 at the height of the second petitioning campaign. Anecdotally linked to Burns's sentiments on seeing a slave ship during his visit to Dundee in 1787, the song's titular 'slave' recalls an arcadian existence in 'Sweet Senegal', before being trepanned by slavers and carried to the snow and frost of Virginia:

> This burden I must bear, while the cruel scourge I fear,
> In the lands of Virginia-ginia O;
> And I think on friends most dear, with the bitter, bitter tear,
> And Alas! I am weary, weary O! (ll. 9–12)[16]

Unfortunately there is no sure evidence that the song was written, rather than collected, by Burns. Kinsley states that 'Burns' part in this song is uncertain' (*K*, p. 1405) and even if it can be attributed, as Gerry Carruthers has recently argued, '[T]his solitary item serves only to highlight how little interest [Burns] took in the pro-abolitionist cause, unlike many other Whigs of radical bent during the period.'[17]

Rather more convincing evidence of Burns's abolitionist sympathies is contained in a letter of July or August 1789 (*L* I, pp. 428–31) to Helen Maria Williams (1762–1827), commenting on her poem of the preceding year *Poem on the Bill Lately Passed for Regulating the Slave Trade*.[18] I will speculate that Williams's poem, and Burns's response to it, offer both a context and a source for the song 'Honest Poverty'. I will focus on a number of allusions which seem to connect the poem and the song, although without claiming to throw much new light on Burns's attitude to slavery, other to confirm that he disapproved of it, albeit in rather vaguely-stated terms. Burns was put in touch with the London-based poet Helen Maria Williams by Dr John Moore, a relative of his Ayrshire patroness Mrs Frances Dunlop. Moore knew Williams through the London Presbyterian and Dissenting literary network in which both played an active part as émigré Scots. Williams's mother hailed from Kilmeny in Fife; she had raised her children in Berwick-on-Tweed after her husband's early death in 1762, before moving to London in 1781, where Helen quickly made a name for herself as a poet and a literary barometer of socially-concerned sensibility. An enthusiast for the French Revolution, she moved to France in 1791 and adopted French citizenship, making her name in the following decade with her popular and partisan chronicle *Letters from France*, her 1797 *Travels in Switzerland*, and a translation of *Paul and Virginia*. Her poetic prominence in the 1780s is evident from the title of William Wordsworth's first published poem 'A Sonnet on Seeing Miss Helen Maria Williams Weep at a Tale of Distress'. But like Burns, Helen Williams's sympathy for the French Revolution would earn her notoriety in polite society in the following decade; James Boswell struck out the epithet 'amiable' from his account of Williams in the second edition of the *Life of Johnson*, and her former acquaintance Hester Piozzi dismissed her in 1798 as 'a wicked little democrat'.[19]

Certainly by 1788 Williams was steeped in Burns's poetry, and after that date Burns was equally well acquainted with hers. In June, Williams wrote to Burns exclaiming that she had fully felt 'the power of your genius':

> I believe no one has yet read oftener than myself your Vision, your Cotter's Evening, the Address to the Mouse, and many of your other poems. My mother's family is Scotch, and the dialect has been familiar to me from my infancy: I was, therefore, qualified to taste the charm of your native poetry, and, as I feel the strongest attachment for Scotland, I share the triumph of your country in producing your laurels.'[20]

In her 'Sonnet on Reading Burns' Mountain Daisy' published in the 1791 second edition of her *Poems*, Williams described the Ayrshire poet as 'nursed "By Genius in her native vigour"'.[21] Williams seems to have been encouraged to write her *Poem on the Bill Lately Passed for Regulating the Slave Trade* by her mentor Rev. Andrew Kippis, who had been elected to the London Committee of the Abolition Society in April 1788.[22] Williams sent a copy of her 364-line poem in tetrameter couplets to Robert Burns, who, unusually, responded with a lengthy and appreciative critique in a letter dated July or early August 1789. 'I know very little of scientific criticism,' he pleaded, 'so all I can pretend to in that intricate art is merely to note as I read along, what passages strike me as being uncommonly beautiful, & where the expression seems to me perplexed or faulty' (*L* I, p. 428).

Although Wylie Sypher is dismissive of Williams for 'smothering her poem in epithet and exclamation',[23] judged by the poetic standards of its age, *The Slave Trade* makes its case with considerable rhetorical power and moral persuasion. After an opening glance at the horrors of the Middle Passage, Williams praised Prime Minister Pitt and the Duke of Richmond for their support of Dolben's Bill, and saluted British legislators for being the 'first of Europe's polished lands, / To ease the Captive's iron bands' (ll. 36–7). Williams hoped that Dolben's Bill would prove the beginning of a process leading inexorably beyond abolition towards emancipation (ll. 151–4) and concluded with a wish that a combination of poetic persuasion and political eloquence would change public opinion and shift international policy in the direction of abolition. In a closing apostrophe to 'Loved Britain', she wished that parliamentarians would be 'Touched by a spark of generous flame' (l. 358), in order to 'teach [other countries] to make all Nature free, / And shine by emulating thee!' (ll. 363–4).

One passage in particular seems to contain an allusion to the case of Burns. At line 231, Williams exonerates the 'generous sailor' who 'dares / All forms of danger, while he bears / The British flag o'er untracked seas'. It is to the 'protecting arm' of the British mariner that we owe the accomplishments of civil society:

> Each cultured grace, each finer art,
> E'en thine, most lovely of the train!
> Sweet Poetry! thy heaven-taught strain –
> *His* breast, where nobler passions *burn*,
> In honest poverty would spurn
> The wealth, Oppression can bestow,
> And scorn to wound a fettered foe.
> True courage in the unconquered soul
> Yields to Compassion's mild control;
> As, the resisting frame of steel
> The magnet's secret force can feel. (ll. 240–51)

One might assume on first reading this passage that the subject of the italicised *His* was the 'generous sailor' evoked in the previous lines, whose protective valour enabled the arts, and poetry in particular, to flourish in Britain, and whose 'honest poverty' led him to refuse to serve in the slave trade. Upon closer scrutiny, however, the lines seem to refer to a *poet* rather than sailor, and, as the italicised pronoun suggests, *one* poet in particular. Henry Mackenzie's epithet for Burns as a 'heaven-taught ploughman' in his 1786 *Lounger* review of the 'Kilmarnock' volume quickly became famous. Williams's phrase 'honest poverty' here probably alludes specifically to line 166 of 'The Cotter's Saturday Night', one of her favourite poems by Burns, although it is noteworthy that the phrase 'honest poverty' doesn't itself appear in Burns's poetry until the 1795 song.[24] If one reads the last word of Williams's line 242 '*His* breast, where nobler passions *burn*' as a pun on the name 'Burns', it seems even more probable that Williams intended a veiled allusion to the Ayrshire poet.

If this is indeed the case, then Williams appears to be referring to Burns's autobiographical account of his own near-employment as a 'Negro driver', as related in the 1787 autobiographical letter to Dr Moore (1729–1802). Writing in the knowledge that Williams would read the letter aloud to Dr Moore, who was currently suffering from an eye complaint, Burns feared that her reading of his candid confessions might undermine her admiration for his poetry; 'then goodnight to that esteem with which she was pleased to honour the Scotch Bard' (*L* I, p. 134). Williams's poem responds by allaying this anxiety, as well as by commenting on Burns's account of the Jamaica affair. In fact she appears to have misread the letter in a manner that sentimentalised Burns's real motives for abandoning the voyage to Jamaica. Like the 'generous sailor', Williams insinuates, Burns as 'heaven-taught' genius courageously preferred 'honest poverty' (in his case as a poet) to complicity in the cowardly mistreatment of fettered African slaves. In fact in the letter Burns had clearly stated that 'poetic ambition' rather than any ethical scruple determined his abandonment of the Jamaica scheme, but Williams prefers to suggest that 'True courage in the unconquered soul / Yields to Compassion's mild control' (ll. 247–8). If the interpretation proffered here is correct, one can understand why Williams was so anxious to send her poem to Burns in order to underline her compliment.

Against the above hypothesis is the fact that Burns himself read and commented on the poem in some detail without apparently picking up on Williams's veiled allusion. This is a problem. However, a rather strange tone of dissimulation runs through Burns's letter to Williams; 'I want to shew you,' he wrote, 'that I have honesty enough to tell you what I take to be truths, even when they are not quite on the side of approbation' (again playing on that word 'honesty') (*L* I, p. 428). One positive fact to emerge from this letter is that Burns was largely in agreement with Williams's abolitionist sentiments.

For instance he refers to 'the unfeeling selfishness of the Oppressor [. . .] the misery of the captive', and to 'the wrongs of the poor African'. Most interestingly, he takes issue with Williams's praise for the 'generous sailor'; 'The character & manners of the dealer in this infernal traffic is a well done though a horrid picture,' he wrote, ' – I am not sure how far introducing the Sailor, was right; for though the Sailor's common characteristic is generosity, yet in this case his is certainly not only an unconcerned witness but in some degree an efficient agent in the business' (*L* I, pp. 430–1). Burns seems to have opted to take advantage of the ambiguity left open by Williams's verse (that is, the *veiled* nature of her compliment to him) in order to interpret the subject of 'honest poverty' as the 'generous sailor', rather than the 'heaven-taught' poet (in other words, himself). Moreover, there is a hint here that Burns's discomfort with Williams's generous exoneration of the sailor serving in the slave trade (that is, he is *not* an 'unconcerned witness' but rather an 'efficient agent in the business') might actually betray an awkward sense of his own potential complicity in planning to serve as a 'Negro driver'. To be fair (mentioned already), in the letter to Moore, Burns had never actually claimed that in choosing a career as poet over slave driver he'd been motivated by 'honest poverty', or anything other than 'ambition'. But Williams's poem put Burns in an embarrassing position: in the face of her compliment, he could neither offer to correct her sentimentalised notion of his motivation for abandoning his Jamaican scheme, nor openly confess any complicity in 'this infernal traffic'.

'Honest Poverty' and Slavery

In conclusion, let us turn back to Burns's 1795 song 'Is There for Honest Poverty' in the light of its strange echoes of Williams's *Poem . . . on the Slave Trade*. On the face of it, it is not surprising that a song dedicated to the triumph of freedom and equality 'o'er all the earth' should find a useful intertextual resource in a poem applauding the first parliamentary measures to regulate the slave trade. What is rather odd though, considering the abolitionist context, is the first stanza's disdain for the 'coward slave', and its apparently untroubled use of 'slave' in an older, 'transferential' sense; particularly when the phrase 'honest poverty', which arrives here for the first time in Burns's poetry, refers directly back to Helen Williams's well-known poem. But Burns's opening stanza appears to turn against Williams's abolitionist definition of 'honest poverty' by preferring the Jacobinical cause of the British labouring poor to any identification with the plight of the 'coward slave':

Is there, for honest Poverty
That hings his head, and a' that;

> The coward-slave, we pass him by,
> We dare be poor for a' that!
> For a' that, and a' that,
> Our toils obscure and a' that,
> The rank is but the guinea's stamp,
> The Man's the gowd for a' that. (ll. 1–8)

According to Kinsley, Burns's principle source for his superb 'guinea's stamp' metaphor here is Wycherley's play *The Plain Dealer* (1677), which he had ordered from the bookseller Peter Hill in 1790. The source text reads:

> [C]ounterfeit honour will not be current with me: I weigh the man, not his title; 'tis not the king's stamp can make the metal better or heavier. Your lord is a leaden shilling, which you bend every way, and debases the stamp he bears, instead of being raised by it. (*K*, p. 1468)[25]

Burns, however, has here changed 'the king's stamp' of his source to 'guinea's stamp', and Wycherley's 'leaden shilling' to a golden guinea, thereby establishing a new range of meaning that would have stuck out prominently in the abolitionist context of the 1790s. Ostensibly of course Burns means that social rank is no gauge of intrinsic human value. But in 1794 'guinea stamp' had another meaning, namely the branding of slaves from the Guinea Coast of West Africa (British slavery was often known as 'the Guinea Trade' given the importance of the region as a source of slaves). The Scottish mercenary John Stedman described this barbarous process in his *Narrative of a Five Year's Expedition against the Revolted Negroes of Suriman* (1796):

> [T]he new-bought negroes are immediately branded on the breast or the thick part of the shoulder, by a stamp of silver, with the initial letters of the new master's name, as we mark furniture or any thing else to authenticate them properly. These hot letters, which are about the size of a sixpence, occasion not that pain which may be imagined . . .'[26]

In Burns's song, by an inversion of the abolitionist's meaning, aristocratic rank is figured as a kind of stamp by which the 'honest man' (l. 15) is *unmarked*: that is, the latter's human value is intrinsic, not 'stamped' like slaves (literally) or aristocrats (metaphorically).

The term 'stamp' is used with regularity in the contemporary literature of slavery and abolition, most notably in William Blake's contemporaneous *Visions of the Daughters of Albion* (1793). (Blake was a friend of Stedman and illustrated the *Narrative*, although it is almost impossible that Burns would have had access to his poem.) In plate 1 of the *Visions*, the American slave owner Bromian boasts

Thy soft American plains are mine and mine thy north & south:
Stampt with my signet are the swarthy children of the sun.
They are obedient, they resist not, they obey the scourge.[27]

Read in the Abolitionist context, though, even Burns' 'the Man's the gowd for a'that' might appear rather loaded; Guinea was of course long the source of British gold as well as of British slaves, and to liken men to gold was to court the notion of a *commodified* humanity (as well as conjuring up a notion of equal human worth, which is Burns's manifest sense). To quote Helen Williams again:

Chained on the beach the Captive stands,
Where Man, dire merchandise! Is sold,
And bartered life is paid for gold. (ll. 252–4)[28]

It is almost as if Burns's powerful hymn to social equality needed to write over, or (in his own words) 'pass by', the object and rhetoric of abolition, as presented in Williams's *Poem . . . on the Slave Trade*. Is it possible that by 1794–5 he resented the poem's praise for William Pitt and the aristocratic Duke of Richmond, 'who, high in birth, / Adds the unfading rays of worth', both of whom had supported Wilberforce in the House of Lords?[29] Or that, by that time, the excitement generated by the petitioning campaign of 1788 seemed like a false dawn, a lost cause? Nevertheless, Burns's opening line 'Is there for Honest Poverty' openly alludes to line 244 of William's poem, an allusion that would have been picked up by those, particularly in the radical camp, who were familiar with it. Burns perhaps simultaneously needed to disavow *and* acknowledge Williams's abolitionist polemic, reflecting both his own compromised involvement in slavery, and the hi-jacking of abolition by Tory politicians.

The remaining four stanzas do not show anything like the same amount of 'leakage' from the abolition debate, except possibly the final stanza:

Then let us pray that come it may,
As come it will for a' that,
That Sense and Worth o'er all the earth,
Shall bear the gree for a' that.
For a' that and a' that,
Its comin yet for a' that,
That Man to Man the warld o'er,
Shall brothers be for a' that. (ll. 37–40)

This is now such a canonical statement of democratic internationalism (despite its exclusion of sisterhood) that it is easy to overlook the specificity of its language in the political discourse of the 1790s. Kinsley notes that the word 'brothers' in line 40 corrects the term 'equals' in Burns's 1795 manuscript of the song (K II, p. 763). The sentimental language of brotherhood replacing 'equality', the religious effect of 'let us pray' (abolitionists like Wilberforce were more likely to pray for the triumph of their cause than Jacobins and democrats), and the optimistic reference to the triumph of 'sense and worth o'er all the earth', suggest that Burns is after all drawing upon the rhetoric of abolition here, just as much as upon the Paineite or republican notion of fraternity. Above all, the final lines contain an unmistakeable echo of that most successful of campaigning slogans, stamped on Wedgwood's medallion of the supplicant Negro: 'Am I not a Man and a Brother?'

At a subliminal level, then, the song struggles with the polemical agenda of Helen Maria Williams's *Poem [. . .] on the Slave Trade*, and as already suggested, this could be because Burns had a bad conscience about his own near-complicity in slavery as a Jamaican 'Negro driver'. Let us close with the suggestion that it does not necessarily follow from this that Burns's difficult attitude to slavery need qualify his radical credentials in 1795, however much it may qualify our admiration for his ethical outlook in general. If we turn to Book 10 of Wordsworth's 1805 *Prelude*, we find a clear statement of the English poet's failure in 1793 to engage with 'the traffickers in Negro blood' (l. 372), not despite, but on account of, his pro-revolutionary sympathies:

> For me that strife had ne'er
> Fastened on my affections, nor did now
> Its unsuccessful issue much excite
> My sorrow, having laid the faith to heart,
> That if France prospered good men would not long
> Pay fruitless worship to humanity,
> And this most rotten branch of human shame
> (Object, as seemed, of superfluous pains)
> Would fall together with its parent tree.[30]

A more homespun expression of Wordsworth's political reasoning is found in a manuscript poem by the relatively unknown William Campbell of Glasgow, held in the Mitchell Library (and it is noteworthy that the same collection contains Campbell's abolitionist poem 'The Negroes Complaint'). In 'To the People of Scotland', Campbell wrote:

> Strange that the African's complaint we hear
> Yet from our Country's wrongs withhold our Ear
> These Wrongs as much respect at least demand
> As those of Negroes in a foreign land.
> Redress them first and then you may of course

Attack the slave trade with redoubled force
But when a remnant of the feudal Laws
Denies us Juries in a civil Cause . . .
To talk of Liberty that noble word
Of all absurdities is most absurd.[31]

Campbell's verse supports Marcus Wood's contention that '[F]or English [and one might add Scottish] radicals the lesson to be learned was simple: bring the sympathy home, and change its colour.' Wood proposes that '[I]t is a grave mistake to assume that Radicals shared an understanding of the minutiae of abolitionist politics, or that they even had an instinctive sympathy with the physical realities of suffering black slaves.'[32] The case of Burns hardly refutes that troubling suggestion, although it fails to do justice to abolitionist poetry written by radicals like S. T. Coleridge, Robert Southey, William Roscoe, James Currie, Edward Rushton, Alexander Geddes, Anne Yearsley or Robert Anderson. My suggestion that radical Burns (like radical Wordsworth) chose to 'pass by' 'the coward slave' on the grounds that abolition had been co-opted by Tory evangelicals and aristocrats deeply hostile to democracy and French revolutionary politics hardly mitigates his opinion. After all, what had the slaves themselves to do with that co-option, and with what historical justice could their spirited resistance to slavery be described as 'cowardly'? In Burns's favour, in her 1788 *Slavery, A Poem* the Tory evangelical Hannah More had taken pains to distinguish the 'fair Freedom' to whom she appealed in the cause of abolition from *political* libertarianism, which she likened to a beast of burden run out of control. It was a distinction that must have been extremely galling to radicals:

Thee only, sober Goddess! I attest,
In smiles chastised, and decent graces dressed.
Not that unlicensed monster of the crowd,
Whose roar terrific bursts in peals so loud,
Deafening the ear of Peace: fierce Faction's tool;
Of rash Sedition born, and mad Misrule.
Whose stubborn mouth, rejecting Reason's rein,
No strength can govern, and no skill restrain;[33]

By contrast Burns's avatar of freedom is proud of his 'hodden gray', self-governing, and openly committed to the republican project of abolishing a corrupt hierarchy in which 'A king' (later changed to 'a Prince' in deference to the sedition laws)[34] 'can mak a belted knight, / A marquis, duke, and a' that'. Beginning at home, 'sense and worth' will eventually encompass the whole world – including the slave economies – and *in the end* all men will be brothers. 'Is There for Honest Poverty' is a signal instance of the 'transferential' eighteenth-century discourse of slavery becoming entangled with a newer abolitionist sense of the term which had emerged in the late 1780s. It is the power of Burns's song, with its characteristic depth of allusion, to capture the ideological tensions afflicting and dividing rival political and humanitarian agendas in the 1790s. The reading in this chapter should confirm that 'Honest Poverty' is much more than 'two or three pretty good *prose* thoughts, inverted into rhyme', as Burns modestly described it in his 1795 letter to Thomson (*L* II, p. 336).[35]

CHAPTER FIVE

Burns and Politics

Colin Kidd

The question of Burns's politics is a vexed one, which Burns's standing as Scotland's national bard has tended rather to obfuscate than to resolve. Over the past two centuries Scots of all political stripes have attempted to appropriate Burns for their pet causes. These ventures have, by and large, remained faithful to the poet's life and work, for there is plausible material enough in Burns's poetry and his letters to present him as, variously, a democrat, a republican, a revolutionary, a socialist *avant la lettre*, a fervent Scottish nationalist, a loyal – if cheekily irreverent – Briton and an internationalist champion of the brotherhood of man.[1] On the other hand, from the early nineteenth century, when, in the wake of the French Revolution, there were worries about the poet's reputation, some of the bard's devotees may have deliberately tried to draw what seemed the controversially radical sting from the poet's politics.[2] As a result, Burns has been successfully portrayed to the world as an apolitical poet of conviviality, carnality and the unchanging rhythms of the natural world. Certainly, the depoliticised Burns of most Burns Suppers is celebrated as the poetic voice of an undiscriminating male boon companionship.

Many scrupulous literary scholars have been rightly dissatisfied with broad-brush and anachronistic generalisations about Burns's beliefs and have attempted to anchor their readings of Burns's politics more securely within the immediate context of eighteenth-century political debate. Was Burns, then, a Whig or a Tory? Indeed, if the former, did his Whiggery extend to the radical extreme of Jacobinism; if the latter, did his Toryism stem from some lingering Jacobite attachment to the lost cause of the exiled Stuarts? Once again, it seems, the range of Burns's sympathies and his adoption of multiple – sometimes ironic – personae in his verse lend plausibility to the various readings of Burns as Whig, radical, Tory and Jacobite. David Daiches has tried to resolve the apparent 'paradox' that Burns was both 'Jacobin and Jacobite' by explaining that Jacobitism was 'an expression of frustrated Scottish national feeling' that drew 'Scotsmen of all shades of the political spectrum', including a radical like Burns.[3] Among the most nuanced analyses of Burns's oddly ambivalent politics is the argument found in the work of several scholars, including Thomas Crawford, William Donaldson and Maurice Lindsay, that Burns started out as a Tory – indulging in Jacobite sentimentalising during the late 1780s and supporting a Tory candidate in the election of 1790 – but was radicalised by the French Revolution to such an extent that by the mid-1790s he had come to endorse the Whig party.[4] Crawford argues for 'the evolution of Burns's political views from the mild Toryism and left-wing Jacobitism of 1789–90 to the Whig partisanship of 1795'.[5] Donaldson further refines this picture of ambiguous political allegiances by showing that 'while apparently a supporter of Government' Burns 'associated with the Whig Opposition', in part through his connection with the Whiggish fourteenth Earl of Glencairn (1749–91); then, when, according to Donaldson, Burns got 'a Tory job', through the good offices of Robert Graham of Fintry (1749–1815), a friend of Dundas, 'he became apparently, an adherent of the Whigs'.[6] Yet there appears to be no clear evidence in Burns's poetry or letters of any *traumatic* repudiation of his previous commitments, or of any *anxious* concern to justify his newly acquired Whig principles.

More recently in Burns the Radical (2002), Liam McIlvanney adds a further complicating dimension to our understanding of Burns's politics by providing a compelling alternative to the identification of the Tory-Jacobite bard.[7] Instead McIlvanney locates Burns in an alternative tradition of dissent and in turn makes it much harder to reconcile his radicalism with his Jacobitism. He demonstrates that Burns subscribed to a brand of Presbyterian politics informed by the legacy of the Covenanting movement of the late seventeenth century and the 'real Whig' politics of those eighteenth-century radicals who considered themselves the heirs of the seventeenth-century commonwealthmen. In this interpretation, Burns's primary allegiance in Scottish historical politics was not to the conservative quasi-Jacobite politics of the episcopalian north-east inherited from his father William Burnes (1721–84), but to the radical Covenanting Presbyterianism forebears of his Ayrshire mother Agnes Broun (1732–1820) (whose grandfather had been shot at Airds Moss).[8] Yet in his letters, and according to the memories other contemporaries had of him, Burns, it seems, made proud – and almost certainly exaggerated – boast of the losses on his father's side in the Jacobite cause.[9] Both openly in his poetry and in private communications, moreover, he mocked the 'idiot race' of 'obscure, beef-witted [and] insolent' Hanoverians[10] – though without questioning the principles of the revolution that had driven the Stuarts from the throne. Whig or Tory? Conservative or radical? Romantic Jacobite or sentimental Covenanter? Contradiction, vacillation and inconsistency appear to be the hallmarks of Burns's politics, and, it seems, modern scholars have contributed as much as Burns himself to the deepening of this scholarly crux. However, a more definitive picture emerges when the focus shifts from

Burns himself to the wider political and ideological context of his times. Undoubtedly, Burns's political loyalties were difficult and cross-grained; but so, it transpires, were the party politics of his times.

It is especially difficult to peer back beyond the left-right rigidities of the French Revolution to the more fluid politics that prevailed between the early 1760s and the late 1780s. Most interpretations of Burns's politics derive, unfortunately, from a fundamental misunderstanding of late eighteenth-century politics. In particular, literary scholars have assumed that the labels of 'Whig' and 'Tory' which were, after all, to be found in Burns's political poetry could be mapped directly onto the political parties existing in the final quarter of the eighteenth century. Here, alas, Burns's own deployment of party names is seriously misleading, at least as a guide to the reality – rather than the rhetoric – of late eighteenth-century partisanship. During the reigns of the first two Hanoverians the Tories as a party had been largely excluded from government but had maintained until the 1750s an organised opposition to the Whig hegemony.[11] However, during the 1750s and 1760s the early Hanoverian party system dissolved.[12] In particular, the Tory party collapsed and atomised,[13] its former adherents adapting to life within a new political system.[14] For much of the third quarter of the eighteenth century politics was not organised around parties; for, in effect, the values of the Whig party – championship of the Glorious Revolution and the Hanoverian succession – were uncontested in public life. British politics was now structured along rather different lines. There were three main types of politicians at large in the House of Commons: first, loyal supporters of government who supported the Crown regardless of the personalities or factions who composed any particular ministry (a pronounced characteristic of Scots members); second, a backwoods squirearchy of independent country members who had no relish for office; and third, active 'party' politicians of a recognisable sort, who used the political factions to which they belonged as vehicles towards the attainment of office, in combination with the consistent phalanx of loyal ministerialists. All of these factions were Whiggish, as were both government and oppositions.[15] Although certain groups, such as the followers of Lord Rockingham (and later Charles James Fox), were more voluble than others in their claims to be the true successors of the Old Corps Whigs, there were no factions in late eighteenth-century British politics that were Tory in outlook. Thus, notwithstanding rhetorical exploitation of ideological issues and the existence of genuine political differences over such questions as American and East Indian policy, opposition tended to be based on the base needs of faction rather than upon the more elevated call of either Whig or Tory principles.

Before 1782 party politics scarcely impinged on Scottish affairs. Most Scottish members returned to Westminster went there as loyal government men and tended to support whatever administration was in power.

After 1782, it seems, party began to take a firmer hold in Scottish politics.[16] However, it was not the party divisions of Whigs and Tories that exerted their grip on Scottish politics, but the curious division from the end of 1783 between Fox-Northites (an amalgam of the most liberal and the most conservative of factions) and Pittites (another oddly indeterminate bloc which advanced both liberal and conservative measures). The defining moment in the consolidation of late eighteenth-century factions into two competing 'parties' was the period of turbulence which followed Britain's defeat in the American War of Independence. Out of the ministerial musical chairs of 1782–4, which had been preceded by the long administration of Lord North (1770–82), there emerged another enduring, but surprising, pattern: the lengthy administration of Pitt the Younger from December 1783 (known as the 'Mince Pie administration' it was not expected to last beyond Christmas 1783) to 1801, opposed by a grouping generally described by historians as the Foxites, or Whigs.[17] However, this sizeable body of opposition comprised not only the remnants of the Rockingham-Fox connection but also the more conservative followers of Lord North to whom the so-called 'Whigs' had attached themselves in the notorious Fox-North coalition of 1783.[18] Thus, according to Donald Ginter (who studied the career of William Adam (1751– 1839), a quondam Northite who became a leading organiser of the Scottish Foxites), the supposedly Whig opposition in the period between 1784 and the early 1790s comprehended 'ultra-conservative Northites' as well as liberal Foxites.[19] This party held together until 1794 when the Portland Whigs – at the conservative end of the party – abandoned the Foxites to join the Pittite government. Of course, the Pittite government which they joined was not a whit less Whiggish in identity than the Whig opposition which they had left. Pittites were not 'Tories'. Both William Pitt the Younger (1759–1806) and his Scottish ally, Henry Dundas (1742–1811),[20] were self-described 'Whigs' – sometimes, revealingly, 'independent Whigs'[21] – and never presented themselves as 'Tories'; though that is how posterity has mythologised them.[22] In the age of Burns 'Tories' existed largely pejoratively (except, ironically enough, in Burns's own poetry). The epithet 'Tory' was a term of political abuse, but it did not come to function as an affirmative badge of party identity until about the second decade of the nineteenth century when the Tory party – with, it must be stressed, no organisational, ideological or personal continuity from the Tory party of the early eighteenth century – was reincarnated.[23] Indeed, historians have speculated that the new Toryism of the early nineteenth century owed as much to the conservatism of the Portland Whigs as to the Pittites.[24] After all, the Pittites embraced various liberal causes. In 1785 Pitt made an unsuccessful attempt to bring in a measure of parliamentary reform, and both Pitt and Dundas were sincere champions of Catholic emancipation, perhaps the principal conservative bugbear of the age.[25] As a result, historians have struggled to find a suitable vocabulary to describe the divisions in British politics during the late eighteenth century,[26] which is possibly why the labels 'Whig' and 'Tory' – inaccurate, if not quite outdated, even then – survive in Burns scholarship.

Whether as a satirist, a song-writer or antiquarian restorer of old verses, Burns turned to political themes again and again throughout his career. The apolitical Burns of the Burns Supper involves misconstruing a profoundly political poet; but, equally, to unmask the Burns of the old bardolaters as a committed but frightened underground Jacobin is to omit the poet's immersion in the messy, perversely divided politics of the 1780s. During the 1780s Burns was an eloquent opponent of Charles James Fox (1749–1806) and the author of a stream of anti-Foxite poems which ridiculed Fox's dissipated lifestyle, for example, in 'The Author's Earnest Cry and Prayer to the Right Honorable and Honorable, the Scotch Representatives in the House of Commons':

> Yon ill-tongu'd tinkler, *Charlie Fox*,
> May taunt you wi' his jeers an' mocks;
> But gie him't het [hot], my hearty cocks!
>   E'en cowe the cadie [rascal]!
> An' send him to his dicing box,
>   An' sportin' lady. (K 81, ll. 109–14)

Not that these attacks on Fox meant that Burns was an opponent of Whig principles. Indeed, if anything it was the egregious Fox–North coalition that, many contemporaries reckoned, was a betrayal of the very idea of political principle: 'Yon mixtie-maxtie, queer hotch-potch, / The *Coalition*' (ll. 125–6).

In his 'Ode to the Departed Regency-bill – 1789' (K 258), Burns sets out his stall on the high-political manoeuvrings that accompanied the recent illness of George III (1738–1820), and clearly aligns himself with the forces of order – the King's Pittite government – against the overweening ambitions of the Foxites, who, hitched to the reversionary interest, had attempted to use the claims of the Prince of Wales to a regency as a ramp to power and high office. Fortunately, Britain had not taken this highway to anarchy:

> No Babel-structure would *I* build
>   Where order exil'd from his native sway
> Confusion may the Regent-sceptre wield
>   While all would rule and none obey. (ll. 41–4)

The message of the 'Ode' is clearly both Pittite (in its particular commitments) and conservative (in its more general political philosophy). Although such allegiances advertised Burns's adherence to a government opposed by that faction which had assumed the mantle of the old Whig party, it is vital that we remember that this neither meant that Burns was properly a Tory nor an enemy of Whig principles; which, in turn, more easily explains why, when in the 1790s Burns began to warm to the Foxites, this readjustment was not attended by any apparent agony of conscience. Burns had sacrificed none of his principles: it was the context that had changed. En route, the depiction of Fox found in 'Sketch Inscribed to the Rt Hon. Ch. J. Fox, Esq' is more balanced and nuanced than in earlier poems. 'A Fragment – On Glenriddell's Fox breaking his chain' (K 527) is a very clever piece of verse which describes how his friend the local Whig Robert Riddell of Glenriddell (1755–94) kept a fox – as appears actually to have been the case, but at the same time so apt and obvious a contemporary political symbol – which, as the poet's imagination accelerates away from the truth of the story, heard so much of the liberties of the people that it became something of an expert on the British constitution. Here again Burns uses the somewhat anachronistic rhetoric of Whigs and Tories, but on this occasion – bar the irony of a friend of the underdog keeping an animal in chains – Burns clearly champions a Whig interpretation of history in which Tories and Jacobites are villains:

> Sir Reynard daily heard debates
>   Of Princes' kings' and Nations' fates;
> With many rueful, bloody stories
>   Of tyrants, Jacobites and Tories:
> From liberty how angels fell,
>   That now are galley-slaves in hell;
> How Nimrod first the trade began
>   Of binding Slavery's chains on Man
> . . .
> How Xerxes, that abandon'd Tory,
>   Thought cutting throats was reaping glory,
> Until the stubborn Whigs of Sparta
>   Taught him great Nature's Magna Charta. (ll. 31–8; ll. 43–6)

In 'Here's a Health to Them That's Awa'' (K 391) Burns sets Foxite sentiments in a Jacobite drinking song. This juxtaposition is perhaps less incongruous than it seems at first sight when one remembers Fox's own dynastic pedigree, well-known Stuart connections and his pointed – if scarcely crypto-Jacobite – christening as *Charles James* Fox less than four years after the Forty-Five. On his mother's side Fox was the great-great grandson of Charles II through the latter's bastard son Charles Lennox, first Duke of Richmond, while Sir Stephen Fox, Fox's paternal grandfather, had served as a page-boy to Charles I at his execution.[27] In the poem Burns champions the Whigs – known by their traditional colours, 'the Buff and the Blue' – as the party of liberty, albeit in a manifestly Scoto-Jacobite idiom:

Here's a health to them that's awa'
Here's a health to them that's awa'
Here's a health to Charlie, the chief o' the clan,
Altho that his band be sma'.
May Liberty meet wi' success!
May Prudence protect her frae evil!
May Tyrants and Tyranny tine [get lost] i' the mist,
And wander their way to the devil! (ll. 9–16)

Nevertheless, this mellowing of anti-Foxite prejudice and apparent disillusionment with Pitt the Younger's own rightwards shift in reaction to the French Revolution does not tell the whole story, at least at the local level.

Burns's most explicit political statements appear in his election ballads, composed for the Dumfries Burghs election in 1790 and the Kirkcudbright Stewartry county election in 1795. However democratic his own ideals, Burns composed his election ballads as an unenfranchised outsider – like the overwhelming majority of his fellow Scots – enthralled by the highly exclusive sport of a tiny élite. So restrictive was the pre-1832 Scottish county franchise that even smaller landholders were unable to vote. The vote in the Scottish counties belonged to freeholders of land valued at forty shillings 'old extent' (a thirteenth-century valuation which took no account, of course, of the subsequent inflation in the value of land) or direct vassals of the Crown holding land worth four hundred pounds Scots. The county of Bute, for example, had only twelve voters, eight of whom were relatives or friends of the Earl of Bute. In the burghs the franchise was restricted to members of the town councils, none of which had more than thirty-three members and most of which had fewer than twenty councillors. Eighteenth-century Scotland was represented in the British parliament by fifteen Members for Scottish burghs. Only Edinburgh had its own MP, while there were fourteen groupings of burghs, five of which contained four burghs and nine five burghs. Examples of these groupings include the Ayr Burghs, a geographically dispersed five-burgh constituency comprising Ayr, Campbeltown, Irvine, Rothesay and Inverary, and the more compact set of Dysart Burghs, which represented the four Fife burghs of Dysart, Kirkcaldy, Burntisland and Kinghorn. In the parliamentary elections for these burgh groupings, the town council of each participating burgh would meet to elect a delegate, and the MP would be decided by the votes of the four or five burgh delegates.[28]

The Dumfries Burghs grouped together in the one parliamentary constituency the towns of Dumfries, Sanquhar, Kirkcudbright, Annan and Lochmaben, all of which were in Dumfriesshire, except for Kirkcudbright, which was in the Stewartry (modern-day Kirkcudbrightshire). In his mock-heroic poem 'The Five Carlins' Burns explores the politics of the five burghs in the Dumfries electoral grouping. At the time of the 1790 election Burns composed a stirring ballad on behalf of the sitting MP, Sir James Johnstone of Westerhall (1726–94), who had been elected for the Dumfries Burghs in 1784. Johnstone has been described as 'one of the most independent members to sit in the House [of Commons] during this period'.[29] His inclinations were Pittite, but he tended to side with the opposition on East India matters.[30] During the competition for the Dumfries Burghs in 1789–90 Burns's primary motivation was, it seems, opposition to the high-handedness in local affairs of the local Whig magnate, the Duke of Queensberry, whose candidate, Captain Miller, managed to unseat Johnstone. Curiously, Burns's 'Epistle to Robert Graham Esq. of Fintry on the Election for the Dumfries String of Boroughs, anno 1790' (K 318) is drenched in the rhetoric of 'Whig' and 'Tory' partisanship:

> The stubborn Tories dare to die,
> As soon the rooted oaks would fly
>   Before th' approaching fellers:
> The Whigs come on like ocean's roar,
> When all his wintry billows pour
>   Against the Buchan bullers – (ll. 73–8)

There is clearly an element of historical game-playing, including references to the Whiggish 'murtherer' (l. 82) of Charles I, to the Covenanters and to Montrose and Dundee as 'Tory' icons. Burns was ostensibly dignifying – and simultaneously subverting in deflationary mock-heroic mode – the matter of the Dumfries Burghs, a local parish-pump contest which he placed in the context of a historic and ongoing two-party struggle in British political life between Cavaliers and Roundheads, Tories and Whigs, and their Pittite and Foxite successors. The victory of the Foxite Whigs at the Dumfries Burghs was, Burns informed his readers, an unheroic and hollow one.

While, as noted above, several Burns scholars have detected a radicalising of Burns's politics between his poems for Westerhall in 1790 and the 'Heron Ballads' composed on behalf of Patrick Heron of Kirroughtree (c. 1735–1803) in the Kirkcudbright Stewartry by-election of 1795, this shift is very difficult to substantiate. If anything Heron, the supposed Foxite, was, it seems, more steadfastly Pittite than Johnstone, the purported Pittite. Heron belonged to a family which had actively opposed the interest of the Earls of Galloway in Kirkcudbrightshire, somewhat unsuccessfully during the 1780s. However, on the death of Alexander Stewart (c. 1739–94), the MP for the Stewartry of Kirkcudbright, Heron was returned for the vacancy in 1795 with the support of Dundas, prompted, it seems, by Dundas's recognition of Heron's stalwart opposition to the Scottish reform movement.[31] When the Earl of Galloway conspired to unseat his local rival in the general election of 1796, a somewhat peeved Dundas was having none of it. Dundas's letter of 31 March 1796 to the Earl of Galloway constituted a robust – albeit prudently oblique – commitment to Heron:

> I have invariably stated that I could not enter into all the local prejudices or parties in the Stewartry of Kirkcudbright, but that having been induced from circumstances and contrary to my intention to take a part at the former election in favour of Mr. Heron, and having acquired from him a fair and unequivocal support, I could not be guilty of such levity as to relinquish his support if he offered himself again. I stated this very distinctly to your lordship in repeated conversations.[32]

Notwithstanding Dundas's support, was Heron a 'Whig', as several scholars have argued?[33] Yes, but only in so far as *all* British politicians in the late eighteenth century, including Pitt and Dundas, were Whigs. Nor was Heron a radical cuckoo in the Pittite nest. On 15 March 1796 Heron voted in parliament *against* the abolition of the slave trade.[34] Local interest politics motivated Galloway's objection to Heron, and larger issues of ideology and party affiliation do not surface in his letters on the Heron problem.[35]

Burns, of course, wrote on behalf of individual candidates, and his election ballads expressed character judgements upon Johnstone, Heron and their opponents rather than definitive subscriptions to the articles of party creeds. Burns's politics operated at three different levels of political culture: with reference to local affairs in Ayrshire and Galloway and to the broader British stage, as well as to the Scottish context so often highlighted by later commentators. To align Burns exclusively with issues of Scottish politics such as Jacobitism and attitudes to the Union of 1707 is to miss both the particularities of parish-pump politics at the constituency level (which, after all, drew a great deal of the poet's attention) and to the *British* issues which divided the heterogeneous parties of his day. These days Burns's lines on the Union of 1707 ('Such a parcel of rogues in a nation' K 375) are quoted, perhaps more often than any other, as an indicator of Burns's political values:

> Fareweel to a' our Scottish fame,
> Fareweel our ancient glory;
> Fareweel even to the Scottish name,
> Sae fam'd in martial story!
> . . .
> O would, or I had seen the day
> That treason thus could sell us,
> My auld grey head had lien in clay

Wi' Bruce and loyal Wallace!
But pith and power, till my last hour,
I'll mak this declaration;
We're bought and sold for English gold,
Such a parcel of rogues in a nation! (ll. 1–4; ll. 17–24)

Yet very little can be adduced from this poem about Burns's political beliefs. As Chris Whatley has shown, Burns lived in an overwhelmingly unionist culture, in which Scottish nationalism was virtually a dead letter.[36] While there were a few grumbles about *how* the Union had been passed – such as the mechanics of patronage and corruption – there was no hostility to the *fact* of Union, nor did nationalist doctrine play a part in the Scottish radical critique of the British state during the 1790s.[37] Burns did not propose the repeal of the Union; rather the passing of Scottish nationhood provided convenient matter for satire and sentiment.

Indeed, what strikes the modern reader is not the substance of Burns's political views, but their tone and register, in particular their obvious indebtedness to the eighteenth-century literature of sentiment.[38] Fine feelings helped to cool the fever of partisanship: this was the message of Addison and Steele's influential magazine *The Spectator* (1711–12), which described the bonds of personal friendship forged between the Tory foxhunting man Sir Roger de Coverley and the Whiggish merchant Andrew Freeport.[39] Similarly, Laurence Sterne, one of Burns's favourite authors (*L* I, p. 141), used *The Life and Opinions of Tristram Shandy* (1759–67) to explore in a sentimental and comic vein the politics of the early eighteenth century.[40] The clearest statement of Burns's politics of sensibility comes in his long anonymous letter, dated 8 November 1788, to the *Edinburgh Evening Courant* (*L* I, pp. 332–5). The letter was provoked by a political sermon delivered on the centenary of the Glorious Revolution by the Reverend Joseph Kirkpatrick (1750–1824), the minister of Dunscore.[41] Burns was no fan of Kirkpatrick's sterile kirkmanship, describing him later in a letter of 1791 as 'one vast constellation of dullness' (*L* II, p. 82). But in early November 1788 what offended Burns about Kirkpatrick was the sneering and vindictively anti-Stuart tone of Kirkpatrick's sermon on the Glorious Revolution:

> Bred and educated in revolution principles, the principles of reason and common sense, it could not be any silly political prejudice that made my heart revolt at the harsh, abusive manner in which the Reverend Gentleman mentioned the House of Stuart, and which, I am afraid, was too much the language of that day. We may rejoice sufficiently in our deliverance from past evils, without cruelly raking up the ashes of those whose misfortune it was, perhaps, as much as their crimes, to be the authors of those evils; and may bless God for all his goodness to us as a nation, without, at the same time, cursing a few ruined

powerless exiles, who only harboured ideas, and made attempts, that most of us would have done. (*L* I, p. 333)

Following the revisionist lead of David Hume on Britain's recent history and the more general accounts of social progress from rudeness to refinement purveyed by the 'philosophical' historians of the Scottish Enlightenment,[42] Burns went on to make a very nuanced and sophisticated apology for the Stuarts which never trespassed onto outright Jacobitism:

> 'The bloody and tyrannical house of Stuart' may be said with propriety and justice, when compared with the present Royal Family, and the liberal sentiments of our days. But is there no allowance to be made for the manners of the times?... At that period, the science of government – the true relation between king and subject, like other sciences, was but just in its infancy, emerging from the dark ages of ignorance and barbarism. The Stuarts only contended for prerogatives which they knew their predecessors enjoyed, and which they saw their contemporaries enjoying. (*L* I, pp. 333–4)

Moreover, Burns the Whig, who rejoiced that the Stuarts had failed in their campaigns, also projects himself as an 'impartial spectator' – of the sort recommended by Adam Smith[43] – when he contemplates the plight of the Stuarts, and as the standard sentimental type, 'the man of feeling', so fashionably delineated by his own literary champion Henry Mackenzie:[44]

> [L]et every man, who has a tear for the many miseries incident to humanity, feel for a family, illustrious as any in Europe, and unfortunate beyond historic precedent; and let every Briton, and particularly every Scotsman, who ever looked with reverential pity on the dotage of a parent, cast a veil over the fatal mistakes of the Kings of his forefathers. (*L* I, p. 335)

To parse Burns's complicated political allegiances, up to the time of the French Revolution at least, requires not only an awareness of the relative absence of clear and consistent ideological contestation in the politics of the 1780s, but also an appreciation of the politics of sentiment, which included a quixotic identification with the underdog, whether a mouse, a louse or a Jacobite. The vogue for the sentimental[45] accounts for some of the apparent whimsicality of Burns's politics. Writing of the bard's political outlook, Thomas Crawford has argued that Burns 'has a natural gift for identifying himself with the men on both sides of a national struggle, and also for standing back and observing the warring factions quite impersonally, and from a distance'.[46] Was this unique to Burns as a man of genius, or was it the outcome of a benign conjuncture in politics and culture? Were Burns's broad-minded and indulgent politics the product, indeed, of an age when clear ideological demarcation between political parties was in abeyance and, moreover, one when the literary world was in thrall to a philosophy which placed a premium on compassion, sincerity, reconciliation and sociability?[47]

However, Burns's politics after 1790 are even harder to construe. In the first place, it is, of course, difficult to gauge the measure of Burns's rapprochement with the Foxites given his apparently willing support for Heron – to all intents and purposes Dundas's man – in 1795. Furthermore, there is the problem – which has riven the world of Burns scholarship over the past decade – of whether Pittite reaction against Jacobin sympathisers eventually drove a reformist Burns underground into a secret world of anonymous and pseudonymous publication from which, it is claimed, some of his radical oeuvre has still to be recovered.[48] Quite apart from the thorny issue of identifying the purported lost poems of Burns, scholars have had to grasp the nettle of Burns's ostensible loyalism during the 1790s. Are scholars entitled to disregard Burns's joining of the Dumfries Volunteers and a loyalist poem such as 'The Dumfries Volunteers' ('Does haughty Gaul invasion threat?') as a sort of 'insurance policy'[49] against official inquisitiveness and suspicion of anything but the most anodyne conservatism? Certainly, the world had changed enormously since the 1780s; but had Burns changed too, and, if so, how far? The evidence points in different directions, and Burns's politics during the 1790s must remain a matter of puzzlement. During the winter of 1792–3 the Board of Excise was sufficiently concerned at Burns's reputation to launch an investigation of his politics. This in turn provoked two anxious letters from Burns to his patron Graham of Fintry which set out the poet's adherence to the British constitution and the revolution principles of 1688, and indicated that his reformist impulses stretched no further than the standard Foxite worry that the executive had corrupted the legislature (L II, pp. 168–9 and 172–5). Moreover, Burns presented himself to Graham as a loyal Briton. The poet conceded that he had at first welcomed the French Revolution. To some loyal Britons, it is important to remember that the early stages of the French Revolution had the appearance of a long overdue reformation of a Catholic despotism.[50] Nevertheless, Burns went on to claim that he had changed his mind when the new French régime began to display the same 'avidity for conquest' (L II, p. 174) as the old régime.

Late eighteenth-century Britain was, as we have seen, a one-party state, and not in any repressive sense. All political positions, whatever their superficial differences, were grounded in a common Whiggery. The very hegemony of an unchallenged set of core Whig shibboleths – the mixed constitution, the Hanoverian succession, the Union – created a tolerant political space in which sentimental Jacobitism, for instance, was indulged as a harmless diversion[51] and in which the sacred revolution principles of 1688 took on a different colouring, perhaps even a different meaning, for different kinds of Whigs, conservative or radical.[52] After all, prior to the French Revolution, even the Pittites had contemplated parliamentary reform – which a decade later was taboo. However, during the 1790s the ground of political orthodoxy narrowed, and Burns, like other free spirits, found that the age of enlightenment and political latitude in which he came of age, had passed. Nevertheless, it remains unproven whether Burns, who was clearly appalled by the turn of events, was unambiguously radicalised by them.

CHAPTER SIX

Burns's Songs and Poetic Craft

Kirsteen McCue

> But by far the most finished, complete and truly inspired pieces of Burns are, without dispute, to be found among his *Songs*. It is here that, although through a small aperture, his light shines with least obstruction; in its highest beauty, and pure sunny clearness. The reason may be, that Song is a brief simple species of composition; and it requires nothing so much for its perfection, as genuine poetic feeling, genuine music of heart.[1]

Thomas Carlyle's description of Robert Burns and his songs, published in the *Edinburgh Review* in 1828, is memorable primarily for the simplicity and beauty of his chosen metaphor: the songs as shafts of pure light – tiny, decisive, yet radiant. Carlyle's comments were rather overshadowed later in the century by Robert Louis Stevenson's opinion that Burns rather wasted the last years of his all-too-short creative life, rarely finding 'courage for any more sustained effort than a song', even if some of them were 'polished and elaborate'.[2] But Carlyle's account is far more understanding of Burns's achievement. At the latest count, in Donald A. Low's edition of the songs, Burns's songs total some 373 sets of lyrics – a major contribution to the genre of Scottish song. And of all of Burns's poetic output, a large number of his songs have gained a place in popular culture which is unrivalled, both in oral and published contexts. Printed collections of 'Scottish', 'Scots' or 'Scotch' songs from his own time until today are filled with songs created, amended, repaired and collected by Robert Burns. In a performance context, and much encouraged by Fred Freeman's 1990s project to record the complete songs,[3] Burns's lyrics are frequently heard, and his version of that most famous song of parting, 'Auld Lang Syne', is sung around the globe on a daily basis.

Where Carlyle's comment is misleading is in its reference to song being a simple medium. Capturing the Romantic notion of the poet as nature's bard, Carlyle suggests that song flows effortlessly from its creator. In this genre, he suggests, no literary skill is required, but just a pure poetic feeling and an emotive musicality. That we like to think of song as the most natural of creative processes is certainly a Romantic construction, but it is one we are loath to put aside. It is well nigh impossible to account, in purely literary critical terms, for the success of a good song lyric, for, in Burns's case, the lyric is most often inspired by a melody. Indeed Burns noted that he had to know a tune intimately before beginning to write a lyric for it (*L* II, p. 242). Arguably, it is the combination of the two elements in performance which exemplifies the success of the song as a whole, but all too often descriptions of such performances, and the atmospheres created by them, reek of artificiality or insincerity. There are fine editorial annotations to the songs by James C. Dick, James Kinsley and Donald A. Low,[4] but aside from the pivotal work of Thomas Crawford,[5] and a tiny number of smaller studies,[6] most critics have avoided detailed discussion of them. Suffice it to say, collecting, amending and writing songs was for Burns a complex process, influenced as much by the songs and tunes he heard and sang himself, as it was by the growing numbers of published collections which fascinated him and which he knew in detail. This chapter aims to follow Burns's path as a songwriter and collector, accounting for these various influences and to show that while Burns is surely the King of Scottish Song, he is working within a vibrant songwriting environment and, moreover, has a distinguished national songwriting and collecting ancestry.

From the very beginning song was to play a central role in Burns's life. As he writes in his 'history of MYSELF' to Dr John Moore (1729–1802) in August 1787 (*L* I, pp. 133–46) his first 'vehicle in rhyme' was a song written on the occasion of his being partnered by one Nelly Kilpatrick when he was fifteen. She was beautiful and it is clear from Burns's retrospective account that he was inspired by sexual longing for her as they worked together in the fields. He describes the 'furious ratann' of his pulse as he 'fingered over her hand, to pick out the nettle-stings and thistles'. But he is also moved by the sound of her voice which he notes, in true romantic style, 'made my heartstrings thrill like an Eolian harp'. Burns set out to win Nelly's love with poetry and so created his first apparently simple love song 'O Once I Lov'd a Bonny Lass', often referred to 'Handsome Nell'(*K* 1):

O, Once I lov'd a bonnie lass,
An' aye and I love her still,
And whilst that virtue warms my breast
I'll love my handsome Nell.

As bonnie lasses I hae seen,
And mony full as braw,
But for a modest gracefu' mien
The like I never saw.

A bonny lass I will confess,
Is pleasant to the e'e,
But without some better qualities
She's no a lass for me.

But Nelly's looks are blithe and sweet,
And what is best of a',
Her reputation is compleat,
And fair without a flaw.

She dresses ay sae clean and neat,
Both decent and genteel;
And then there's something in her gait
Gars ony dress look weel.

A gaudy dress and gentle air,
May slightly touch the heart,
But it's innocence and modesty
That polishes the dart.

'Tis this in Nelly pleases me,
'Tis this enchants my soul;
For absolutely in my breast
She reigns without controul.

Even in this first creation Burns is setting forth a number of characteristics which are to become central to his love lyrics: Scots language combines with polished English, beauty embodies love, simplicity and modesty rise above sophistication, and, moreover, purity of reputation is the finest of attributes. While she's not directly compared with one of higher social standing, Nelly's rural and thus 'natural' genealogy sets her upon an equal, or even higher, pedestal to any woman of 'gentle air'. Even within her own environment Nelly is 'decent and genteel'. The first appearance of this song is in Burns's *Commonplace Book*, where, in the first entry dated April 1783, he gives the background to the song, the lyric in full and his own comments on it. In characteristically modest mode Burns congratulates himself on the honesty of his heart and the sincerity of his tongue, but is nonetheless critical. The first stanza, he notes, is 'too much in the flimsy strain of our ordinary street ballads', and 'the expression is a little awkard [sic] and the sentiment too serious'.[7] He is thus clearly aware of the performance and chapbook publication of street ballads. He also gives the melody to which the song is set as the reel 'I Am a Man Unmarried'. It transpires that this melody has, until recently, eluded Burns's song editors. Dick's edition of the songs gives no melody, and Kinsley prints the melody which is published with Burns's song in the sixth and final volume of James Johnson's *Scots Musical Museum* (no. 551) in 1803. In the *Museum* Burns's lyric appears with an untitled tune, a slow air, which is at odds with this original choice of a reel and thus creates quite a different atmosphere when sung. Neither William Stenhouse in 1853 nor John Glen in 1900 were able to trace the tune 'I Am a Man Unmarried',[8] but in the 1990s, while working on Andrew Crawford's ballad collection, Emily Lyle found it.[9] Though none of the twentieth-century editions of Burns print a chorus for this song, Lyle points out that the *Commonplace Book* includes a refrain beginning 'Fal lal de dal &c.' after the first verse, and this matches perfectly the lyric as noted down in the 1820s by Crawford from the singing of John Smith of Lochwinnoch. The melody 'I Am a Man Unmarried' is in a four-part form (with two obvious 'halves' or sections) and is typical of most Scottish tunes popular during this period. Here the main part of the melody (for the verse) comprises two opening sections, which are virtually identical, and which consist of the opening two-bar theme repeated four times. Burns's four-line stanza matches this neatly with his *abab* rhyme scheme mirroring the structure and internal 'chimes' of the first part of the tune. The second part of the melody is then a rousing sing-a-long chorus again with two strains, the latter ending slightly differently than the former. This matches the refrain as noted by Burns in his *Commonplace Book* and also the original lyric notated by Crawford. Lyle notes that the song at this time had 'quite wide currency'[10] and is found often with a lyric entitled 'The Roving Batchelor' in Scottish chapbooks or pamphlets.[11] Like Burns's lyric 'The Roving Batchelor' appears to have been a song of wooing, though quite unlike Burns's effusive love lyric in nature. Burns's first song reveals an emotional creative inspiration, shows that he is able to use a tune to create a lyric, and illustrates that his songs connect to both a contemporary performance and a printed song culture.

Burns's general knowledge of songs at the time of creating 'Handsome Nell' would undoubtedly have been limited. His major songwriting and collecting took place after his visit to Edinburgh in 1786 and in collaboration with James Johnson (c. 1750–1811) (*The Scots Musical Museum*, 1787–1803) and thereafter George Thomson (1757–1851) (*A Select Collection of Original Scotish Airs*, 1793–1846), two of the major song editors and publishers of the period. But his retrospective account of his first song is written at a time when his thirst for knowledge about song culture was developing apace. Only four songs appeared in Burns's first *Poems Chiefly in the Scottish Dialect* published in Kilmarnock in 1786, but the following year his first Edinburgh edition with the same title included ten songs.[12] Seven of them are love songs, mostly in a pastoral style and one of which ('Green Grow the Rashes') is a transformation of a bawdy song well known to Burns and his peers. Two are jovial drinking songs with Masonic connections (K 27 and 115), and the last is the politically-charged yet comic 'When Guildford Good our Pilot stood', lambasting the British government's foreign policy at the outbreak of the American Revolution (K 38). Dick's later categorisation of Burns's songs shows a similar pattern, with the love songs far outweighing all the others, but Burns's skills for political comment and his talent for writing songs which celebrate convivial or fraternal socialising are notable even from the start.

A look at this first group of songs allows us to see just how many influences are at work on Burns's songs. 'It Was Upon a Lammas Night'(K 8), 'Behind yon Hill where Stinchar Flows' (K 4) and 'From Thee Eliza I Must Go'(K 9) all have strong associations with English song tradition, mostly through the histories of their respective melodies.[13] 'Behind yon Hill' uses the tune 'My Nanie O' which had appeared in a London broadside before being used by Allan Ramsay earlier in the eighteenth century; and 'Corn Rigs', also connected to Ramsay and the tune for Burns's 'It Was Upon a Lammas Night', dates back at least as far as John Playford's *Choyce Ayres* of 1681 and Thomas Durfey's *Wit and Mirth* of 1698, two important English collections. Burns's letters mention the importance and influence of collections of English and Irish songs and he refers to one such collection – generally believed to be Joseph Ritson's *Select Collection of English Songs* – in his letter to Moore as being his 'vade mecum' (L I, p. 138).[14] Two of the ten songs – 'Behind yon Hill' and 'Again Rejoicing Nature Sees' (K 138) – have connections with lyrics included in David Herd's *Ancient and Modern Scots Songs, Heroic Ballads &c., Now First Collected into One Body* of 1769 (then in two volumes in 1776). While Burns seems not to mention Herd in his correspondence, it is generally accepted by Burns's song editors that Herd's influence is notable especially in Burns's creation of new lyrics from fragments ('Ay Waukin O' – K 287 – is a fine example). Six of the ten songs have melodies which were printed in James Oswald's *Caledonian Pocket Companion*, a music-only fiddle collection published in twelve parts between 1743 and 1759. Burns owned a copy and, in statistical terms, the *Companion* was the major repository of tunes for Burns's songs.[15] In four of these ten songs Burns's original choice of tune is later amended, either by Burns's own alteration of the lyric or by a publisher/ editor who chooses a different melody entirely. In the case of 'Now Westlin' Winds' (K 2) Burns starts with the tune 'I Had a Horse & I Had Nae Mair', as noted in his *Commonplace Book*,[16] but then chooses 'Port Gordon', which he most probably finds in Oswald's *Companion*, as a better match. However, his lyric never appears in print with this tune. James Johnson matches it with the virtually unsingable 'When the King Comes o'er the Water' (but which he mistakenly calls 'Come, Kiss With Me') in his *Scots Musical Museum* of 1792 (no. 351). Then in his second volume of *A Select Collection of Original Scottish*

Airs in 1801 (no. 93) George Thomson combines an altered lyric beginning 'Now Westlin' Winds and Sportsmens' Guns' with the Irish tune 'Ally Croaker'. Editors have been cruelly treated by literary critics and Burnsians alike for making such choices, especially after Burns's death. But it was standard practice at this time for editors and songwriters to jump between tunes, and the simple, common structure of so-called 'traditional' melodies with their repetitive sections of similar lengths aided this process.[17]

In Burns's first poetic editions the songs appeared simply as lyrics without tunes. Included as a group at the end of the collection, they are mostly marked out in the index as a 'Song' or 'A Fragment' and are printed with a tune title above the lyric proper, much in the style of earlier collections of songs. Most notable of these was Allan Ramsay's *Tea Table Miscellany* (hereafter *TTM*) first published in four parts between 1723 and 1737.[18] By the mid-1790s this collection was in at least its eighteenth edition and it was both hugely popular with the reading public, and a truly inspirational source for Burns.[19] Ramsay's 'works' and his 1720s pastoral comedy *The Gentle Shepherd* (which features several of his most famous songs) are mentioned in Burns's correspondence (*L* I, p.138), and editorial work on Burns's songs identifies the *TTM* and William Thomson's *Orpheus Caledonius* (1725 or 1733) as two of his most influential song publications.[20] *Orpheus Caledonius* was a London-produced music book which appeared hot on the heels of Ramsay's *TTM* and pinched many of Ramsay's songs and associated tunes without permission.[21] It is mentioned frequently in contemporary sources on music, and was clearly widely distributed and very popular. Burns recommends several of its songs to James Johnson for inclusion in the *Museum* (*L* II, pp. 368–71).

Burns's knowledge of and respect for the work of 'the immortal Allan' is clear (*L* I, p. 414).[22] Even although it is one of his first creations, 'Corn Rigs' (beginning 'It was upon a Lammas night') is one of Burns's best known and best loved songs. It was inspired by two sources: the first was a fragment which Burns included in his 'Notes on Scottish Song' written into a friend's copy (Robert Riddell (1755–94)) of Johnson's *Museum* where he lists it as being 'an old song' with the chorus:[23]

O corn rigs and rye rigs,
O corn rigs is bonie;
Whare e'er ye meet a bonie lass,
Preen up her apron, Johnie.

The second source, given beside this fragment in his 'Notes', is Ramsay's 'My Patie is a Lover Gay'. This song is the finale of Ramsay's *Gentle Shepherd* where Peggy, who has just discovered her aristocratic roots and thus secured her betrothal to the high-class shepherd Patie, sings of her triumphs with 'the newest' song that she has. Ramsay chooses the tune 'Corn Rigs are Bonie' and there is clear reference to the old fragment. A close comparison of Ramsay's pastoral song (*TTM* published Kilmarnock, 1788) and Burns's new creation to the same tune (*K* 8) reveal the extent of Ramsay's influence on Burns and show how both songwriters adapt existing materials to make new songs:

Burns

It was upon a Lammas night,
When corn rigs are bonie,
Beneath the moon's unclouded licht,
I held awa to Annie:
The time flew by, wi' tentless heed,
Till 'tween the late and early;
Wi' sma' persuasion she agreed,
To see me thro' the barley.

The sky was blue, the wind was still,
The moon was shining clearly;
I set her down wi' right good will,
Amang the rigs o' barley:
I ken't her heart was a' my ain;
I lov'd her most sincerely;
I kiss'd her owre and owre again,
Amang the rigs o' barley.

I lock'd her in my fond embrace;
Her heart was beating rarely:
My blessings on that happy place,
Amang the rigs o' barley!
But by the moon and stars so bright,
That shone that hour so clearly!
She ay shall bless that happy night,
Amang the rigs o' barley.

I hae been blithe wi' Comrades dear;
I hae been merry drinking;
I hae been joyfu' gath'rin gear;
I hae been happy thinking:
But a' the pleasures e'er I saw,
Tho' three times doubl'd fairly,
That happy night was worth them a',
Amang the rigs o' barley.

Ramsay

My *Patie* is a lover gay,
His mind is never muddy,
His breath is sweeter than new hay,
His face is fair and ruddy.
His shape is handsome, middle size;
He's stately in his wawking;
The shining of his een surprise;
'Tis heav'n to hear him tawking.

Last night I met him on the bawk,
Where yellow corn was growing,
There mony a kindly word he spake,
That set my heart a glowing.
He kiss'd, and vow'd he wad be mine,
And loo'd me best of ony;
That gars me like to sing sinsyne,
O *corn rigs are bonny*.

Let maidens of a silly mind
Refuse what maist they're wanting,
Since we for yielding are design'd,
We chastly should be granting;
Then I'll comply, and marry *Pate*,
And syne my cockernony;
He's free to touzle aire or late,
Where corn rigs are bonny.

Chorus
Corn rigs, an' barley rigs,
An' corn rigs are bonie:
I'll ne'er forget that happy night,
Amang the rigs wi' Annie.

Ramsay's Peggy is a shepherdess who has been brought up in a rural setting, with no idea of her impressive ancestry until the last moments of the play, so she is able to walk the line between untouched simplicity and newly discovered refinement most comfortably. Arguably this is one of the reasons why Ramsay's lyric was so popular, for the theatrical audience and the clientèle for song publications wished to experience such apparent rural simplicity.[24] Ramsay concentrates on Peggy's description of Patie's physical attributes and the lovers' meeting in general terms. His second verse sets the scene: an evening in the corn fields, pretty words, thumping hearts and kisses – all enhanced by the dance-like rhythms of the tune. The tune is simply full of joy, with its bouncy two beats in a bar and lots of quavers or running notes, which suggest youthful skipping and Peggy's bubbling excitement. Indeed Thomas Crawford has commented that Peggy's four key songs in *The Gentle Shepherd* are, not surprisingly, set to the most popular tunes.[25] Ramsay chooses only song verses, connecting to the 'original chorus' simply by reference to the corn rigs in verses two and three. He adapts the crude lifting of the apron, in the 'original' chorus, changing it to the suggestive preening up of Peggy's 'cokernony', or the tuft of hair at the top of her head (pushed forward usually by the way the hair is tied up). Ramsay's 'moralitas' in his final verse accounts for women's place in society and Peggy's delight and ultimate contentment with her lot. Any sense of class difference is lost with Burns, for his lyric drops any notions of 'gentility' and becomes truly democratic. Burns uses the sensuousness of the fragment and Ramsay's second and third verses as his starting point. And Peggy's final 'saucy' verse, in which she admits that the female sex is designed purely for physical enjoyment and 'touzling', persuades Burns to create a song celebrating physical love. Patie's shining eyes and the 'heavenly' tones of his voice in the first verse potentially inspire Burns's supreme choice of moonlight, to which he refers in all but his final verse. The mood created by the unclouded skies and clear quality of the light enhance the physical sensations of being in Annie's company. Moreover, Burns creates a chorus, as suggested by the old fragment. This allows a repetition of the second half of the tune, which reaches upwards melodically, and also ensures that the narrator is able to reiterate his joy at spending the night in the 'rigs wi' Annie'. Burns's final verse, very much from a male narrator's perspective, emphasises that physical love far outweighs all man's other social entertainments. Notably Ramsay's reference to 'touzling' rather enhances the frisson of sexual excitement in his song, especially in the context of Peggy's newfound aristocratic status. While Burns's lyric captures the excitement of the lovers' physical activity, it does so with modesty and graciousness: a sparkle in the eye, rather than a touzling of the cokernony! This shows Burns, as Carol McGuirk has argued, at a certain maturity even in this early work.[26] It also makes George Thomson's decision to continue to print Ramsay's lyric in preference to Burns's rather unusual, for Thomson, to whom Dick refers as 'the egregious Thomson',[27] was a stickler for correct morals and polite manners in his editorial practice. It was Thomson, most often, who requested 'cleaner' versions of lyrics for inclusion in his *Select Collection*. Interestingly posterity has favoured Burns's song, which is now far better known than Ramsay's.

Examination of these very early songs then reveals much about Burns's songwriting methods, and about the ancestry of songwriting and collecting which informed him. Having established his methodology it was only natural, when Burns met James Johnson in Edinburgh in April 1786, that he would become the key collaborator on a project which has proved to be the most significant collection of Scottish songs in history.[28] At Johnson's request Burns threw his energy enthusiastically into *The Scots Musical Museum*:

> An Engraver, James Johnson, in Edinr has, not from mercenary views but from an honest Scotch enthusiasm, [had (*deleted*)] set about collecting all our native Songs and setting them to music; particularly those that have never been set before. – Clark, the the [sic] well known Musician, presides over the musical arrangement: and Drs Beattie & Blacklock, Mr Tytler, Woodhouselee, and your humble servt to the utmost of his small power, assist in collecting the old poetry, or sometimes for a fine air to make a stanza, when it has no words. –

As this letter to James Hoy (1747–1828) of Gordon Castle illustrates (*L* I, p. 163), Johnson's six-volume venture was truly a 'home to the Muses'. Johnson's muses were living men and women of social standing who portrayed a fine blend of creative and antiquarian skills. Working for the *Museum* involved variously collecting, amending, rewriting and writing anew. So gentlemen poets like Blacklock, Beattie, Burns and a host of others, scoured the countryside for materials, worked their way through existing published sources of songs, swapped and shared ideas with one another by letter or in person, and created song lyrics from scratch for tunes which, in their opinion, needed to be preserved. Sometimes attributed for their work, and sometimes labelled 'anonymous', they helped create a repository of 'national song'. Murray Pittock suggests – in discussion of the festivities of Alloway Kirk in 'Tam o'Shanter' – that Burns 'reinscribes the denominating force of music, dance, and song in Scottish nationhood, hidden, repressed, but there to be discovered'.[29] But Johnson's project suggests that Scottish song culture was very much alive and visible. It was an opportunity for a generation to become actively involved in the songs of their nation – in their collection and preservation – even if that often meant persuading themselves of ancient lines of descent when there were clearly none, or where, like popular drama of the time, a great deal of disguise, or cross-dressing took place. Hamish Mathison's exploration of the *Museum* project illustrates clearly that this was where political lyrics and staunch Jacobite songs and tunes also demanded inclusion, and where Burns's prowess as creator of political lyric comes to the fore.

It was the involvement with Johnson's project that inspired Burns to engage head-on with other writers and collectors of the eighteenth century. He immersed himself in key texts on songs which allowed him to examine the history of Scotland's music, and thus to think about the role of song within this. He also became concerned with the classification of and theoretical approaches to songwriting and collecting – knowing the work of Ramsay, Riston, Aikin and Tytler amongst others. Burns's newfound friendship with Robert Riddell of Glenriddell, owner of Friar's Carse and close neighbour of Burns from his arrival at Ellisland Farm in 1788, also plays an important part. A keen musician, by the time of their meeting Riddell had already produced a volume of music for the piano forte or harpsichord – which included 'traditional' Scottish instrumental pieces and 'two Songs in the Old Scotch Taste' – published coincidentally by James Johnson in c. 1785.[30] Such literary influences and friendships consequently shaped and enhanced Burns's methods of songwriting, of 'refining' and 'improving' songs, as evidenced particularly in his correspondence to George Thomson in the 1790s. And as Nigel Leask has recently mapped out, Burns's own professional development as an exciseman in the last years of his life sits comfortably alongside his creative project of listing and measuring songs, of gauging this element of Scottish culture.[31]

Both Johnson's and shortly thereafter George Thomson's song publishing projects pushed Burns's songwriting and collecting to new heights – he is thought to have produced at least 220 of Johnson's 600 songs[32] and around 150 of Thomson's c. 550 songs, including some for his Irish and Welsh collections.[33] But in addition to their nationalist antiquarian agenda these collections also established Burns's songs as musical creations. Both collections were created very much with performance in mind and were particularly aimed at polite young women, who were working at home on improving their skills as singers, pianists or flautists. And, moreover, these two collections worked at different ends of the musical spectrum: Johnson designed his cheaper, pocket-sized collection, with simpler settings mostly by local Edinburgh musician Stephen Clarke, to accommodate all abilities;

Thomson's expensive coffee-table-sized volumes with settings by the best of European composers (including most famously Haydn and Beethoven) were aimed at the musically skilled amateur or even the professional performer. Burns is often thought to be the supreme folklorist, so these first publications of his songs with their 'classical' settings can sit uncomfortably with his posthumous iconic image.

Suffice it to say, Burns remains closely linked to 'folk' performance, and thus his songs are able both to straddle contemporary societal structures and to exemplify the inextricable links between oral and printed cultures. Indeed Burns's most famous song, 'Auld Lang Syne' (K 240) is a fine example. Variants of the lyric are traced far back into the sixteenth century where the refrain 'And auld kyndnes is quyt foryett' is found in the Bannatyne manuscript of 1568.[34] Lyrics which include the title 'Auld Lang Syne' or 'Old Long Syne' or the phrase 'should auld acquaintance' appear in publications and private manuscript miscellanies throughout the seventeenth century and versions are found in both James Watson's *Choice Collection of Comic and Serious Scots Verse* published in Edinburgh between 1706 and 1711 and in Ramsay's *TTM*, as well as in editions of Ramsay's 'works', such as Burns would have seen. But Burns's references to the song are all to do with its performance. He first mentions it in his letter to Mrs Dunlop of 7 December 1788, when he notes that the old song 'has often thrilled thro' my soul' and he completes the letter by enclosing the song and celebrating the 'native genius' of its anonymous creator whom he says is a 'heaven-inspired Poet' (*L* I, pp. 341–5). Burns is keen to emphasise his oral sources more and more, and certain of his songs gain a new authority as a result. His letter to George Thomson in early September 1793, sending the same lyric, states quite clearly that he has notated it from a performance (*L* II, pp. 246–7):

> One Song more, & I have done. – Auld lang syne – The air is but mediocre; but the following song, the old Song of the olden times, & which has never been in print, nor even in manuscript, until I took it down from an old man's singing; is enough to recommend any air.

The song appeared in 1796 in Johnson's *Museum* with an air or melody that Burns referred to as 'mediocre' and not the 'common Scotish country dance' which was also associated with it (*L* II, p. 329). It would be facile to say here that 'the rest is history', for Burns's version of the song was to gain unrivalled popularity across the globe by means of a complex process of social singing (most probably with Masonic connections) and theatrical performance during the early decades of the nineteenth century. It was also in combination with a quite different melody chosen by George Thomson after Burns's death. So this is yet another example of a fine lyric with multiple melodic combinations, and one, moreover, which Burns claims not to have authored, though that is not what the world now thinks. And how can we be sure, when the methods of creating song lyrics are so complex and multi-layered, that some of the fine lyrical skill here is not that of Burns? His choice of description of the old man is surely specific – was the 'heaven-inspired Poet' not one and the same as the 'heaven-taught ploughman' himself?

Questions of authorship are tricky when dealing with songs of this period. Burns's consummate artistry comprises not just an innate sense of melody and a fine set of lyrical skills; it also embodies his ability to act as a vehicle through which the lyrics of one metamorphose into those of another. More than any other songwriter of the period Burns has a special empathy with his sources: a fine awareness of when to touchup a lyric, or when to leave it well alone. Of all his peers Burns thus earns the right to place the crown of Scottish song firmly on his head – posterity, and the fine quality of his best songs, has ensured that it has stayed there. Writing songs is far from easy, but it is the apparent simplicity of Burns's final product that belies his art and ensures, as Carlyle states, that his light continues to burn most brightly.

CHAPTER SEVEN

Burns and Robert Fergusson

Rhona Brown

In his role as unofficial first biographer to Robert Fergusson (1750–74), Robert Burns was concerned with preserving the memory of a comet-like literary genius, and also projected dismay at his own imagined fate as a 'Bard unfitted for the world' (K 143, l. 6). On one hand, according to Robert Crawford, 'Burns's praise is an exercise in confident wishful thinking. His paeans to his precursor are bound up with his own aspirations as a poet.'[1] Equally, Crawford claims that Fergusson's paradigm 'both terrified and inspired'[2] the Ayrshire poet. Burns saw Fergusson as his 'elder brother' (K 143, l. 3) both in 'misfortune' (l. 3) and in 'the muse' (l. 4) and he refers to the work of Fergusson more frequently than to any other writer. Burns's first editor and biographer, James Currie, posited 1782 for his subject's first acquaintance with Fergusson's poetry, but Matthew P. McDiarmid argues plausibly for 1784.[3] McDiarmid points to Burns's 'Kilmarnock' edition, so soaked in Fergussonian influence, published in 1786 and largely showcasing Burns's productivity from 1784 to 1786. As McDiarmid says, 'The marvellously creative period, 1784 to 1786, was not a delayed reaction to the spark of Fergusson's genius, but rather a direct explosion from it.'[4]

Burns first cites Fergusson in his 'Epistle to J. Lapraik, An Old Scotch Bard' (K 57), which is dated 'April 1st, 1785', where he is described as 'bauld an' slee' (l. 80). In his epistle 'To W. Simson, Ochiltree' (K 59), written only a few weeks later in 'May – 1785', Burns is more sombre in his remembrance of Fergusson's poetic bequest. Fergusson's work, according to Burns, assures him of a 'deathless fame' (l. 18). The next stanza is entirely devoted to Fergusson's tragedy:

> (O *Fergusson*! thy glorious *parts*,
> Ill-suited *law*'s dry, musty arts!
> My curse upon your whunstane hearts,
>   Ye Enbrugh Gentry!
> The tythe o' what ye waste at *cartes*
>   Wad stow'd his pantry!) (ll. 19–24)

In stark opposition to Fergusson's labour at '*law*'s dry, musty arts' and his empty 'pantry' is the Gentry's luxurious extravagance. Burns expounds a theme that would become a favourite in his corpus: the assiduous dignity of the poor set in rhetorical opposition to the idleness of the aristocracy. Here, according to Carol McGuirk, Burns follows a literary template provided by Fergusson. In their poetic obsession with consumerism in its various forms, '[b]oth set scenes of riotous consumption – displays of food, flesh and finery – against scenes of rural self-sufficiency.'[5] For Burns, then, the antithesis presented in 'To W. Simson' is didactic. While Fergusson is no archetype of 'rural self-sufficiency', his poverty and diligence are heavy reminders of the destructive cycle of consumption.

His poetry laments his predecessor's fate, but Burns's prose illustrates command of Fergusson's literary legacy. Burns's letter to Dr John Moore, written on 2 August 1787, provides a portrait of the poet's fond esteem for Fergusson:

> Rhyme, except some religious pieces which are in print, I had given up; but meeting with Fergusson's Scotch poems, I strung anew my wildly-sounding, rustic lyre with emulating vigour. (*L* I, p. 143)

After abandoning hope of continuing as a poet, Burns languishes until Fergusson gives him the impetus and, it is implied, the tools to renew his approach to his craft as a Scottish bard. Despite Burns's appreciation of his 'Scotch' inheritance, his often-quoted lines 'On Fergusson I' (1787) (*K* 143) are written in deferential Augustan English:

> Curse on ungrateful man, that can be pleas'd
> And yet can starve the author of the pleasure!
>
> O thou my elder brother in misfortune,
> By far my elder Brother in the muse,
> With tears I pity thy unhappy fate!
> Why is the bard so unfitted for the world,
> Yet has so keen a relish of its Pleasures? (ll. 1–7)

In this short tribute, the poet becomes 'author', not simply of diverting literature, but of 'pleasure' itself and again, as in 'To W. Simson', Burns utilises antithesis to edify and instruct. While the heedlessness of the public to Fergusson's plight is again reprimanded, the poet is presented as separate from common humanity: Burns presents himself and Fergusson as sentimental ideals; as 'brothers in the muse' who are, like Henry Mackenzie's Harley in *The Man of Feeling*, 'unfitted for the world'. Appropriately, Burns gives Fergusson's 'unhappy fate' the tribute of 'tears', and Fergusson becomes the human embodiment of Burns's much-pitied mountain daisy, roughly annihilated in the flowering of a young life.

In a second poem 'On Fergusson' (1787) Burns continues his lament in fitting tenor:

> Ill-fated Genius! Heaven-taught Fergusson,
>   What heart that feels and will not yield a tear,
> To think Life's sun did set e'er well begun
>   To shed its influence on thy bright career.
> O why should truest Worth and Genius pine
>   Beneath the iron grasp of Want and Woe,
> While titled knaves and idiot-greatness shine
>   In all the splendour Fortune can bestow? (K 144, ll. 1–8)

Consistently portrayed as unappreciated and yet full with literary promise, Fergusson's biographical legacy becomes a broad lesson on justice from which humanity should learn. And while it is Fergusson's 'Scotch poems' that stimulate Burns's 'emulating vigour', these reverent neoclassical English tributes to his predecessor demonstrate the scope of Fergusson's poetic bequest to Burns, illustrating that both poets, while scintillating in vernacular Scots, could utilise 'standard' English with gravitas and aplomb.

Besides poetic tributes, Burns also provided a physical memorial of his precursor, erecting a monument at Fergusson's grave in Edinburgh's Canongate Kirkyard. This gesture, which put Burns in substantial and enduring arrears, demonstrates his severe devotion to his antecedent while liberating Fergusson's memory from time's wilderness. In his inscription for the stone, Burns refers to Fergusson as 'Scotia's' 'Poet' (K 142, ll. 3 and 4).[6] Of the many ways in which Burns honours his 'Poet' of 'Scotia', however, nowhere is his impulse more sincere or durable than in his poetic assimilation of Fergusson's legacy. From Fergusson, Burns inherits themes, rhyme schemes and reinvigorated verse forms, as well as cultural and political idioms. If Burns did indeed discover Fergusson's work in 1784, the 'Kilmarnock' edition, published two years later, demonstrates that his 'emulating vigour' was immediate and explosively constructive. In short, Fergusson was a vibrant catalyst in the making of the 'Kilmarnock' edition and, therefore, in the making of Burns, Scotland's poet.

Burns opened all of his collections with 'The Twa Dogs. A Tale' (K 71), naturally according to McGuirk, as it 'introduces many of his central concerns, emphasizing the ties that connect all living beings, and yet also expressing dismay and some anger at the enormous gulf between the busy and the idle, the needy and the privileged'.[7] Here, then, is an immediate link with the Burnsian Fergusson. Like his antithetical portrayal of an 'Ill-fated Genius', labouring under the 'iron grasp of Want and Woe' while the 'Enbrugh Gentry' fritter their income at 'cartes', Luath, the '*ploughman's collie*' (l. 23) eloquently outlines his industrious cotter family's material impoverishment and simultaneous spiritual wealth, while Caesar, 'the *gentleman* and *scholar*' (l. 14) who is 'keepet for his Honor's pleasure' (l. 8) exposes his aristocratic owners' idle, empty existence. While the poem's central concerns are reminiscent of Burns's construction of Fergusson's biography, its theme and structure are borrowed from Fergusson's 'Mutual Complaint of Plainstanes and Causey, in their Mother Tongue' (1773),[8] 'A Drink Eclogue' (1773)[9] and, most significantly, 'The Ghaists: A Kirkyard Eclogue' (1773).[10] In 'Mutual Complaint of Plainstanes and Causey', Edinburgh's pavement debates with its causeway as to which receives the heavier traffic, while in 'A Drink Eclogue', home-spun 'Whisky' and imported 'Brandy' dispute which is the more worthy beverage. Both are, like 'The Twa Dogs', humorous vignettes which hold solemn debates on eighteenth-century life behind apparently simple exteriors.

But 'The Twa Dogs' borrows more than structure and style from Fergusson's most politically-barbed poem, 'The Ghaists'. Luath and Caesar find their counterparts in George Herriot and George Watson, two ghosts raised from their beds in Greyfriars Kirkyard to debate the recently-proposed and soon-to-be-defeated Mortmain Bill. Fergusson's characters are apposite: the Mortmain Bill, which obligated the trustees of Scottish benefactors to invest their funds in a British governmental pool, was seen as an affront to patrons such as Herriot and Watson, who had bestowed resources for the schooling and maintenance of the sons of poor and deceased Edinburgh merchants: their 'hospital' schools would be directly blighted by the Bill. In addition to the financial injury caused by the Mortmain Bill, many Scots – including Fergusson – were outraged that Scottish funds would be administered in London, and a petition ensured the Bill was never passed.

The parallels between 'The Twa Dogs' and 'The Ghaists' go further than simple characterisation. In 'The Twa Dogs', Caesar and Luath depict an odious cleft between the wealthy and the deprived. While Caesar's idle owners have little to do to generate riches, Luath's must engage in brutalising labour. Caesar finds the treatment of tenants abhorrent:

> I've notic'd, on our Laird's *court-day*,
> An' mony a time my heart's been wae,
> Poor *tenant-bodies*, scant o' cash,
> How they maun thole a *factor*'s snash;
> He'll stamp an' threaten, curse an' swear,
> He'll *apprehend* them, *poind* [impound, confiscate] their gear,
> While they maun stand, wi' aspect humble,
> An' hear it a', an' fear an' tremble! (ll. 93–100)

Caesar presents his own kind as spoilt, obnoxious children, 'stamping' and 'threatening', 'cursing' and 'swearing' to gather their 'gear'. While Luath has fluently articulated his tenant farming family's 'sair disasters' (l. 79) as they are 'fash'd' (l. 71) with the gruelling toil of 'biggan a dyke' (l. 72) or 'Bairan a quarry' (l. 73), Caesar's owner 'rises when he likes himsel' (l. 53) while he 'draws a bonny, silken purse' (l. 56). Burns's rhetorical stroke, however, means that the reader's – and indeed Luath's and Caesar's – sympathy remains firmly with the cotter's family. While Luath's description of his family's accustomedness to teetering on 'poortith's brink' (l. 103) to such an extent that it 'gies them little fright' (l. 106) suggests a sad form of learned helplessness, their warm familial affection provides a concrete coping device:

> The dearest comfort o' their lives,
> Their grushie weans, an' faithfu' wives;
> The *prattling things* are just their pride,
> That sweetens a' their fireside. (ll. 111–14)

Family life is the sweetness in the tenant's apparently sour life; the love of his wife and children mean that he can 'thole a *factor*'s snash'. With the biblical lesson of the rich man's attempts to enter Heaven firmly in mind, Burns's message is, of course, that the tenant's priorities are correct and, indeed, Christian, while the factor is damned.

In Fergusson's 'The Ghaists', a similar device is employed. After remembering the 'blest days' (l. 33), 'Whan royal Jamie sway'd the sovereign rod' (l. 32), Herriot examines the gentry's selfish strategies:

> They raise provisions as the stents they raise,
> Yoke hard the poor, and lat the rich chiels be,
> Pamper'd at ease by ither's industry. (ll. 70–3)

For both Burns and Fergusson, the aristocracy are 'pamper'd' by the 'industry' of the poor. In 'The Ghaists', the situation is bleak and its actors deeply sinister; the rich, 'if they get their private pouches lin'd, / Gie na a winnelstrae for a' mankind' (ll. 105–6) as they 'Laugh in their sleeve, and get a place at court' (l. 114). In 'The Twa Dogs', the tenants are 'maistly wonderfu' contented' (l. 84) because their families provide spiritual wealth and succour. While Fergusson's poem ends on a serious note, with the ghosts wishing to 'fleg the schemers o' the *mortmain-bill*' (l. 134), Burns's ends humorously, with the dogs shaking 'their lugs' (l. 235) with relief as they 'Rejoic'd they were na *men* but *dogs*' (l. 236). Although 'The Twa Dogs' and 'The Ghaists' bear the same didactic message concerning the dishonour and voracity of titled mankind, each piece retains an individual spirit. While Burns may borrow political sentiment from 'The Ghaists' in 'The Twa Dogs', its gentle narrative humour is also comparable to Fergusson's 'Mutual Complaint'. His literary inheritance from Fergusson is inclusive; Burns exploits it to create his own profoundly distinctive poetic brand.

Burns's 'The Brigs of Ayr' (K 120) is another poem 'suggested' by Fergusson's 'Mutual Complaint' but, as Thomas Crawford observes, it also owes considerable debt 'to Allan Ramsay's "The Twa Books", which contains the lines: 'For as auld-fashioned as I look, / Maybe I am the better book'.[11] Like 'The Twa Books', Burns's 'The Brigs of Ayr' is a debate concerning the merits of old and new, with Ayr's ancient bridge debating its strengths with its newly-built counterpart. Ostensibly a simple, witty tale, Burns's poem nevertheless soberly explores the advantages of improvement in all its forms. Crawford elaborates:

> The New Brig equates progress with the architecture of Robert Adam, whom the Town Council paid for a plan of a bridge, according to the Ayr burgh accounts; and the advancement is seen as identical with Reason, with anti-celibacy, with the mean between two extremes. Reaction, on the other hand, is manifest in Gothic architecture, Roman Catholicism, the celibacy of nuns, and the Calvinist fanaticism of the later seventeenth century.[12]

With his poet's fantasy of a dawn dispute between inanimate father and son, Burns channels Enlightenment debates on 'Reason' and 'progress', and 'The Brigs of Ayr', like 'The Twa Dogs' and 'The Ghaists', concerns non-human observations of very human faults. After rekindling cherished memories of 'my dear-remembered, ancient yealings [contemporaries in age]' (l. 150), 'To whom our moderns are but causey [street]-cleaners' (l. 155), the Auld Brig mourns a lost Scottish past of apparently 'plain' but intense religious passion:

> Nae langer Rev'rend Men, their country's glory,
> In plain, braid Scots hold forth a plain, braid story:
> Nae langer thrifty Citizens, an' douce,
> Meet owre a pint, or in the Council-house;
> But staumrel [stammering], corky-headed, graceless Gentry,
> The herryment and ruin of the country,
> Men, three-parts made by Taylors and by Barbers,
> Wha waste your weel-hain'd [preserved] gear on d—d *new Brigs* and *Harbours*!
>   (ll. 166–73)

The Auld Brig champions icons of the Scottish past: Calvinist and Roman Catholic preachers and their 'douce' congregations, apparently moderate social pleasures and a romanticised concept of meritocracy. In a typically Burnsian rhetorical stroke, this idealised past is contrasted to the base present: now that 'staumrel, corky-headed, graceless Gentry' are in control, they have brought about the 'ruin of the country'. Again, as in 'The Twa Dogs', the 'weel-hain'd' labour and capital of ordinary people such as 'Taylors' and 'Barbers' are squandered by ignominious aristocrats, and, as in 'The Ghaists', the poor are 'yoked hard' for the benefit of their self-styled 'betters'. Most tellingly, their efforts are wasted; their money is utilised to create mere material show, providing Ayr's *new Brigs and Harbours*'.

The New Brig responds to its counterpart's blustering language with Enlightenment ratiocination and moderation. After refusing to bedaub the names of the Auld Brig's 'Priesthood' (l. 176), recognising that such pronouncements are perilous, as '*Corbies* and *Clergy* are a shot right kittle' [roused] (l. 177), the New Brig contrasts the corruption and extremism of the past to the moderate, Enlightened present:

> Nae mair the Council waddles down the street,
> In all the pomp of ignorant conceit;
> Men wha grew wise priggin [haggling] owre hops an' raisins,
> Or gather'd lib'ral views in Bonds and Seisins.
> If haply Knowledge, on a random tramp,
> Had shor'd them with a glimmer of his lamp,
> And would to Common-sense for once betray'd them,
> Plain, dull Stupidity stept kindly in to aid them. (ll. 184–91)

In an ironic echo of the Auld Brig's lament of 'Nae langer . . .', the New Brig celebrates the death of past conventions. And again, the New Brig utilises a watchword of Enlightenment in its argument: while the Auld Brig mourned the 'plain' preaching of the past, the New Brig equates plainness with 'dullness' and 'Stupidity', and rejoices in the reign of 'Common-sense'.

Tellingly, Burns gives the New Brig the last word in his debate of tradition and progress, embracing 'Common-sense' and apparently allying himself with the improvers of the Scottish Enlightenment. The poem's ending introduces harmony, moderation and reason:

> Last, white-rob'd Peace, crown'd with hazle wreath,
> To rustic Agriculture did bequeath
> The broken, iron instruments of Death,
> At sight of whom our Sprites forgat their kindling wrath. (ll. 231–4)

Exploiting Augustan literary machinery, Burns ends 'The Brigs of Ayr' on a conciliatory note. The 'Sprites' of the new and old bridges are silenced by the solemn presences of 'Peace', 'Agriculture' and 'Death', as the poet rejects irrational indulgences in the supernatural. In his witty deconstruction of the uncanny, Burns presents himself as the Enlightened gentleman poet; as 'the Bard in a Rational Society'.[13]

In Fergusson's 'Mutual Complaint of Plainstanes and Causey', the reader witnesses a similar night-time conversation between Edinburgh's pavement and causeway. Although both characters have kept their places in the capital for 'thir hunder years and mair' (l. 21) and see themselves as comrades who bear 'sun-shine and [. . .] weety weather' 'together' (ll. 23–4), they indulge in a traditional Scottish flyting as replicated in Burns's 'The Brigs of Ayr'. Their debate concerns not progress and tradition, but which of them suffers most at the hands of their traffic. 'Causey' insists it is he, as he endures 'the brunt / Of Highland chairman's heavy dunt' (ll. 60–1). The response of 'Plainstanes' illustrates parallels of both tone and technique with 'The Brigs of Ayr':

> For whin-stanes, howkit [dug] frae the craigs [crags],
> May thole [endure] the prancing feet of naigs,
> Nor ever fear uncanny hotches [jerks]
> Frae clumsy carts or hackney-coaches,
> While I, a weak and feckless creature,
> Am moulded by a safter nature. (ll. 63–72)

In this humorous retort, 'Plainstanes' celebrates his 'weakness' and 'fecklessness' as positive attributes, while Fergusson presents a comic illustration of poetic decorum: 'Causey' has earned the honour of bearing the weight of 'clumsy carts' because he is made of 'doughtier' materials. Despite comparable approaches in 'Mutual Complaint' and 'The Brigs of Ayr', the poems' endings diverge. While Burns silences his bridges with majestic personifications, Fergusson proposes an idiosyncratic solution to his debate:

> But first, I think it will be good
> To bring it to the *Robinhood*,
> Whare we shall hae the question stated,
> And keen and crabbitly debated. (ll. 129–32)

Plainstanes and Causey agree to present their case to 'the *Robinhood*', the debating society of which Fergusson was a member, for discussion and resolution. While this is undoubtedly humorous, particularly for Fergusson's local audience, it perhaps illustrates one source for the preponderance of debate poems in the oeuvres of Fergusson and Burns. While providing social interaction and a rehearsal ground for literary compositions, Fergusson's Cape Club and Robinhood Society and Burns's Tarbolton Bachelors' Club, like Ramsay's Easy Club earlier in the century, were influential on literary production. Fergusson's and Burns's dispute poems offer poetic expression of the social life of clubs in eighteenth-century Scotland, as well as imperative negotiations of society at large.

Burns's smiling exploration of the supernatural, as seen in 'The Brigs of Ayr', is visible too in 'Halloween' (K 73), which also takes cues from Fergusson's 'Hallow-Fair' (1772).[14] From Fergusson, Burns inherits an ancient poetic tradition of festivity and brawl poetry, encapsulated in both poets' use of the reinvigorated 'Christ's Kirk on the Green' stanza-form. 'Halloween' and 'Hallow-Fair' are united in their focus and subject matter: rather than exploring supernatural beliefs, both Fergusson and Burns describe the human rituals carried out at Halloween; namely drinking, carousing and gaming. Fergusson's poem demonstrates that the chaos of the evening, rather than any supernatural visitation, is the real cause of terror for his narrator:

> Good fock, as ye come frae the fair,
>   Bide yont frae this black squad:
> There's nae sic savages elsewhere
>   Allow'd to wear cockade.
> Than the strong lion's hungry maw,
>   Or tusk o' Russian bear,
> Frae their wanruly fellin paw
>   Mair cause ye hae to fear
>   Your death that day. (ll. 100–7)

In 'Hallow-Fair', the drunkards gathered in Edinburgh for play are to beware, not of ghosts and witches, but of the City Guard, the capital's police force, made up of ex-soldier Highlanders. This 'squad' is 'blacker', according to Fergusson, than any of the Devil's work. Fergusson's aim here is, of course, to generate humour – the City Guard become villains in the poet's corpus comparable to the foppish 'macaronies' and the Scotophobic Samuel Johnson – but there are also serious aspects to this Halloween brawl. Fergusson describes the noise and tumult generated by the celebration as akin to 'a' the tongues at Babylon, / Confus'd that day' (ll. 71–2). Rather than utilise the watchwords of Enlightenment, as Burns does, Fergusson employs the artillery of the Tory Augustan humanist. As F. W. Freeman suggests:

> If in so many town poems Auld Reikie is equated with order and tranquillity, purity and health, fair weather or indoor warmth, modern Edinburgh is its antithesis: counterpastoral, or, specifically, as in 'Hallow-Fair', 'Babylon', an image familiar to the reading public since the days of Roundhead and Cavalier. Modern Whig Edinburgh was, in the rhetoric of Mackenzie of Rosehaugh, Colvil, Pitcairne and William Meston, the new Babylon: 'Babel', 'Babylon of Confusions', 'Whore of Babylon', 'Whore of Babel', and so on.[15]

Fergusson, with his Tory world-view, fears the progress personified by Burns's New Brig; the actual grounds for fright in 'Hallow-Fair' are people and the disorder they create. Where Burns's Enlightened poetic eye looks to the future with optimism, Fergusson's Tory, Jacobite and humanist eye looks back, to a simpler time of order and harmony.

In Burns's 'Halloween', the ruling sentiment is, as in 'Hallow-Fair', human festivity and carnival. While Burns frames his poem with ghost stories from local Ayrshire folklore, his text contains none of Fergusson's apprehension; instead, its narrator looks delightedly on the scene of celebration which passes before him:

> Wi' merry sangs, an' friendly cracks,
>   I wat they did na weary;
> And unco tales, an' funnie jokes,
>   Their sports were cheap and cheary:
> Till *buttr'd Sons*, wi' fragrant lunt,
>   Set a' their gabs a steerin;
> Syne, wi' a social glass o' strunt,
>   They parted aff careerin
>   Fu' blythe that night. (ll. 244–52)

In his role as a rational, Enlightened bard, Burns simply enjoys the human spectacle in 'Halloween' and, while he is detached from his characters just as Fergusson is in 'Hallow-Fair', Burns displays a sanguinity and confidence which is inspired by, but qualified in, Fergusson's work. According to McGuirk, these differences between the two poets are explained by the fact that 'Burns is simply not as afraid of the dark as Fergusson': 'Fergusson's poems never open out, like so many of Burns's, into a vision of the better world that's 'comin yet, for a' that' . . . Fergusson's Scotland is a darker place. He is less hopeful, more haunted, than Burns.'[16] Many of Burns's most renowned poetic celebrations of humanity's social pleasures, however, find their roots in Fergusson's work. Burns's 'The Holy Fair' (*K* 70), with its comically irreverent portrait of an open-air Presbyterian communion or 'Occasion' in Mauchline, derives from Fergusson's description of Edinburgh's summer horserace in 'Leith Races' (1772).[17] Both poets' narrators begin their poems wandering in the summer countryside, when they are met by female personifications. Fergusson's muse and guide, who 'loups like HEBE o'er the grass' (l. 25) identifies herself as 'Mirth', who 'ne'er was kend / To grumble or look sour' (ll. 32–3); and in the bargain struck between poet and muse, Fergusson utilises ballad and folksong tradition in tandem with neoclassical literary tropes. Burns, on the other hand, meets 'three *hizzies*, early at the road' (l. 12). Two, quiet and solemn, are 'Superstition' and 'Hypocrisy', while 'Mirth's' Burnsian counterpart is 'FUN – your cronie dear, / The nearest friend ye hae' (ll. 37–8). Whereas 'Mirth' in 'Leith Races' guides the poet through a scene of festivity which he presents in the carnivalesque 'Christ's Kirk' metre, Burns's poem is more complex. The skulking presence of 'Superstition' and 'Hypocrisy', loitering behind the scenes, reminds the reader that Burns's poem is designed to satirise the excesses of organised religion. In this case, Fergusson's inheritance is recontextualised to be meaningful in Burns's Presbyterian milieu: the native religion of the heart is, according to Burns, superior to the artificiality of Christian worship. These Rousseauist concepts of native dignity and natural goodness are close to Burns's poetic heart, appearing throughout his corpus in myriad ways. In this, too, he translates literary inheritances from his predecessor. In 'Scotch Drink' Burns describes whisky as his muse, borrowing both his theme and outrageously drunken rhymes from Fergusson's 'Caller Water' (1773).[18] Similarly, Burns's 'To a Haggis' extols homely Scottish food in a manner similar to Fergusson's 'Caller Oysters' (1772)[19] and 'Good Eating' (1773).[20] Fergusson's 'The Farmer's Ingle (1773) and Burns's 'The Cotter's Saturday Night' are often compared, with the former clearly a model for the latter. Many of the themes of luxury and virtue, as discussed already, pertain. There is, however, at least one significant difference between the two poems. Fergusson chooses the relatively prosperous farmer as his patriarch, while Burns's central figure is a cotter, occupying a role traditionally lower in the agricultural hierarchy. Here is another moment where Burns transposes a Fergussonian idea to late eighteenth-century Ayrshire accommodating it to his own typical and altogether more fragile economic milieu.

Fergusson and Burns both died prematurely. Each imagined their own deaths in their poetry, Burns in 'A Bard's Epitaph' (K 104) and Fergusson in 'The Author's Life'.[21] Burns describes his 'life's mad career, / Wild as the wave' (ll. 15–16), while Fergusson sees his existence as 'the flowing stream / That glides where summer's beauties teem' (ll. 1–2). As Burns surveys 'this grave' (l. 18), Fergusson imagines forsaking 'winter's sad decay' (l. 9) to 'center in my parent lake' (l. 10). Just as Fergusson's 'flowing stream' lends water to Burns's wild, poetic 'wave', Burns also bestows gifts on Fergusson, providing literary memorials more enduring than the stone he erected in Canongate Kirkyard. While Burns undoubtedly thrives on Fergusson's poetic legacy, his predecessor's 'real service', according to McDiarmid, was to 'help Burns to be his original self'.[22] Fergusson and Burns are allied but unlike; they are, in Burns's words, true 'brothers in the muse'.

CHAPTER EIGHT

Burns and Romantic Writing

Fiona Stafford

In Jane Austen's *Sanditon*, Burns is pressed into service by Sir Edward Denham, who regards him as the perfect ally in his attempt to impress the increasingly sceptical Charlotte Heywood. Though initially sympathetic to Sir Edward's display of sensibility, Charlotte finds herself beginning 'to stagger' under the barrage of quotations and bewildering sentences. Sir Edward evokes Scott, only to dismiss him for his 'want of passion', before moving on to uphold Burns as the quintessential man of feeling – 'Burns is always on fire. – His Soul was the Altar in which lovely Woman sat enshrined, his Spirit truly breathed immortal Incense which is her due.' As the conversation takes a distinctly predatory turn, Charlotte retorts that although she had read Burns with great delight, she was 'not poetic enough to separate a Man's Poetry entirely from his Character' and that 'poor Burns's known Irregularities' greatly interrupted her enjoyment of his poetry.[1] In this brief comic exchange, Austen is playing with the relationship between life and lines, as her fictional characters deploy quotation and literary reference to develop or impede their mutual acquaintance. Her choice of Burns for this self-conscious literary exploration could hardly have been more appropriate. As the author of some of the best known love lyrics of the age, Burns was an obvious favourite for Austen's character, and the poem on 'Highland Mary' that Sir Edward recalls had already succeeded in melting the generally unyielding heart of the formidable Edinburgh critic, Francis Jeffrey.[2] Equally important, however, was the knowledge that by 1817, Burns's poetry had become inseparable from ideas about his life. Indeed, the comic allusions to Burns have a dark undertone in Austen's unfinished satire on the contemporary vogue for sea-water therapies, for his final illness had been hurried on by the treatment prescribed for him on the Solway. Responses to literature, as Austen knew only too well, were determined as much by thoughts of an author's death as by knowledge of his life. Burns's story was so familiar to readers of the period that she had no need to waste her own failing energy on spelling out the references. His very name was the perfect shorthand for a dying author who had scores to settle with the medical profession. Burns had not been helped much by doctors in the months of his premature decline, but his posthumous reputation had been heavily coloured by the biography which James Currie had published as an introduction to the first substantial edition of his *Works* in 1800. Charles Lamb, who idolised Burns in his youth, was not alone in being surprised to find the biography of his favourite poet 'interspersed with dull pathological and *medical* discussions' from the Liverpool doctor who assembled the surviving poetry and letters.[3] Others, however, including Lamb's friend, Coleridge, were much more intrigued by medical matters and greeted Currie's work as 'a masterly specimen of philosophical biography'.[4] Medical knowledge might not have been able to cure Burns's illness, but it seemed to be providing some sort of explanation for his decline.

Currie's edition of Burns reached a wide audience and did much to create a memorable image of the man behind the poems and songs, even in the minds of those most dismayed by the biography. For Wordsworth, Currie's 'Life' was a 'revolting account of a man of exquisite genius, and confessedly of many high moral qualities, sunk into the lower depths of vice and misery!'[5] It nevertheless furnished him with the haunting lines in 'Resolution and Independence' that conjure up the young Burns, walking 'in glory and in joy / Following the plough', and make the decline of the older poet into 'despondency and madness', seem all the more bleak.[6] Keats, a trained medical practitioner himself, was similarly troubled by the famous 'fate of Burns', but more inclined to attribute it to the very society Currie presented as the fertile ground of the poet's healthy growth. Keats looked aghast on the severe Presbyterian culture that seemed so stifling to a man of vigorous natural tendencies, commenting indignantly, 'I would sooner be a wild hog than be the occasion of a Poor Creatures pennance before those execrable elders.'[7] Clearly, not all contemporary readers responded to the revelations about Burns's life in the same way – but few could have missed them altogether. Whether or not Jane Austen's readers were more likely to share Sir Edward Denham's admiration for Burns's 'illimitable Ardour' or Charlotte Heywood's unease over the notorious 'Irregularities', there is little doubt that during the early nineteenth century, Burns's own character, emotion and personal experience were widely believed to be immediately evident in his work.

When Austen created the brief conversation about Burns's life and art, she was making fun of fashionable attitudes, even as she addressed a serious contemporary concern. Burns came under frequent discussion in the London literary circles that she encountered during 1815 and 1816, but his life attracted interest throughout the islands. After the copyright on Currie's Burns expired, a new edition appeared in Edinburgh, in 1815, with additional letters from the poet's brother and friends, that defended his memory against the disapproving interpretations of his first editor. Alexander Peterkin, introducing the new collection, charged anyone who had known Burns to 'come forth . . .

and tell the truth, and to vindicate his memory from unqualified dishonour'.[8] The question of Burns's life had become a standard topic of debate.

When Crabb Robinson visited Anna Letitia Barbauld and Joan Aikin in Islington in May 1816, he read them Wordsworth's newly published denunciation of intrusive literary biography, *A Letter to a Friend of Robert Burns*, commenting in his diary, 'Wordsworth is a pure man, and therefore his indulgence of the irregularities of Burns is most amiable.'[9] Crabb Robinson was clearly on Charlotte Heywood's side of the debate over Burns's life and art and, like Austen's heroine, found his delight in the poems complicated by knowledge of the poet's private affairs. Others thought differently, however, including Sir Egerton Brydges who found evidence in Burns's letters that 'the impulse of the true poet towards his occupation is generally irresistible, even to the neglect of all, to which prudence and self-interest imperiously direct his attention.'[10] According to this argument, the passions that led to the creation of the most affecting poetry also tended to produce embarrassments of every kind: in other words, Burns's 'irregularities' were inseparable from his 'genius'.

When Crabb Robinson pondered over whether Wordsworth was right to be covering 'as with a mantle' the great poet's 'infirmities', he was articulating the same question that Austen raised in *Sanditon* and that numerous contemporary readers of Burns felt obliged to address. For even poems as wonderful as 'Scotch Drink' or 'Tam o' Shanter' had taken on a somewhat different tone when read in the light of Currie's account of Burns's descent into alcoholism. The love lyrics that were being sung everywhere began to strike some admirers as less than sincere, once they became aware of the poet's rapid succession of passions ('He felt & he wrote & he forgot', as Charlotte Heywood observes).[11] Indeed, the issues surrounding a poet's life and art were directly addressed in one of the greatest manifestos of Romantic literature, where Shelley argued passionately that a great writer's personal shortcomings were mere 'dust in the balance' to be 'washed in the blood of the mediator and the redeemer Time'.[12]

If the poems were immortal, did it matter that the life of their creator had not conformed to contemporary standards of morality? What right had biographers to make judgments on the man, when his real significance lay in his writing? Shelley was reiterating the point made by Wordsworth in his defence of Burns ('Our business is with their books, – to understand and to enjoy them')[13] and by Byron in *Don Juan*:

> All these certes are interesting facts,
> Like Shakespeare's stealing deer, Lord Bacon's bribes,
> Like Titus's youth and Caesar's early acts,
> Like Burns (whom Dr Currie well describes),

Like Cromwell's pranks; but although truth exacts
These amiable descriptions from the scribes
As most essential to their hero's story,
They do not contribute much to his glory.[14]

The indignation of Wordsworth, Shelley and Byron, each of whom had reason to feel unease over the biographical question, reveals only too clearly that the contemporary appetite for juicy lives of poets was keen. Such concerns are not peculiar to the Romantic age, however, since biographical issues still prove troubling to readers repelled by personal aspects of a favourite author. Admirers of T. S. Eliot's poetry may be unsettled by suspicions about his anti-Semitism, while enjoyment of Ted Hughes's work has been marred for some by thoughts of his complicated relationships. Like so many modern critical preoccupations, debates over the writer's life are part of the rich legacy of the Romantic period, which saw the birth of less idealised biography and more self-expressive poetry than that of earlier ages. Central to both developments was Robert Burns – man and poet.

This chapter is not concerned primarily with the importance of Burns for literary biography, but rather with his influence on writers of the Romantic period. In order to understand the very varied literary responses to Burns, however, it is necessary to recognise that even contemporary reactions were conditioned by notions about the man behind the poetry. The immediate success of *Poems Chiefly in the Scottish Dialect*, published in Kilmarnock in July 1786, meant that Burns's reading public was influenced almost at once by the critical acclaim of Henry Mackenzie, whose famous *Lounger* essay appeared in December, fixing the label of the 'heaven-taught ploughman' to the poetry. Nor was the image constructed entirely from without – Mackenzie and other early readers were responding directly to Burns's presentation of himself in the epigraph as 'The Simple Bard', whose verses had always been a comforting diversion from the hard work of agricultural labour.

When the second edition of Burns's *Poems* appeared in Edinburgh the following year, it included a dedication to the 'Noblemen and Gentlemen of the Caledonian Hunt', with whom the poet claimed 'the common Scottish name'.[15] Despite this more elaborate appeal to his 'illustrious Countrymen', however, Burns still reminded readers of his rural upbringing: 'I was bred to the Plough, and am independent.' Although Burns asserted the essential equality of mankind in his poems, his insistent self-portrayal as a ploughman meant that some were inclined to read his work through the distorting lenses of social superiority. His Scottish dialect struck many as the language of the lower classes, as is abundantly evident in the double-edged adjectives that characterise the early reviews – 'uncultivated', 'common' 'untutored', 'simple', 'provincial'. The qualities that seemed most to confirm the truthfulness of his work also placed him in the awkward situation of being simultaneously elevated and patronised. Burns's immediate literary success was immense, but the image of the simple bard, picked up and promoted by influential critics, remained. His early death then prompted a host of obituaries and memoirs, in which the humble origins of the poet were described in detail for readers trying to make sense of the natural genius who had dawned, dazzled and disappeared so suddenly. Any writer who encountered Burns's work after 1796 was therefore influenced by not only the sentimental image of the heaven-taught ploughman, but also the fuller analyses which followed his melancholy end.

The response of the younger generation of Romantic writers – Byron, Shelley, Mary Shelley, Keats or Clare – was thus inevitably different in kind from those who had experienced the excitement generated by the 'Kilmarnock' edition. Cowper, Wordsworth, Coleridge, Lamb and Scott were all reading Burns before his death in 1796 and greeted *Poems, Chiefly in the Scottish Dialect* in the way that only fellow writers can react to a remarkable new talent. Cowper's admiration for the 'very extraordinary volume' mingled with frustration over Burns's 'uncouth dialect' and Dorothy Wordsworth's spontaneous amusement at 'To a Louse' in December 1787 were entirely free of the later biographically-informed pall.[16] For Byron, Keats and the Shelleys, on the other hand, Burns's unhappy story was already finished by the time they began to appreciate his genius: from the beginning, they knew that the corpus was complete. Their reading of Burns was necessarily coloured by the controversy over his life, while his significance for their own work was often linked to related literary questions. Mary Shelley's posthumous tributes to her husband, for example, drew strength from the 'many volumes [. . .] filled with the life of the Scottish plough-boy', because they seemed a guarantee of the truth of his poetry: 'We welcome with delight every fact which proves that the patriotism and tenderness expressed in the songs of Burns, sprung from a noble and gentle heart.'[17]

If biographical knowledge made it difficult for later Romantic readers to respond to Burns's poetry without preconceptions, it nevertheless seems often to have enhanced their sense of Burns's emotional truth. Carlyle's emphasis on Burns's 'sincerity' was the culmination of three decades of reading Burns in terms of his life as well as his art. The widely held assumption that Burns's poetry represented the spontaneous responses of a peculiarly tender heart meant that the life story was increasingly read as confirmation of the poetry. Hazlitt's pithy summary – 'He had an eye to see, a heart to feel' – grew directly from the Romantic obsession with the details of a humble poet's life, loves and local community.[18] Burns was inseparable from his surroundings and Hazlitt saw his unfiltered experience as the key to his success: 'For the artificial flowers of poetry, he plucked the mountain-daisy under his feet.' Burns was a man with his feet firmly on the ground and his poetry was quite distinct from much of what poured from the London presses. Instead of imitating literary convention, he felt his environment, recreating his responses in poetry.

Admiration of this kind might have meant that Burns was regarded as a poet of merely mimetic skills, rather than as a fountain of creativity, but new aesthetic ideas had made feeling and sincerity seem essential to the creation of truly imaginative poetry. Though Hazlitt pronounced Burns somewhat deficient in 'inventive power' compared with Shakespeare, other influential critics were turning to his work as an expression of creative genius. For Coleridge, one of the defining features of genius was an ability to represent familiar objects in such a way as to awaken in others a 'kindred feeling' and 'freshness of sensation'. This rare quality was to be found in Shakespeare, of course, but it was also characteristic of Burns:

> Who has not a thousand times seen snow fall on water? Who has not watched it with a new feeling, from the time that he has read Burns' comparison of sensual pleasure
> > To snow that falls upon a river
> > A moment white – then gone for ever![19]

As Coleridge grappled to distinguish between writers who were merely talented, and those possessed of true genius, he placed Burns firmly in the latter category. Burns shared with Wordsworth the capacity to 'carry on the feelings of childhood into the powers of manhood; to combine the child's sense of wonder and novelty with the appearances, which every day [. . .] had rendered familiar'. The capacity to feel profoundly and consequently to create moving poetry was, for Coleridge, a mark of the truly creative writer, of the human mind most akin to the divine.

By the late eighteenth century, feeling had come to be regarded as fundamental to the creation of true poetry – an aesthetic development with far-reaching consequences. As M. H. Abrams recognised long ago, Romantic poetry embodied a new expressive impulse, which rapidly came to be defined by contemporary commentators as 'the imaginative process which modifies and synthesises the images, thoughts, and feelings of the poet'.[20] Rather than being judged primarily according to the accuracy of its imitation of human nature, or by its capacity to please and educate readers, poetry became prized for its revelation of 'the mind and heart of the poet himself'. Poetry of any real value depended on profound emotion and, conversely, poetry with the capacity to move the hearts of readers could be taken as evidence of the innermost feelings of the poet. Burns, the 'man of feeling', composed deeply affecting poems, which were in turn read as evidence of his own sensitivity and reliance on emotion as the key to human action – 'The heart ay's the part ay, / That makes us right or wrang' (*K* 51, ll. 69–70).

The idea that poems expressed the 'spontaneous overflow of powerful feelings' was articulated most memorably by Wordsworth, whose own aesthetic beliefs had drawn strength from the congenial example of Burns. In 1799, the year before he composed the Preface to *Lyrical Ballads*, Wordsworth was in Germany, reading Burns with renewed admiration. He wrote excitedly to Coleridge, praising the 'presence of human life' in Burns's poetry and its capacity to stir profound feelings – 'His "Ode to Despondency" I can never read without the deepest agitation.'[21] When Wordsworth was setting out their poetic ideals in prose in the summer of 1800, however, he emphasised not only the connection between poems and feelings but also the kind of environment in which the essential passions of humanity could best be discovered. Many of the poems in the first volume of *Lyrical Ballads* of 1798 had been set in the countryside, but the new, expanded edition was even more marked by the presence of pastoral poems and rural figures. As Wordsworth explained to his readers, 'Low and rustic life' was chosen for his attempts to create a kind of poetry that aspired to permanence, because in that situation, 'the essential passions of the heart find a better soil in which they can attain their maturity, are less under restraint, and speak a plainer and more emphatic language'.[22] Another reason, of course, was that the poetry of Burns, which embodied just the kind of spontaneous feeling and universally recognisable human situations that Wordsworth championed, was also the product of an unassuming rural community.

Currie's four-volume edition of Burns, with its detailed account of Burns's upbringing on a Scottish farm, appeared in 1800 just as Wordsworth was preparing his new edition for the press. When Coleridge arrived in Keswick, in July, he was fresh from a week in Liverpool, where he had spent time discussing the new Life of Burns with its author, James Currie.[23] Much of what was being revealed about Burns confirmed ideas that Coleridge and Wordsworth had been developing since the beginning of the *Lyrical Ballads* project and so, as Wordsworth worked hard on his Preface, Coleridge's recent encounter with Currie was very timely. If Currie's edition prompted Wordsworth into fresh engagement with Burns in 1800, however, it was acting on an admiration that had hardly grown stale. Wordsworth's profound sympathy with Burns's poetry was well-established, as evident not just through remarks in letters, but also in his own poetry. The dismay visible in 'Lines Written in Early Spring', published in 1798, where Wordsworth describes how 'much it grieved my heart to think / What man has made of man', finds an obvious antecedent in Burns's 'Man's inhumanity to man / Makes countless thousands mourn!' (*K* 64, ll. 55–6).[24] In this poem, 'Man was made to Mourn', Burns had portrayed himself as a young poet, learning from the figure of 'the reverend sage' (l. 10) beside the Aire, a framework similar to that adopted by Wordsworth in 'The Ruined Cottage', 'Old Man Travelling', 'The Last of the Flock', the Matthew Poems and later in 'Resolution and Independence'.

Burns's ability to move his readers by unflinchingly addressing unpalatable aspects of the human condition made him an inspiring model for Romantic writers. Their emphasis on feeling in poetry grew not just from abstract ideas about aesthetics but rather from a growing uneasiness about human suffering and a new readiness to sympathise and promote fellow-feeling. Although the 'Kilmarnock' edition was praised by early reviewers for its comic observation of rural manners, it was also full of insights into the distresses afflicting ordinary people. Man's inhumanity to man is lamented in many poems through a pervasive concern for the oppressed. Fears of ageing, dispossession and death run through 'To a Mouse', 'To a Mountain-Daisy' or 'To Ruin', and even the more defiant tone of the 'Epistle to Davie' is thrown into relief by the darkness beneath the bravura. Burns's heart was not enflamed by pretty women alone, but warmed to pity or righteous indignation when confronted by human suffering. Although some of his admirers, like Austen's Sir Edward, were moved only by Burns's beautiful love songs, many were more deeply affected by the poet's confessions of despondency over the plight of man.

For radical writers in the early 1790s, Burns's work offered memorable comment on human rights. Readers who greeted the Fall of the Bastille as the beginning of a new world of freedom and equality could find their political opinions embodied in the poetry of Burns. The 'Kilmarnock' edition opens with the dialogue between the gentleman's Newfoundland and the ploughman's collie, but it is immediately clear from Caesar's description of his master's idle habits, affected tastes, restless travelling, parade and pomp that the sympathies of 'The Twa Dogs' lie firmly with the 'poor tenant-bodies'. Burns's distaste for the 'lordling's pomp' (K 72, 'The Cotter's Saturday Night', l. 169) and emphasis on the superior blessings of 'health and peace and sweet content' (K 72, l. 175) (to be found in the cottage more often than the palace) imbued his first collection of poems with a radical undercurrent that was to become more visible to readers in the decade after its publication. Though in 1786 'A Dream' could risk a light-hearted reference to being 'indicted Treason' (K 113, prefatory epigraph) poets ten years later would not feel free to publish satirical addresses to the king offering political advice and biting comment on the royal family.

Burns's emphasis on having been bred to the plough and on being an independent man takes on a more clearly political dimension when the 'Edinburgh' edition is read alongside his private correspondence of 1787. His friend, Mrs Dunlop, warned him to leave out 'The Dream' from any new edition of his *Poems*, because it was not being well received by readers in London. Burns refused to compromise by flattering the wealthy and powerful, however, and wrote back resolutely, 'I set as little by kings, lords, clergy, critics, &c as all these respectable Gentry do by my Bardship' (*L* I, p. 108). He was, nevertheless, 'resolved to study the sentiments of a very respectable Personage, Milton's Satan – Hail horrors! Hail infernal world!' (*L* I, p. 108). Beneath the witty indignation, Burns was foreseeing his own self-destruction, as he did in numerous letters and poems, but his admiration of Milton had a political as well as personal significance. To celebrate Satan in the same breath as dismissing those at the top of the contemporary social hierarchy was to reveal the same kind of response to *Paradise Lost* as that of Blake, Godwin, Byron or Shelley. For Burns as for his radical heirs, Milton's Satan was the champion of the oppressed and the eloquent opponent of tyranny. The poems in the 'Kilmarnock' edition often wrap their radical sympathies in comedy, but the sentiments of the song beginning 'Is there for honest Poverty' could hardly be less equivocal: 'the rank is but the guinea's stamp / The Man's the gowd for a' that'. Burns used rhetorical questions with the same force that Blake adopted in *Songs of Experience* for poems such as 'Holy Thursday' – and both poets were fully aware of the radical potential inherent in what appeared to be a simple song. The heaven-taught ploughman, as Liam McIlvanney has demonstrated in detail, might more accurately have been known to Romantic readers as 'Burns the Radical'.

As concerns about the violent course of the French Revolution became compounded with fears of an invasion, prompting the British government to introduce a clampdown on any cultural activity deemed seditious, the radical expressions of the early 1790s were largely forced underground. Burns's poetry nevertheless continued to be a source of inspiration for writers with radical sympathies, providing models for expressing ideas of equality without risking charges of sedition. Poems such as 'The Jolly Beggars' were too dangerous to emulate, but Burns's overriding sympathy with the poor and suffering offered ways of exposing the wrongs of society less directly and of emphasising what was common to all humanity. The expression of feeling in poetry was not a purely aesthetic question, and so for many Romantic poets the recent fashion for sensibility provided the foundations for a new kind of literature that was profoundly political and moral in purpose.

If writers of the previous generation, such as Sterne and Sheridan, had been inclined to extract comedy from the excesses of sensibility even as they extolled its pleasures, Burns presented poems of feeling without mocking his low-born subjects. The humour of his work is never directed unkindly at those beneath him, nor does he make fun of the love-struck, unfortunate or broken-hearted. Seamus Heaney has drawn attention to the sympathy that pervades even comic poems such as 'The Death and Dying Words of Poor Mailie', observing that Burns 'retains a certain protectiveness towards those very things which bring out the verbal scamp in him'.[25] Burns caught the comedy of everyday misfortune, but his amusement never destroyed the underlying sympathy, which co-existed with a sense of the tragedy inherent in the commonplace.

This capacity to present deep feeling without absurdity was of enormous importance to writers of the 1790s who had become increasingly disenchanted with Godwinian rational argument and were beginning to recognise the persuasive power of sympathy. By 1800, Wordsworth was presenting deep feeling as essential to poetry, but his aesthetic ideas were part of the radical impulse that continued to inspire his work, despite his own conflicted feelings about contemporary France. 'Simon Lee', for example, adopts the form and metre of several of Burns's songs, but its initially light, timeless tone is punctured by the startling exposure of the indignities of old age. Neither are readers invited to mock the Old Cumberland Beggar or Michael, but to recognise the same truth that Burns had set out in 'A Man's a Man for a' That' or the 'Epistle to Davie' – that 'we have all of us one human heart'.[26]

When Wordsworth defined the poet as 'a man, speaking to men', he could have been referring specifically to Burns just as much as setting out his own ideal.[27] Burns's down-to-earth verse epistles and various addresses were those of a man proud of his independence and repelled by condescension. His use of local language was not merely unapologetic, it was often quite defiant, as in the 'Epistle to John Lapraik', with its overt contempt for the misplaced loftiness of 'your Critic-folk' (*K* 57, l. 55). Although the epistle, with its literary allusions and evocations of Scottish tradition is more complicated than it appears, its immediate, colloquial force had a special resonance for writers whose own language did not conform to the kind of English that became the established standard in the later eighteenth century. Poets such as Robert Anderson, who composed in Cumberland dialect and published his collections in Carlisle, hailed Burns as 'Prince o' the mirthfu' rhyming thrang' in the moving homage composed during Burns's final illness in 1796.[28] Anderson adopted Burns's verse forms, tone and above all, his fearless use of dialect. Here was a poet who demonstrated that the familiar local vernacular could be the language of poetry – and what's more, he had convinced the most respected critical judges of the day.

Indeed, it is hard to overestimate the importance of Burns's success for writers who belonged to the lower classes of eighteenth- and nineteenth-century society. In his autobiography, James Hogg recalled hearing 'Tam o' Shanter' from the lips of 'a half daft man', when he was working as a young shepherd in the Scottish Borders: 'I was delighted! I was far more than delighted – I was ravished! I cannot describe my feelings.'[29] For the young Hogg, it was a life-changing moment – 'This formed a new epoch of my life. Every day I pondered on the genius and fate of Burns. I wept, and always thought with myself – what is to hinder me from succeeding Burns?'

Burns had the power to move people at every level of British society, but his meaning for aspiring poets who had to work hard to survive was especially exciting. Burns had shown the world that a man who spent his life engaged in strenuous physical labour, who spoke with the distinctive accent of his provincial neighbourhood, could publish poetry that moved the hearts of men and women, high and low, rural and urban, Scottish and English.

Not everyone, however, was as thrilled as Hogg by Burns's capacity to inspire poetic outpourings in the lower classes. John Lockhart identified the phenomenon as the 'most incurable' mania of a mad age, lamenting the way in which Burns's celebrity had 'had the melancholy effect of turning the heads of we know not how many farm-servants and unmarried ladies', with the most unfortunate results: 'Our very footmen compose tragedies, and there is scarcely a superannuated governess in the island that does not leave a roll of lyrics behind her in her band-box.'[30] The heavy humour preceded his attack on Keats, the young poet whose promising career in medicine had been blighted by the outbreak of poetical mania. Posterity has not found Lockhart's judgement persuasive, but he was quicker than many of Keats's admirers to recognise the influence of Burns. When Keats attended Hazlitt's lectures in January 1818, he heard Burns being singled out for special praise as a working man, equally at home with the plough or pen, who yet possessed Shakespearean qualities. Six months later, in the very summer that Lockhart's essay appeared, Keats was in Scotland, making the tough pilgrimage to Burns's birthplace.

Keats had walked all the way from Hampstead, paying tribute to Wordsworth en route, and his excitement over reaching Burns country is palpable in the surviving letters: 'We came down upon everything suddenly – there were in our way, the 'bonny Doon', with the Brig that Tam o' Shanter crossed – Kirk Alloway, Burns's Cottage and then the Brigs of Ayr.'[31] Keats recognised the Ayrshire landmarks even though he was seeing them for the first time, and knew that friends in London would pick up the Burnsian references just as easily. Keats had set off in the hope that it would give him 'more experience', 'rub off more Prejudice', introduce him to 'grander mountains' and generally 'strengthen' his poetic range 'than would stopping home among Books', but everywhere he went, the memory of his reading was there to intensify or aggravate his responses (I, p. 342). Keats's journey north was part of his personal programme of poetic growth: by visiting the landscapes of the best native poets, he sought to expand his own creative horizons. Above all, it was a way of breaking away from his normal way of life. Keats approached Alloway with the expectation of 'annulling self' – an idea that he would develop some months later when trying to define the 'poetical Character', which 'has no self – it is every thing and nothing' (I, pp. 323, 386–7).

Instead of finding immediate inspiration in the cottage, however, Keats was almost paralysed by Burns's memory:

> His Misery is a dead weight on the nimbleness of one's quill – I tried to forget it – to drink Toddy without any Care – to write a merry Sonnet – it wont do – he talked with Bitches – he drank with Blackguards, he was miserable. – We can see horribly clear in the works of such a man, his whole life, as if we were God's spies. (I, p. 325)

Keats's ironic allusion to *King Lear* reveals the desperation he felt in Alloway, when confronted with the reality of Burns's life. Nothing in his reading had prepared him for the conflict of emotions which subsequently informed the strange 'Lines written in the Highlands after a Visit to Burns's Country'. The long lines, apparently recalling the experience of 'footing slow across a silent plain', are also reminiscent of the alternating four-stress/three stress lines of Burns's 'Man was Made to Mourn', especially when read aloud (I, p. 344). Keats was using Burns's poetry to recreate the feelings of 'a man whose spirit had gone forth / To find a bard's low cradle-place about the silent north!' but neither the cottage nor Burns figures directly in Keats's poem, which turns instead to terrifying thoughts of personal deprivations – 'Oh horrible to lose the sight of well-remembered face, / Of brother's eyes, of sister's brow, constant to every place'. Whether thoughts of Burns brought to mind the permanent separation of death, or some other deep fear may be unclear, but the startling shift from exultation to despondency is not. The 'great birthplace' produced the most unsettling sensations in Keats, who ends the poem with an uncharacteristic prayer that 'man may never lose his mind on mountains bleak and bare'. Keats had come to Scotland full of optimism, but what he discovered in Alloway was that 'One song of Burns's is of more use to you than all I could think of for a whole year in his native country' (I, p. 325).

Unlike many of the Romantic pilgrims who trudged across south-west Scotland, Keats realised that direct imitation of Burns was futile; but the aftermath of his tour was nevertheless astonishingly productive. In the year following his return to Hampstead, Keats composed all his finest poems, including 'Hyperion', with its cold, northern settings. Though he avoided Scottish forms and dialect except for comic purposes, echoes of Burns continued to sound in poems and correspondence, as in the letter to Haydon, attacking contemporary judgments of the arts, which evokes the 'Second Epistle to John Lapraik'. Keats's consoling message to Haydon, that 'any thing really fine in these days will be felt' shows that ideas he had set out tentatively the year before ('We read fine things but never feel them to the full until we have gone the same steps as the Author') had now become a firm conviction (II, p. 219; I, p. 279). His trip to Scotland – and the profound emotions experienced as he went the same steps as the poets he most admired – had confirmed his faith in the power of feeling and its foundational role in art. If Burns had 'an eye to see, a heart to feel', then he possessed the most important attribute of the great artist.

In August 1820, battling with consumption and contemplating his trip to Rome, Keats tried to reassure Fanny Brawne, 'If I return well from Italy I will turn over a new leaf for you. I have been improving lately, and have very good hopes of "turning a Neuk" and cheating the Consumption' (II, p. 330). It is easy to imagine Keats invoking the tender tone that made Burns the favourite poet of the would-be lovers in his own courtship, but in this late letter the affectionate evocation of Burns's 'To Miss Ferrier' is shrouded by the prospect of a separation likely to prove permanent. Keats was remembering Burns's moment of grateful creative recovery in the light of his own rapidly diminishing powers. If Burns's own life and premature death was anything but reassuring, however, Keats could take comfort from the knowledge that Burns's best moments had proved enduring. For the poet who feared that his name was writ on water, the thought of Burns, whose words had already proved immortal was immensely consoling. Burns's initial success had shown that anything really fine would be felt immediately, but his posthumous fame proved that it could continue to be felt.

For poets compelled to pour feeling into verse, but troubled by the difficulty of capturing fleeting feelings in adequate language, Burns's proven capacity to arrest the transitory was especially heartening. Poetry might be an outpouring of powerful emotion – an effusion, or lava-flow – but the very violence of the creative moment inevitably brought on thoughts of bursting, fading, cooling and even exhaustion. Writing itself sometimes seemed a way of deadening the vital passionate moment. Wordsworth's persistent emphasis on feeling being 'recollected in tranquillity' was part of a pervasive anxiety about the mercurial nature of powerful emotions and their resistance to being brought to order. But everyone agreed that the poetry of Burns embodied genuine feeling and, crucially, made it live for ever. Again and again, people turned to Burns to find suitable words for expressing their own feelings, confident that his lines were able to stand the test of time. When Mary Shelley was seeking to comfort her old friend, Edward John Trelawny, she turned at once to Burns and, quoting the 'Lament for James, Earl of Glencairn' from memory, commented, 'Such feelings are not the growth of a moment. They must have lived for years.'[32] Burns's lines, learned by heart, provided a language through which she could express emotions that were not only deep but lasting. If Burns himself had been accused of having felt, written and forgotten, the work he left behind him continued to be felt by readers, who wrote and remembered.

CHAPTER NINE

Burns the Critic

Corey E. Andrews

> Conceal yoursel as weel's ye can
> Frae critical dissection;
> But keek thro' ev'ry other man,
> Wi' sharpen'd, sly inspection. (*K* 105, 'Epistle to a Young Friend', ll. 37–40)

Robert Burns's view of critics seems clear enough – like many of his peers he had little kind to say. Perhaps his best known animadversion can be found in the following passage from 'To Robert Graham of Fintry':

> Vampyre booksellers drain him to the heart,
> And scorpion critics cureless venom dart: –
> Critics – appall'd, I venture on the name –
> Those cut-throat bandits in the paths of fame;
> Bloody dissectors, worse than ten Monroes:
> He hacks to teach, they mangle to expose. (*K* 335, ll. 35–40)

Critical dissection is a pre- and post-mortem procedure, hacking away at the poet's corpus: 'Dead even resentment for his injur'd page, / He heeds or feels no more the ruthless critic's rage!' (ll. 50–1). Transcending the stings of 'scorpion critics' appears to inform Burns's writing process, where honest sentiment provides creative direction and freedom from critical injury.

Ironically enough, this view of Burns's poetics was popularised by his earliest critics, Henry Mackenzie most prominently. In his *Lounger* review, Mackenzie wrote that Burns's verse displayed 'a high tone of feeling, a power and energy of expression particularly and strongly characteristic of the mind and the voice of a poet'.[1] The majority of Mackenzie's review consisted of carefully-selected quotations, intended to exemplify the 'high tone' and 'energy of expression' which distinguished Burns's poetry. The most memorable coinage from the review appears near its conclusion, where Mackenzie remarks 'with what uncommon penetration and sagacity this heaven-taught ploughman, from his humble and unlettered station, has looked upon men and manners'.[2] The polarities of informed, critical correctness versus inspired, artless composition have dominated discussions of Burns from the start. Burns's poetry offers frequent asseverations on the subject, contrasting learned 'poets' and fun-loving 'rhymers' with little doubt of his preference; he declaims quite bluntly in the epistle 'To James Smith' (K 79) that 'I rhyme for fun' (l. 30). 'Rhyming for fun' suggests a deliberate refusal of critical instruction for verse or life. His 'Epistle to Davie' (K 51) states that 'It's no in books, it's no in Lear, / To make us truly blest' (ll. 61–2), while his 'Epistle to J. Lapraik' contends that:

> I am nae *Poet*, in a sense;
> But just a *Rhymer* like by chance,
> An' hae to Learning nae pretence. (K 57, ll. 49–51)

The dismissal of 'Learning' finds its apogee in Burns's spirited lines in the 'Epistle to J. Lapraik' on 'Critic-folk', whose useless knowledge makes them fit candidates for a place in the *Dunciad*:

> What's a' your jargon o' your Schools,
> Your Latin names for horns an' stools?
> If honest Nature made you fools,
> What sairs your Grammers? (ll. 61–4)

Such education changes the lives and nature of the young scholars who hope to become 'Critic-folk' like their teachers. In fact, the students undergo a Circean transformation:

> A set o' dull, conceited Hashes
> Confuse their brains in Colledge-classes,
> They gang in Stirks [steer], and come out Asses. (ll. 67–9)

Summing up the argument in the 'Epistle to J. Lapraik', Burns issues a direct challenge to critics' authority and their judgment of literary value:

> Your Critic-folk may cock their nose,
> And say, 'How can you e'er propose,
> You wha ken hardly verse frae prose,
>   To mak a sang?'
> But, by your leaves, my learned foes,
> Ye're maybe wrang. (ll. 55–60)

This dichotomy between 'learned foes' and 'heaven-taught' poets has greatly oversimplified the largely ignored issue of Burns's own critical practice. In his prose and letters, one can find wide-ranging discussions of poetry and song, along with detailed analyses of literary forms and modes. Burns's critical writings belie the deliberate oppositions of critic and poet and reveal a writer deeply invested in his craft, using critical axioms and sentimental topoi to refine his work.

As Carol McGuirk has observed, Burns's efforts were often hampered by external perceptions of his creativity: '[I]n their eagerness to experience Burns as a poet of nature, his admirers ignored [his] efforts to assert an articulate critical authority.'[3] For Burns, criticism was less about displaying correct learning or taste than discovering sources for emulation. Successful emulation resulted from critical analysis and creative transposition, studying primary texts for sources, ideas and strategies for future writing. Such a vigorous and surprisingly cohesive attitude about the craft of writing forms the heart of Burns's criticism, an uncollected commentary randomly dispersed throughout his prose. This body of work also pointedly refutes his supposed 'want of Learning' and reveals a predominantly practical reader intrigued with the process of poetic creation.

The commonplace book of 1783–5 reveals Burns's early infatuation with language and the beginnings of his critical practice. Paratactic constructions abound as the young would-be poet lists the 'scraps and observations' that will comprise the book itself: a miscellany of random thoughts, poems and proverbial insights. He hopes a 'curious observer of human-nature' may someday be interested in 'how a ploughman thinks and feels under the pressure of Love, Ambition, Anxiety, Grief, with the like cares and passions'.[4] The critical view is raw and energetic, on a par with the debate-minded approach of the Tarbolton Bachelor. Noting that 'there is certainly some connection between Love, Music, and Poetry', he claims that:

> I never had the least thought or inclination of turning Poet till I got once heartily in Love, and then Rhyme and Song were, in a manner, the spontaneous language of my heart. The following composition was the first of my performances, and done at an early period of life, when my heart glowed with honest warm simplicity [. . .] The performance is, indeed, very puerile and silly: but I am always pleased with it. (p. 3)

He then proceeds to copy and critique 'O Handsome Nell', announcing that '[L]est my works should be thought below criticism; or meet with a critic who, perhaps, will not look on them with so candid and favourable an eye; I am determined to criticize them myself' (p. 6). He is rather hard on the song: the first stanza he finds 'quite too much in the flimsy strain of our ordinary street ballads', the fourth is 'indifferent', the last line of the fifth 'halts a little', the 'short syllables' of the second and fourth lines of the sixth 'hurt[s] the whole', while the seventh has 'several minute faults'. In the face of such finical criticisms, Burns does admit that he 'composed it in a wild enthusiasm of passion, and to this hour I never recollect it, but my heart melts, and my blood sallies at the remembrance' (p. 6).

A similar critical appraisal can be found in Burns's introduction to 'My Father Was a Farmer', which he describes as a 'wild Rhapsody miserably deficient in versification, but as the sentiments are the genuine feelings of my heart, for that reason I have a particular pleasure in conning it over' (p. 13). Burns echoes this view in another prose introduction for an early poem, in this case 'My Nanie, O', stating that

> Shenstone observes finely that love-verses writ without any real passion are the most nauseous of all conceits: and I have often thought that no man can be a proper critic of Love composition, except he himself, in one, or more instances, have been a warm votary of this passion. (p. 16)

He defends the weaknesses of 'My Nanie, O' in a way highly characteristic of his early critical practice: '[A]s I have been all along, a miserable dupe to Love, I put the more confidence in my critical skill in distinguishing foppery and conceit, from real passion and nature' (p. 16). Although such experience presumably qualifies him to be a 'proper critic of Love composition', he asserts that 'whether [it] will stand the test, I will not pretend to say' (p. 16). However, he can testify without reserve that 'it was, at the time, real' (p. 16).

Focusing on the reality of the feelings expressed in the song finds its counterpart in numerous other works transcribed in the commonplace book, such as 'O Thou Great Being' (written to express the poet's 'most dreadful distemper, a hypochondria, or confirmed melancholy') (p. 10), 'The Wintry West' (composed after a 'tract of misfortunes' [p. 12]), and 'O Thou Unknown, Almighty Cause' (originating after 'fainting fits, and other alarming symptoms of a pleurisy or some other dangerous disorder, which indeed still threaten me, first put nature on the alarm' [p. 23]). As G. Ross Roy has observed, the fact that such 'pedestrian performances' were included in the commonplace book 'points to a still-forming critical faculty in the poet'.[5]

Such extra-textual information provokes some critical interest, but it is Burns's view of poetry itself that exerts the most fascination throughout the commonplace book. Among several forgettable poems and songs in the book are some of Burns's best-known works, sometimes copied without preamble but at times supplied with a critical introduction. Such is the case with 'Green Grow the Rashes', which he tells us was written 'in the genuine language of my heart'.[6] Unlike the works listed above, 'Green Grow the Rashes' presents a distinctly different critical relationship between the poet and the subject of the work. Instead of being the expression of inner turmoil, the song exists as an emblem of respite, ease and the refusal of the practical: 'The wisest man the warl' saw / He dearly lov'd the lasses, O' (p. 21).

In a short paragraph following the song, Burns extols the value of the valueless, celebrating the new role that the poem creates for its creator: that of poet, commentator on the commonplace. He states emphatically that:

> I do not see that the turn of mind, and pursuits of such a one as the above verses describes, one who spends the hours and thoughts, which the vocations of the day can spare, with Ossian, Shakespeare, Thomson, Shenstone, Sterne, etc . . . I say I do not see that the turn of mind and pursuits of such a one are in the least inimical to the sacred interests of Piety and Virtue, than the even lawful, bustling, and straining after the world's riches and honors. (pp. 22–3)

The defiance evident in so much of Burns's poetry is fully-developed in this passage, which highlights the fundamental opposition he sees between poets and the rest of the avaricious world.

Later characteristic attitudes are also apparent in the commonplace book. For instance, national identity assumes prominence near the end of the book, where Burns represents his critical 'turn of mind' as resolutely Scottish. In the long prose paragraph leading into 'When First I Came to Stewart Kyle', he begins the first of many critical disquisitions on his Scots predecessors, 'the excellent Ramsay, and the still more excellent Fergusson', whose works issue a national mandate for the poet himself:

> We have never had one Scotch poet of any eminence, to make the fertile banks of Irvine, the romantic woodlands and sequestered scenes on Aire, and the healthy mountainous source, and winding sweep of Doon, emulate Tay, Forth, Ettrick Tweed etc. (pp. 46–7)

As much critical maxim as personal exhortation, Burns's wish falls on wilfully deaf ears: '[T]his is a complaint I would gladly remedy, but Alas! I am far unequal to the task both in native genius and education. Obscure I am, and obscure I must be, though no young Poet['s] . . . heart ever beat more fondly for fame than mine' (p. 47). Such lines point to an emerging sense of both a creative subject and a critical style.

More decidedly critical is the poet's take on 'Old Scotch Songs', a lengthy metrical analysis extending to several pages. Burns begins by noting that:

> There is a certain irregularity of syllables in the Old Scotch Songs, a redundancy of syllables with respect to that exactness of accent and measure that the English Poetry requires . . . There is a degree of wild irregularity in many of the compositions and fragments which are daily sung . . . by my compeers, the common people – a certain happy arrangement of Old Scotch syllables. (pp. 48–9)

In his defence of Scottish folk prosody, Burns contends that 'wild irregularity' actually produces a much more pleasing effect upon the listener than monotonous, albeit metrically correct verse. If considered impartially, this assertion, he argues, has critical weight:

> [L]et them both be sung before a real Critic, one above the biasses of prejudice, but a thorough Judge of Nature, how flat and spiritless will the last appear, how trite, and lamely methodical, compared with the wild-warbling cadence, the heart-moving melody of the first. (p. 48)

As he had been invigorated by the examples of Ramsay and Fergusson, Burns encourages other 'Scotch poets' to work with their national body of work. He finds song to be particularly well-suited to the task:

> It might be possible for a Scotch Poet, with a nice, judicious ear, to set compositions to many of our most favorite airs, particularly that class of them mentioned above, independent of rhyme altogether. There is a noble sublimity, a heart-melting tenderness in some of these ancient fragments. (p. 49)

David Daiches remarks of this passage that 'these are not the comments of a "Heaven-taught ploughman," who breaks spontaneously into song without fully knowing what he is doing.'[7] Burns's careful observance of metrical pattern leads Daiches to describe him as a 'careful craftsman . . . particularly interested in the problem of setting words to music'.[8] Indeed, as Daiches notes, the commonplace book itself points the way 'to Burns's remarkable later activity in rescuing, rehabilitating, and recreating Scottish folk song'.[9]

Burns's remarks in the commonplace book are prescient on this topic, indicating an early and pronounced interest in song-collecting. Such songs, he states, are suitable and indeed 'noble' for poetic emulation:

> [T]hese old Scottish airs are so nobly sentimental that [. . .] one would compose to them; to south the tune, as our Scotch phrase is, over and over, is the readiest way to catch the inspiration and raise the Bard into that glorious enthusiasm so strongly characteristic of our old Scotch poetry.[10]

Along with the assured nature of his technical discussion of Scottish song, Burns exhibits a generous critical view of 'common people' as compeers and fellow performers of a national art-form. The commonplace book, however, records not only the result of Burns's critical analysis, but also his self-conscious review of his own acts of writing. This is precisely what distinguishes Burns, a young poet thirsting for fame, from his 'common' compeers.

Serving as a critical double-take, Burns's commonplace book reminds its readers and author of Burns's new poetic role, one that allows him to document not only his poems but also his 'scraps and observations'. Indeed, the commonplace book records more than 'scraps and observations', also chronicling tastes, talents and most importantly, Burns's critical ideas about the work at hand. This self-aware critical stance evolves throughout his prose, becoming most evidently enunciated and performed in the letters.

Always alert to the character of the recipient, modulating tonality, style and content, the letters are Burns's most transparently designed artworks. The letters repeatedly force one to pay attention to the way language is shaped to fit both reader and occasion. They are predominantly performances: Burns employs several personae that speak and embody the poet's distinct selves, variously adapted for specific recipients. 'Clarinda' (Agnes Machehose 1758–1841) most famously, but also Frances Dunlop (1730–1815), Dr John Moore (1729–1802), Henry Erskine (1746–1817) and Peter Hill (1754–1837), among many others: all demanded and received a different Burns. However, as Kenneth Simpson has argued, '[I]t is equally true that in many of his letters Burns, to meet the needs of his own personality, assumed distinctive voices.'[11] Jeffrey Skoblow makes a related point: '[Burns] knows precisely to whom he speaks, and precisely what passes for lingua franca – and badge of membership – among such parties.'[12]

For a poet fond of the verse epistle and dramatic monologue, letters became another extension of creative practice, allowing the early love of language greater occasion for often self-indulgent play. When he practises 'critic-craft', he presents a more serious and self-conscious persona. On such occasions one senses what the stakes were: the evidence (and defence) of his difference. The fullest description of this character trait appears in Burns's autobiographical letter to Dr Moore, from August 1787; in an often quoted passage, Burns lists the works that triggered his transformation from 'the most ungainly, aukward being in the parish' to his present celebrated self (*L* I, p. 138). Including Pope, Shakespeare, Addison, Steele and Ramsay along with scientific and philosophical works, Burns constructs an impressive roster clearly meant to impress the letter's recipient.

Of all these works, however, he attributes his knowledge of 'critic-craft' to his reading of 'a select collection of English songs' (*L* I, p. 138). Burns recollects that 'I pored over them, driving my cart or walking to labor, song by song, verse by verse; carefully noting the true tender of sublime from affectation or fustian. I am convinced I owe much to this for my critic-craft such as it is' (*L* I, pp. 138–9). However self-deprecatory, Burns believed that such critical practice did indeed differentiate him from others. He states further in this letter that even before the publication of the 1786 'Kilmarnock' edition, 'I can truly say that pauvre Inconnu as I then was, I had pretty nearly as high an idea of myself and my works as I have at this moment' (*L* I, p. 144). The source of this confidence lies in his critical awareness:

> It is ever my opinion that the great, unhappy mistakes and blunders . . . of which we see thousands daily guilty, are owing to their ignorance, or mistaken notions

of themselves. To know myself had been all along my constant study. – I weighed myself alone; I balanced myself with others; I watched every means of information how much ground I occupied both as a Man and as a Poet. (*L* I, p. 144)

Such self-assessment was accurately premonitory: 'I was pretty sure my Poems would meet with some applause' (*L* I, p. 144).

For Burns, however, such premonitions did not preclude the hard work of the poetic craftsman. As he wrote to Henry Erskine in 1789, '[T]he rough material of Fine Writing is certainly the gift of Genius; but . . . I firmly believe that the workmanship is the united effort of Pains, Attention & Repeated – trial' (*L* I, p. 359). To Dr Moore also in 1789, he expressed the concern that such intensive familiarity with the work might create an unavoidable blindness on the writer's part: 'The worst of it is, against one has finished a Piece, it has been so often viewed and reviewed before the mental eye that one loses in a good measure the powers of critical discrimination' (*L* I, p. 350). Perhaps an offshoot of his famously touchy personality, Burns's attentiveness to possible criticisms appears throughout the drafting, distribution and publication of his works. The letters demonstrate just how extensively Burns circulated his works in order to gauge the critical reactions of friends and patrons. Though he could politely acknowledge harsh criticism, he seemed to seek the generous response of a friend. He wrote to Mrs Dunlop in 1788 that:

> Your Criticisms are truly the work of a FRIEND. – They are not the blasting depredations of a canker-toothed caterpillar-Critic; nor are they the fair statement of cold Impartiality, balancing with unfeeling exactitude the pro & con of an Author's merits; they are the judicious observations of animated Friendship, selecting the beauties of the Piece. (*L* I, p. 323)

Although his observations on Dunlop's criticisms have an idyllic ring, Burns recognised the need for abrasive critique as well. A miscellaneous piece from 1791, entitled 'Literary Scolding – Hints', offers a litany of linguistic insults Burns kept in store for future flyting:

> Thou Eunuch of language . . . Thou servile echo of fashionable barbarisms – Thou Quack, vending the nostrums of Empirical elocution . . . Thou Ignisfatuus, misleading the steps of benighted Ignorance – Thou Pickleherring in the puppet-show of Nonsense. (*L* II, p. 93)

To fellow poets, especially Scots poets, he could occasionally be quite harsh. Writing to Mrs Dunlop in 1789 about a poem by the late John Mylne, Burns complained that 'the piece has a good deal of merit, but it has one damning fault – it is by far too long' (*L* I, p. 382). He continues with an aside that illustrates his own sense of self-worth, particularly when compared with the work of lesser Scots competitors: '[M]y success has encouraged such a shoal of ill-spawned monsters to crawl into public notice under the title of Scots poets, that the very term Scots poetry, borders on the burlesque' (*L* I, p. 382).

Burns offers a more charitable critique of a fellow poet in a letter to Peter Hill from 1788, in which he discusses James Cririe's 'Address to Loch Lomond' at some length. It is noteworthy that Cririe's 'Address' is wholly in English, perhaps arousing Burns's critical ire to a lesser degree. In fact, Burns begins his critique of Cririe's poem quite humorously by stating that 'were I impannelled, one of the Author's Jury to determine his criminality respecting the Sin of Poesy, my verdict should be "Guilty! A Poet of Nature's Making!"'(*L* I, p. 325). Once he begins in earnest, Burns's criticisms display the mind of a serious close reader at work, tracking down allusions and suggesting alterations in diction, prosody and style. He notes Cririe's method of composition, a technique that he approves and practises:

> It is an excellent method for improvement, and what I beleive [sic] every Poet does; to place some favorite classic Author, in our own walks of study & composition, before us a Model. Tho' your Author has not mentioned the name, I could have, at half a glance, guessed his Model to be Thomson. (*L* I, p. 325)

Using Thomson as a model may be productive for poetic improvement, but it can also lead to 'servile copying'. Burns finds that Cririe has fallen into this trap: 'Will my brother Author forgive me, if I venture to hint, that his imitation of that Immortal Bard is in two or three places rather more servile than such a genius as his required' (*L* I, p. 325). Indeed, Burns identifies a direct plagiarism of Thomson on the poem's first page, but such theft accounts to only a misdemeanor in Burns's critical court. He forgives such minor faults in view of Cririe's overall use of Thomson's poetic model:

> I have read Thomson at the same time, & I think the versification of the Address, in simplicity, harmony, & elegance, fully equal to the Seasons. Like Thomson too, he has looked into Nature for himself: you meet with no copied description. (*L* I, pp. 325–6)

Burns applies key critical terms that had been employed for his own poetry: harmony, natural descriptiveness and simplicity. This last is especially pleasing to Burns; he notes that 'one particular Criticism I made, at first reading; in no one instance has he said too much. – He never flags in his progress, but like a true Poet of Nature's making, kindles in his course' (*L* I, p. 326). Burns's critical refrain – 'a true Poet of Nature's making' – derives in large part from the poem's indebtedness to Thomson, its regional natural setting, and its application of a familiar georgic mode. The poem's relation to other georgic formulae is noted – 'A thunder-storm is a subject which has been often tried, yet our Poet in his grand picture has interjected a circumstance, so far as I know, entirely original' (*L* I, p. 326) – as is its inclusion of pastoral lovers:

> He has contrived to enliven his Poem with a little of that passion which bids fair, I think, to usurp the modern muses altogether. I know not how far this episode is a beauty upon the whole, but the Swain's wish to carry – 'Some faint idea of the vision bright,' to entertain her 'partial listening ear,' is a pretty thought. (*L* I, pp. 326–7)

Burns's largely positive critique extends for two pages, focusing on the poem's 'beautiful' imagery and the poet's 'noble ray of poetic genius'. It is interrupted with an apology to Hill – 'I forget that while I am thus holding forth with the heedless warmth of an Enthusiast, I am perhaps tiring you with nonsense' (*L* I, p. 327) – that does not halt Burns's critical appraisal. The poem's description of monuments constructed near Loch Lomond for local notables John Napier, George Buchanan and Tobias Smollett is 'one of the most elegant Compliments I have ever seen' (*L* I, p. 327). Burns finds Cririe's depiction of an unsatisfied sportsman to be 'equal to any thing in The Seasons' (*L* I, p. 327) and quite congenial to his feelings about hunting. Burns ends his letter to Hill by requesting that 'I should like to know who the Author is; but whoever he be, please, present him with my grateful thanks for the entertainment he has afforded me' (*L* I, p. 327).

A similarly lengthy, generous critique is found in a letter Burns wrote to Helen Maria Williams in late July 1789. Burns thanks Williams for 'a most elegant poetic compliment; then for a polite, obliging letter; and lastly, for your excellent poem on the Slave-Trade' (*L* I, p. 427), which has prompted his four-page enclosure recording his line-by-line reactions to the poem. While polite, Burns's criticisms in the letter are exceedingly detailed in their attention to syntax, imagery and metre. He professes to 'know very little of scientific criticism' (*L* I, p. 428), yet what emerges is Burns's profound, teacherly awareness of the tools of his craft.

As in his letter to Hill about Cririe's poem, Burns writes to Williams as a fellow poet who offers professional advice on the construction of her poem. He accords her the respect owed to a colleague as he describes his method of criticising a work of poetry:

> Your poem I have read with the highest pleasure. I have a way, whenever I read a book, I mean a book in our own trade, Madam, a poetic one, and when it is my own property, that I take a pencil and mark at the end of verses, or note on margins and odd paper little criticisms of approbation or disapprobation as I peruse along. I will make no apology for presenting you with a few unconnected thoughts that occurred to me in my repeated perusals of your poem. I want to shew you that I have honesty enough to tell you what I take

to be truths, even when they are not quite on the side of approbation; and I do it in the firm faith that you have equal greatness of mind to hear them with pleasure. (*L* I, p. 428)

As in his critique of Cririe's poem, Burns proves himself a close reader who is sensitive to originality and clarity of expression. He notes that 'the simile of the hurricane is likewise fine; & indeed, beautiful as the Poem is, almost all the similes rise decidedly above it' (*L* I, p. 428). Similarly, he states that 'Verse 46th I am afraid is rather unworthy of the rest: "to dare to feel," is an idea that I do not altogether like' (*L* I, pp. 428–9). He is also rather attentive to syntax: 'Either my apprehension is dull, or there is something a little confused in the apostrophe to Mr. Pit. – Verse 55th is the antecedent to verses 57th & 58th but in verse 58th the connection seems ungrammatical . . . Try it in Prose' (*L* I, p. 429). Metaphorical confusion is corrected – 'Verse 110th is, I doubt, a clashing of metaphors: to load a span, is, I am afraid, an unwarrantable expression' (*L* I, p. 430) – while beautiful imagery and expressions are commended – 'Verse 100th is exquisitely beautiful' (*L* I, p. 430).

Williams's debts to Thomson are also analysed and catalogued. As he had in Cririe's poem, Burns does not find instances of 'servile copying' but instead creative transposition of familiar episodes or conceits. A passage on home is praised by comparison with Thomson's model – 'That whole description of Home may vie with Thomson's description of Home, somewhere in the beginning of Autumn' (*L* I, p. 430) – as is her description of a thunderstorm. The latter, however, receives a much more positive endorsement than Cririe's version of the same:

A Tempest, is a favorite subject with the Poets, but I do not remember any thing, even in Thomson's Winter, superiour to your verses from the 344th to the 351st. – Indeed that last Simile, beginning with, Fancy may dress &c. & ending with the 350th verse is, in my opinion, the most beautiful passage in the whole Poem. – it would do honor to the greatest names that ever graced our Profession. (*L* I, p. 431)

Burns also discusses the poem's subject matter in a substantive way, repeatedly remarking on 'nobly-executed pictures of Oppression' (*L* I, p. 430). He claims that 'the address to the advocates for abolishing the slave-trade [. . .] is animated with the true life of Genius' (*L* I, p. 430), noting that 'the character & manners of the dealer in this infernal traffic is a well done though a horrid picture' (*L* I, p. 430). Appearing right after the portrait of the slave trader is an extended panegyric on the British sailor, a figure which is described in a uniformly positive fashion. Responding to this passage, Burns remarks that:

> I am not sure how far introducing the Sailor was right; for though the Sailor's common characteristic is generosity, yet in this case his is certainly not only an unconcerned witness but in some degree an efficient agent in the business. (*L* I, pp. 430–1)

This apt observation fully illustrates the depth of Burns's criticism, where close attention is paid to the poem in all its formal and contextual registers.

Burns ends the critique with an apology, fearing that 'I am got so much in the cant of criticism, that I begin to be afraid lest I have nothing except the cant of it; and instead of elucidating my Author, am only benighting myself' (*L* I, p. 431). His assessment of the outcome of his critique could not be more inaccurate; Burns's letter to Helen Maria Williams stands as one of his most accomplished, charitable works of criticism. He presents a thorough, kind, yet constructive examination of Williams's poem in its entirety, offering multiple ideas for revision and praising the work's distinctive properties. The letter ends with an address to Williams that reveals the close connection Burns felt between his critical intentions and his conscience: 'I will not beg your pardon, Madam, for these strictures, as my conscience tells me that for once in my life I have acted up to the duties of a Christian in doing as I would be done by' (*L* I, p. 431).

Sadly, Burns never received the kind of honest, understanding critical response that he proved capable of giving. His later criticism shows an increasing distance between his own criticisms and those he received; as Simpson has remarked, 'Burns recognised the widening gap between the creative impulse . . . and the legislative nature of Scottish criticism.'[13] Nowhere was this legislative critical style more readily encountered than in the person of George Thomson (1757–1851), the most antagonistic correspondent of Burns's later years. In fact, much of volume two of the collected letters comprises replies to Thomson's overly hands-on approach to collaboration on the song collection. Writing to Thomson in 1793, Burns expressed a thinly-veiled exasperation with these repeated critical battles:

> Give me leave to criticize your taste in the only thing in which it is in my opinion reprehensible: (you know I ought to know something of my own trade) of pathos, Sentiment & Point, you are a compleat judge; but there is a quality more necessary than either, in a Song, & which is the very essence of a Ballad, I mean Simplicity – now, if I mistake not, this last feature you are a little apt to sacrifice to the foregoing. (*L* II, p. 196)

Negotiating such critical disputes forms the bulk of his letters to Thomson and informs the body of his criticism of Scottish song, some of Burns's best work as a practising critic.

The Notes on Scottish Song from an interleaved copy of *Scots Musical Museum* documents Burns's annotation and evaluation of a whole body of work. Thomas Crawford has argued that Burns's growing interests in Scottish song

> did not take place simply and easily, but in a roundabout manner and after setbacks and recessions, and they happened as the result of the whole man's struggle to understand, and, if possible, to master, divided and distinguished worlds.[14]

Indeed, one senses within the *Notes* the emerging dimensions of a hard-won critical practice, particularly Burns's governing perception of the value of song. This value becomes increasingly nationalist, though not to the exclusion of English interests or techniques.

His critical assessments rarely stray from evaluations of musicality, lyrical quality, fitting of lyrics and melody, and distinctions of taste. For example, on 'Bess the Gawkie' he observes that

> this song shews that the Scotish [sic] Muses did not all leave us when we lost Ramsay and Oswald . . . It is a beautiful song and in the genuine Scots taste. We have few pastoral compositions, I mean, which are the pastoral of Nature, that are equal to this.[15]

He develops and employs a rather specific critical vocabulary; of 'The Banks of the Tweed,' he explains that 'this song is one of many attempts that English composers have made to imitate the Scottish manner, and which I shall, in these strictures, beg leave to distinguish by the appellation of Anglo-Scotish productions' (p. 2). His critical verdict for 'The Banks of Tweed' is direct and definitive, showing an unequivocal judgment of the song's music and lyrical content: '[T]he music is pretty good, but the verses are just above contempt' (p. 2).

Although he concedes that other songs in the collection are 'tolerable Anglo-Scotish productions', his key critical argument is effusively nationalist: '[I]t is singular enough that the Scotish Muses were all Jacobites' (pp. 4–5). This statement is fully supported by the critic's ethos. He writes that

> I have paid more attention to every description of Scots songs than perhaps any body living, and I do not recollect one single stanza, or even the title of the most trifling Scots air, which has the least panegyrical reference to the families of Nassau or Brunswick; while there are hundreds satirizing them. (p. 5)

Burns continues dryly, '[T]his may be thought no panegyric on the Scots poets, but I mean it as such. For myself, I would always take it as a compliment to have it said, that my heart ran before my head' (p. 5). This critical note ends with Burns's oft-quoted comparison between the 'gallant though unfortunate house of Stewart' and the 'obscure beef-witted insolent race of foreigners' then on the throne (p. 5).

For Burns, Scottish song is defined within and by national culture; it is integrated within this space despite content or style. For this reason, much of Burn's critical discussion focuses on the song's provenance in both melody and lyric. His discoveries are usually anonymous and national: '[T]he first half stanza is much older than the days of Ramsay' (p. 17). Elsewhere, he finds that 'the old words of the song are omitted here, though much more beautiful than those inserted here' (p. 17). Some observations border on the anthropological: '[T]his beautiful song is in the true old Scotch taste, yet I do not know that ever either air or words, were in print before' (p. 49). He is not always laudatory; about 'She Rose and Let Me In', he complains that 'I believe it was Ramsay, took it into his head to clear it of some seeming indelicacies, and made it at once more chaste and more dull' (pp. 20–1). To Frances Dunlop in 1788, he confessed that

> the songs in the 2nd Vol. of the Museum, marked, D, are Dr. Blacklock's; but as I am sorry to say they are far short of his other works, I, who only know the ciphers of them all, shall never let it be known. (*L* I, p. 337)

He elsewhere remarks about 'I'll Never Leave Thee' that 'this is another of Crawford's songs, but I do not think in his happiest manner. What an absurdity to join such names as Adonis and Mary together!' (p. 22).

Perhaps the most telling of his criticisms involves his own contributions to a project to which he devoted a considerable amount of time and scholarly energy. About 'To the Weaver's Gin Ye Go', he states that

> Here, once for all, let me apologize for many silly compositions of mine in this work. Many beautiful airs wanted words; in the hurry of other avocations, if I could string a parcel of rhymes together any thing near tolerable, I was fain to let them pass. He must be an excellent poet indeed, whose every performance is excellent. (p. 24)

To Thomson in 1792, Burns tried to convince the editor to accept his version of 'Nanie O' for inclusion, but conceded that '[D]on't let it enter into your head, that you are under any necessity of taking my verses' (*L* II, p. 153). Far from asserting his authority as the project's co-editor, Burns avers that 'I have long ago made up my mind as to my own reputation in the business of Authorship; & have nothing to be pleased, or offended at, in your adoption or rejection of my verses' (*L* II, p. 153). His letter ends with a prayerful wish for good creative partnership: '[M]y wish is, not to stand aloof [. . .] but cordially join issue with you in the furtherance of the work. – GUDE SPEED THE WARK! AMEN!!!' (*L* II, p. 155).

Such exclamatory remarks as the last defy Burns's previously held and hotly-defended distinctions of his own creative and critical difference. One remarkable feature of Burns's contribution to Scottish song is its anonymous character, marked by a deliberate cloaking of his contributions. Carol McGuirk has noted that: 'the lyrics of "a significant percentage of the published repertory of Scottish National Song" – in fact, about 35% of all Scots folksongs published before 1800 – were actually written by Robert Burns.'[16] The fact that Burns actively denied credit for such a significant body of work is remarkable, but it should not be regarded as an unwillingness to acknowledge the literary and musical quality of Scottish song. As has been suggested, Burns's critical career begins and ends with Scottish song, a body of work greatly amenable to commentary, scholarship and creative contribution. As such, it provoked Burns's best criticism by allowing him to incorporate his own writing – both creative and critical – into a much larger national enterprise sustained by such energies.

CHAPTER TEN

Burns, Scott and Intertextuality

Alison Lumsden

Walter Scott (1771–1832) met Burns only once in his life. The meeting took place in 1787 at the home of Adam Fergusson when Scott was only fifteen years old and is documented in Lockhart's biography where Scott himself recalls the incident. As he recounts it, Burns is looking at a print by Bunbury of a soldier lying dead on the snow. Nearby stands his dog, and his widow with a child in her arms. The print, and some lines of poetry inscribed beneath it, apparently moved Burns to tears. Only the young Scott, of course, could provide the answer to Burns's question of who had written the affecting lines of poetry: they were taken from Langhorne's poem 'The Justice of the Peace'.[1]

Recalling the incident in 1827 for Lockhart, who was then writing his biography of Burns, what strikes Scott most is the memory of Burns the man:

> There was a strong expression of sense and shrewdness in all his lineaments; the eye alone, I think, indicated the poetic character and temperament. It was large and of a dark cast, and glowed (I say literally *glowed*) when he spoke with feeling or interest. I never saw such another eye in a human head, though I have seen the most distinguished men in my time.[2]

Equally interesting here, however, is the fact that the meeting involves an intertextual reference of a sort; Bunbury's print is given additional layers of interpretation by the words from Langhorne written beneath it; words for which Scott provides a context, and which work together with the visual image to produce emotion and meaning for Burns. The meeting between Burns and Scott, therefore, has at its heart an intertextual experience, demonstrating the ways in which one text can provide meaning for another by offering layers of textual and sub-textual resonance. It is the nature of another intertextual meeting between Burns and Scott that this chapter considers; the ways in which reference to Burns's work in the Waverley novels also offer additional meaning and resonance in these fictional texts.

To recognise the essentially intertextual nature of Scott's work is, of course, to say nothing new; this was, indeed, a major theme of the Fourth

International Scott Conference in Edinburgh (1991) where the title 'Scott in Carnival' prompted several papers on the essentially dialogic nature of Scott's work and the consequent role of intertextuality in constructing the fabric of his fiction.[3] However, it is only with the work of the Edinburgh Edition of the Waverley Novels in uncovering all the direct allusion and embedded references to other authors that the full extent of Scott's dialogue with a myriad of his literary predecessors can fully be appreciated. In fact, what the notes to the Edinburgh Edition show is that Scott's fiction is constructed via a mesh of allusion; where Scott can find a literary precedent he will undoubtedly use it and, with what seems to be an ability to recall what he has read almost verbatim, he draws on the whole wealth of his own reading from childhood onwards when he comes to construct the webs of intertextual meaning which constitute the Waverley texts. As Ainsley McIntosh recognises, the range of allusions in Scott's work 'bear witness to a memory indelibly impressed with the results of a mind avidly engaged in the pursuit of literary studies from an early age'.[4] The effect of such intertextuality, argues Sheena Sutherland, is that allusion functions to create 'broader implications in relation to the novel[s] as a whole, establishing connecting contexts and thereby instituting a variety of different coded subtexts'.[5]

Scott himself, however, attaches less significance to the allusions that pepper his texts. Describing, for example, his use of the mottos that frequently introduce chapters in his fiction, he states:

> The scraps of poetry which have been in most cases tacked to the beginnings of chapters in these Novels, are sometimes quoted either from reading or from memory, but, in the general case, are pure invention.[6]

We have learnt, however, to be cautious about what writers say of their own practice and this is particularly true of Scott whose relationship to his work is continually one of evasion; even here, perhaps, in the Introduction to *Chronicles of the Canongate* where he is ostensibly admitting authorship of the Waverley Novels for the first time, but is in fact simply constructing a new series of masks for himself.

Researching the processes of production of a Waverley Novel for the Edinburgh Edition in fact suggests that Scott took significant care with both the mottos and the allusions in general that are included in his texts; frequently, for example, we find Scott asking for particular texts which will provide background material for the novel he is at the time writing, and often he will ask James Ballantyne to fill in a particular reference if he does not himself have it to hand. As Scott's ideas evolve, mottos in particular are frequently changed. As Claire Lamont has indicated, the shifting nature of the mottos to 'The Highland Widow' are particularly pertinent to our present purposes: the title for this novella, she explains, comes from a song called 'The Highland Widow's Lament' which was first published in Johnson's *Scots Musical Museum* in 1796 and was contributed by Burns, who undoubtedly wrote part of it. In its published form Scott uses stanzas one and five of Burns's text as the motto to the second chapter. Lamont suggests, however, that the relationship between the two texts was originally more prominent:

> When Scott started to write the tale the manuscript (f.30) shows the title 'The Highland Widow' followed by one stanza of 'The Highland Widow's Lament' as a motto (stanza 5 of Burns's text). That motto was deleted in the manuscript and replaced with four lines from Coleridge's 'Christabel' [. . .] The motto from 'The Highland Widow's Lament', increased to two stanzas, was moved to the beginning of the second chapter . . . where its connection with the title of the tale is less obvious.[7]

In this instance, revision obscures what is clearly an intertextual relationship between Burns and Scott but it also reinforces the fact that in Scott's work allusion is not merely decorative or incidental but something to which he gives considerable care.

Intertextuality also offers a kind of dialogue with authors of an earlier period. As Christopher Worth has argued in a discussion of *Woodstock*, intertextual utterances, like all others, 'are not neutral or transparent, but [are] already filled with ideology and meaning from their previous uses and contexts, the connotations of the other. They bring with them their history'.[8] Just as Scott's notes, Introductions and introductory chapters create layers of dialogue in his texts, so too as Scott alludes to the work of others the meanings of those earlier texts – however we as readers might choose to interpret them – accrue to his own works of fiction to offer yet more levels of interpretative value.

It is no surprise that Burns's work operates as an important intertext for Scott. Burns is frequently quoted in Scott's letters and his *Journal* also includes over twenty references to Burns.[9] These references are used to elucidate, to add emphasis, to express feeling, and even on rare occasions within this sad document, to add humour. They give some indication of the resonances that Burns's work might offer the Author of Waverley and this is also implied by his most significant critical commentary on Burns: his review of R. H. Cromek's 1808 *Reliques of Robert Burns*.[10] This essay offers as much a critique of Burns the man and his work as it does of Cromek's *Reliques*, and it leads Scott into a discussion of what he perceives to be the character of Burns in general, again giving some indication of what Burns the man, if not Burns the poet, represented for Scott: 'Burns was, in truth, the child of passion and feeling,' he writes. His is a 'powerful but untamed mind':[11]

> Burns neither acknowledged adversity as the 'tamer of the human breast,' nor knew the golden curb which discretion hangs upon passion. He even appears to have felt a gloomy pleasure in braving the encounter of evils which prudence might have avoided, and to have thought that there could be no pleasurable existence between the extremes of licentious frenzy and of torpid sensuality. [quoting Burns he writes] 'There are two only creatures that I would envy. – A horse in his wild state traversing the forests of Asia, – and an oyster on some of the desert shores of Europe. The one has not a wish without enjoyment; the other has neither wish nor fear.' When such a sentiment is breathed by such a being, the lesson is awful: and if pride and ambition were capable of being taught, they might hence learn that a well-regulated mind and controlled passions are to be prized above all the glow of imagination, and all the splendour of genius.[12]

On the face of it, this description seems to offer a well-rehearsed, and slightly censorious, version of Burns. However, it is interesting to note that it is surprisingly similar to a comment that Scott makes about Byron in a review of *Childe Harold* Canto 3, when he suggests that 'A powerful and unbridled imagination is ... the author and architect of its own disappointments' and that Byron should 'tame the fire of his fancy, and descend from the heights to which she exalts him, in order to obtain peace of mind and tranquillity'.[13] However, Scott admired Byron as much as he admired Burns, stating in his *Journal*, 'I have always reckond Burns and Byron the most genuine poetical geniuses of my time and a half a century before me',[14] and it is clear that in both instances the potentially destructive nature of their characters, or at least the tendency to passion, is intrinsic to their art, and part of what Scott describes as 'sensibility'. His review continues to elaborate upon the virtues of this:

> The traits of sensibility which, told of another, would sound like instances of gross affectation, were so native to the soul of this extraordinary man, and burst from him so involuntarily, that they not only obtained full credence as the genuine feelings of his own heart, but melted into unthought of sympathy all who witnessed them. In such a mood they were often called forth by the slightest and most trifling occurrences; an ordinary engraving, the wild turn of a simple Scottish air, a line in an old ballad, were, like 'the field mouse's nest' and 'the uprooted daisy,' sufficient to excite the sympathetic feelings of Burns. And it was wonderful to see those, who, left to themselves, would have passed over such trivial circumstances without a moment's reflection, sob over the picture, when its outline had been filled up by the magic art of his eloquence.[15]

It is not hard to find examples of ways in which Scott seems to have learnt from the example of Burns in this respect, since his own fiction is full of details of this sort which work together to produce emotional effect. While there are of course too many to detail here, we can consider the ways in which emotion is evinced, for example, in a novel like *The Heart of Mid-Lothian*.[16] One of the most moving episodes in the text is a cottage scene with Jeanie and her father, just after Jeanie has received the letter asking her to meet Staunton. Davie Deans, we are told, chides his daughter for having neglected her household tasks:

> 'Why, what meaneth this, Jeanie?' said the old man – 'The brown four-year-auld's milk is not seiled yet, nor the bowies put up on the bink. If ye neglect your wardly duties in the day of affliction, what confidence have I that ye mind the greater matters that concern salvation? God knows, our bowies, and our pipkins, and our draps o' milk, and our bits o' bread, are nearer and dearer to us than the bread of life.' (p. 131)

In a sense reiterating the importance of the commonplace that he has praised in Burns, Scott here uses minor household objects – bowls, pots, drops of milk – to build up an emotional resonance. It is then, perhaps, hardly surprising that Burns is directly evoked only a page later, when again domestic detail is described in order to produce sympathy between reader and Davie. We are told, '[T]he poor old man added to his usual supplication, a prayer that the bread eaten in bitterness . . . might be made as nourishing as those which had been poured forth from a full cup and a plentiful basket and store' (p. 132).[17]

In spite of his rather priggish assessment of Burns's character it would seem that Scott the writer also recognises that Burns's 'powerful and untamed mind', his 'uncontrolled passion' is intrinsic to the nature of his art; for Scott the Romantic writer, at least in the Cromek review, the merit of Burns's artistic capacities lay in his native sensibilities. It seems that Burns's art for Scott is essentially affective; it is not an art that necessarily appeals to the intellect, but one which produces a sympathetic and emotional response from the most commonplace of circumstances. Writing of 'Tam o' Shanter' he suggests that 'No poet, with the exception of Shakespeare, ever possessed the power of exciting the most varied and discordant emotions with such rapid transitions',[18] and this quality is one that he reproduces in his own art.

In this review, however, Scott also allows some anxiety about Cromek's enterprise, suggesting that admirable work has already been done by Dr Currie's edition. This too is revealing, for again it gives us some insight into how Scott viewed Burns. While on the whole praising Currie's collection Scott identifies in it something of a squeamishness, a 'fastidious and over-delicate rejection of the bard's most spirited and happy effusions' as he calls it.[19] Referring to *Poems Ascribed to Robert Burns the Ayrshire Bard*, he suggests that this octavo, published in Glasgow in 1801, 'furnishes valuable proofs of this assertion'.[20] 'It contains,' he goes on, 'among a good deal of rubbish, some of his most brilliant poetry. A cantata in particular, called *The Jolly Beggars*,' he writes, 'for humorous description and nice discrimination of character, is inferior to no poem of the same length in the whole range of English poetry.'[21] He praises the poem for its depiction of ordinary life and continues, '[T]he festive vagrants are distinguished from each other by personal appearance and character, as much as any fortuitous assembly in the higher orders of life.'[22] Again, the influence of such depictions can apparently be seen in Scott's fiction. While we could find many examples of the depiction of ordinary life in his work, the example which seems most directly related to the 'festive vagrants' is the description of *Redgauntlet*'s Wandering Willie (whose name, as discussed below, in a sense owes something to Burns).

This connection seems obvious if we compare the description of the fiddle player in 'The Jolly Beggars' (K 84) with the depiction of Wandering Willie in Scott's text. The fiddler's song is given as follows:

> I am a Fiddler to my trade,
> An' a' the tunes that e'er I play'd,
> The sweetest still to WIFE or MAID,
>   Was whistle owre the lave [others] o't.
>
> At KIRNS [churns] an' WEDDINS we'se be there,
> An' O sae nicely's we will fare!
> We'll bowse [booze] about till Dadie CARE
>   Sing whistle owre the lave o't.
>
> Sae merrily's the banes we'll pyke [pluck],
> An' sun oursells about the dyke;
> An' at our leisure when ye like
>   We'll whistle owre the lave o't.
>
> But bless me wi' your heav'n o' charms,
> An' while I kittle [tune] hair on thairms [animal gut strings]
> HUNGER, CAULD, an' a' sic harms
>   May whistle owre the lave o't. (ll. 133–48)

Like Burns's figure, Scott's is itinerant, one of the 'wandering train' (l. 275) described in the poem, and scorns the idea of '"a bein nook in ... a braw house"',[23] preferring, as his wife puts it, to '"die the death of a cadger's powney in a wreath of drift"' (p. 82). Both he and his wife are described in detail, with the kind of discrimination Scott admires in Burn's poem,[24] and of course Willie, like Burns's fiddler, is engaged to play at 'Kirns an' Weddins'. It is not hard to see how Scott's description of Wandering Willie draws on Burns, and indeed the connection is made explicit when Willie claims to be '"the best fiddler that ever kittled thairm with horse-hair"' (p. 80). In the Cromek review, then, Scott recognises Burn's talent for depicting all the strata of Scottish society, and again this seems to be a quality that he imports into his own fiction.

Scott was clearly fond of this poem and laments in his Cromek review that it, along with 'Holy Willie's Prayer' which he describes as 'a piece of satire more exquisitely severe than any which Burns afterwards wrote, but unfortunately cast in a form too daringly profane to be received into Dr Currie's collection'[25] are absent from Cromek's volume; the collection is, he suggests, 'more properly gleanings than relics – the refuse and sweepings of the shop, rather than the commodities which might be deemed contraband'.[26]

Scott's description of Burns in the Cromek review gives us some general indication of what he admired in it, and is suggestive of the ways in which it may have influenced his fiction, re-emerging in it in both his means of producing emotion, and in his depiction of character. However, the work of the Edinburgh Edition has helped to establish the full extent of the references in his fiction, allowing us to trace specific allusions to Burns and the ways in which they appear. But what kind of 'history', to borrow Worth's phrase, do these allusions bring to Scott's work? What sorts of dialogue might he be constructing with his poetic predecessor by referencing Burns's work in his own? Some understanding of this may be reached by considering these allusions in detail.

In the twenty-four volumes of the Edinburgh Edition published so far there are in fact 104 allusions to Burns's work. Of these, six comprise the repeated lines on the 'land o' cakes' from 'On the Late Captain Grose' which figure on the title pages of several of the texts; fourteen references form mottos to chapters and the remaining references are embedded within the text. To give an indication of how these are distributed we can observe that *The Heart of Mid-Lothian* takes the lead with sixteen references; *Redgauntlet* follows with eleven, *The Pirate* has nine and perhaps somewhat more surprisingly *The Fortunes of Nigel*, less immediately obvious as a Scottish novel but nevertheless inherently about the state of Scotland within the Union, has eight references. *Chronicles of the Canongate* has six, *The Bride of Lammermoor* and *The Tale of Old Mortality* five each. *Castle Dangerous* has two references. Somewhat surprisingly, *Waverley* has only three direct references, and one fairly oblique reference to Burns; similarly *Rob Roy* has direct references only to 'Is There for Honest Poverty' and 'Auld Lang Syne' where Scott may have had Burns's versions in mind, and an oblique allusion to an event similar to that described in 'The Cotter's Saturday Night'. Perhaps predictably, the non-Scottish and medieval novels allude far less to Burns with *Ivanhoe* containing two references and *Ann of Geierstein*, *Kenilworth*, *Peveril of the Peak* and *Count Robert of Paris* containing only one reference each. No text edited so far, however, is without reference to Burns.

These references are drawn from a range of Burns's work although it is clear that Scott has some favourite texts which come most naturally to mind. There are, for example, twenty references to 'Tam o' Shanter', that text which Scott describes as exciting discordant emotions, and, in spite of the fact that it was 'too daringly profane' for Dr Currie, 'Holy Willie's Prayer' is alluded to six times. 'Love and Liberty' (or 'The Jolly Beggars') is also appealing, figuring four times in the tally; 'Halloween' seems to provide something of a supernatural backdrop figuring again four times. It should be noted here, that these references take the form of both direct allusions to Burns and more oblique reference, encompassing everything included within the Edinburgh Edition's practice of acknowledging direct allusion, references where the wording of the original varies slightly from Scott's quotation, and general rather than direct verbal indebtedness, indicated by the Edinburgh Edition's instruction to the reader of its notes to 'compare'. This total also refers in places to references to traditional song where Scott may or may not be referring to Burns's versions. However, Scott was to write in his *Journal* that 'No one but Burns ever succeeded in patching up old Scottish songs with any good effect' (p. 342) and there is often compelling evidence to suggest that it is Burns's lyrics that he has in mind. A note to *Redgauntlet*, for example, reminds us that Scott is likely to be referring to Burns's version of 'Here Awa', There Awa', Here Awa' Willie' as it had the first line 'Here awa', there awa' wandering, Willie'. This was republished in George Thomson's *A Select Collection of Original Scottish Airs* (1793), but in this version the comma between Burns's words 'wandering' and 'Willie' was omitted thus producing the sobriquet 'Wandering Willie'.[27]

The notes to the Edinburgh Edition then, reinforce the reader's impression that there is a significant dialogic relationship with Burns operating in Scott's fiction. However, if we leave number crunching aside, precisely what kind of meaning is produced in the Waverley Novels by this conversation with Burns's texts? It is impossible, of course, to examine all the allusions to Burns's work that have been identified here but by looking at a few examples we might go some way to answering this question. I will now turn, therefore, to the ways in which references to Burns operate in two of the Waverley Novels; those which I have been most directly involved in editing, *The Heart of Mid-Lothian* and *The Pirate*.

Of the sixteen references to Burns in *The Heart of Mid-Lothian* five are to 'Holy Willie's Prayer', one is to 'The Ordination' and one is to 'The Holy Fair'. Of the five references to 'Holy Willie' all are either spoken by or occur in relation to David Deans. Speaking of Reuben Butler's future, for example, Deans suggests that 'the lad may do weel, and be a burning and a shining light' (p. 79). Later, after Effie's arrest, he tells Reuben, 'I have been ower proud of my sufferings in a gude cause, Reuben, and now I am to be tried with those whilk will turn my pride and glory into a reproach and a hissing' (p. 102). This, of course, recalls Holy Willie's own observation that God

> lets this fleshy thorn
> Buffet [his] servant e'en and morn
> Lest he o'er proud and high should turn. (K 53, ll. 55–7).

Later on the same page David tells Reuben that he has been 'sae honoured and exalted in [his] youth' (p. 102) again recalling Willie's question: 'What was I, or my generation, / That I should get such exaltation?' (ll. 13–14). A further reference occurs as discussed above, when Jeanie and David sit down for their meal.

So what do these allusions to 'Holy Willie's Prayer' in relation to David Deans imply? At one level they support Tony Inglis's observation that Scott's mind is working associatively in this text so that 'Scott is drawing ... on the banks and cells of memory where *this* has lodged, and *this* and *this*, in significant proximity to one another.'[28] Taking as his subject a Covenanter and religious fanaticism in general, in other words, certain texts seem to push themselves naturally to the forefront of Scott's mind, a fact borne out by David Hewitt's and my own recognition upon editing the text that many of the other allusions in it draw directly from Covenanting literature so that 'David Deans is marked as the tradition-bearer, transmitting Covenanting experience and legend into the eighteenth century.'[29]

However, given that Scott describes this poem in his Cromek review as one of Burns's 'most exquisitely severe satires' we should question if these references have other implications, perhaps suggesting a more severe condemnation of Deans's extremist religious position than many readings would imply. *The Heart of Mid-Lothian* has, of course, also been read as entering into a dialogue with Scott's earlier Covenanting novel *The Tale of Old Mortality*, as a more sympathetic representation of the Covenanters than that novel proposed. However, while this may indeed be true of the text as a whole the references to 'Holy Willie' which characterise Scott's presentation of Deans in the earlier part of the text might suggest that Scott begins by reiterating something of the dangers of fanaticism and the hypocrisies of an extremist religious position that marked the earlier text. Mr Middleburgh's condemnation of Deans as 'a Deanite', with 'opinions peculiar to [himself]' (p. 176) in fact reinforces this view and the frustration it evokes in the more moderate magistrate.

In fact, *The Heart of Mid-Lothian* is essentially a chronicle in structure; it is a novel about change. In its controversial fourth volume Scott stretches out its time scheme beyond 1745 in order to illustrate the evolution of opinion in Scotland and the softening of religious fanaticism – exemplified by Deans of course – within the parameters of modernity.[30] Later references to Burns in the text reinforce this view. The references to 'The Ordination' and 'The

Holy Fair' in fact both occur in the last volume of the novel and are used to evoke a shifting of Deans's opinions in the light of his experiences. In both instances these references are more direct than those to 'Holy Willie' taking the form of mottos rather than embedded allusions; that from 'The Ordination', predictably enough, introduces the chapter where Reuben is to be ordained into the parish of Knocktarlitie, while that from 'The Holy Fair' opens the following chapter which describes the celebrations which ensue. While both of these intertexts may also be satires, they are satire of a more gentle and compassionate nature than that which is to be found in 'Holy Willie', more accommodating of the foibles of human nature, and this is surely consistent with David's changing views: by this stage in the text he is prepared to turn a blind eye to the grey areas that surround Reuben's election to the position of minister, and while he can hardly approve of the 'clattering pint-stoop' and 'yill-caup commentators' implied by the motto from 'The Holy Fair' he 'escaped any risk of being scandalised, by engaging with one of his neighbours' in a discussion of the Highland Host (p. 405).

These references to Burns in *The Heart of Mid-Lothian*, then, reinforce a sense of changing opinion both in David Deans and in Scotland as a whole; while they may not precisely evoke the passion Scott implies in his Cromek review they certainly imply intensities of emotional response and belief beyond that which might be immediately apparent on the surface of the text. Elsewhere, a reference to 'Tam o' Shanter' also implies intensities of experience beyond those acknowledged by the dominant Enlightened voice found within the novel.

This is exemplified most clearly in a reference to the poem that occurs at the close of Jeanie's night visit to Arthur's Seat. 'Her juvenile exercise as a herdswoman, had put "life and mettle" in her heels,' we are told, 'and never had she followed Dustiefoot, when the cows were in the corn, with half so much speed as she now cleared the distance betwixt Muschat's Cairn and her father's cottage at Saint Leonard's' (p. 163). The immediate meaning may seem bizarre, for it creates, of course, a connection between Jeanie and the dance of the witches in the Kirk of Alloway. However, there is a broader implication for it surely suggests not that Jeanie herself is demonic, but that the experience she has fled from may be so; the chapter opens with a discussion of changing attitudes to witchcraft and Jeanie's night walk ends with an embedded suggestion that aspects of experience beyond the liminal may not be as distant as the Enlightened voice of the narrator has initially implied.

In this incident, then, 'Tam o' Shanter' operates to provide something of a mediation between systems of belief; between the values of Enlightenment Scotland and those of an earlier age. The poem also operates in this way in *The Pirate*, a text which deals more overtly with the negotiations involved in changing ways of life and the conflicts of belief systems which such negotiations imply.³¹ As with the 'Holy Willie' references discussed earlier, allusions to 'Tam o' Shanter' in *The Pirate* are clustered together and act as an intertext to Mordaunt Merton's walk in the storm between Jarlshof and his father's home at Stourburgh:

> There were ten 'lang Scots miles' betwixt Stourburgh and Jarlshof; and though our pedestrian did not number all the impediments which crossed Tam o' Shanter's path, – for, in country where there are neither hedges nor stone inclosures, there can be neither 'slaps nor stiles,' – yet the number and nature of the 'waters and mosses' which he had to cross in his peregrination, were fully sufficient to balance the account, and to render his journey as toilsome and dangerous as that of the celebrated retreat from Ayr. (p. 60)

In one sense these allusions may be merely topographical implying the treacherous nature of the terrain that Mordaunt must negotiate to reach home. As Scott himself says in his *Journal*, '[I]n younger days I used to enjoy a Tam-of-Shanter ride through darkness wind and rain, the boughs groaning and cracking over my head, the good horse free to the road and impatient for home and feeling the weather as little as I did'.³² But 'Tam o' Shanter' is unusually foregrounded here; not only is the title of the poem mentioned, but, somewhat uncommonly for Scott, each of the direct allusions appears within inverted commas. And if that is not enough, we are reminded of the context of them by mention of the 'celebrated retreat from Ayr'. This foregrounding suggests that the poem has greater significance for Mordaunt and the text as a whole than that of mere topographical similarity. *The Pirate* is, it can be argued, a novel that deals with agricultural change and resistance to it; in fact it offers a similar negotiation between Enlightenment views on the progress of history and the older belief systems of an oral folk culture to that found in Burns's poem. Moreover, these ideas are of clear significance in the context of Mordaunt's walk, for while he is making his way home his heart in fact lies with the older traditions and ways of life that Jarlshof embodies. So too, just as these tensions are figured in 'Tam' via the protagonist's brush with the supernatural, Mordaunt's journey from Jarlshof to Stourburgh also embodies a tension between a world where the words of the hag Norna of the Fitful Head are still paid heed to and one where they are deemed irrelevant, again reinforcing the dynamic that lies at the very heart of this text.

Elsewhere in *The Pirate*, two poignant allusions to Burns also help figure the competing structural directions of the text. One of these occurs at the point where Mordaunt nearly drowns in his attempt to rescue Cleveland the Pirate. Minna and Brenda watch aghast and Scott writes:

> Minna grew as pale as death, while Brenda uttered successive shrieks of terror. But though there were some nods, winks, and hints, that auld acquaintance were

not easily forgot, it was, on the whole, candidly admitted, that less than such marks of interest could scarce have been expected, when they saw the companion of their early youth in the act of perishing before their eyes. (p. 162)

While Brenda's shrieks may be dismissed by the onlookers, the reference to 'Auld Lang Syne' reminds us that old acquaintance is not easily forgotten and of course prefigures Brenda's marriage to Mordaunt at the end of the text. Reference to Burns elsewhere, however, also suggests the tragic and more fatalistic conclusion that is also embodied in the novel, and which again signifies an older set of belief systems. Speaking of the sisters Norna states that 'To know them once, is to love them forever' (p. 96). For Norna of the Fitful Head, our destinies are predetermined, written in the stars and knowable through the intervention of pagan gods; the fate of the sisters and their lovers reflect this. While Brenda and Mordaunt may find happiness, Minna and Cleveland, of course, indeed must part forever at the end of the text.

These examples suggest that the magic art of Scott's own eloquence may lie in his ability to exploit his vast knowledge of literature to weave meaning by reference to other texts. By allusion to Burns and others The Wizard of the North casts his net wide to create a polyphony of meanings within the creative space of the Waverley Novels, reinforcing the tensions between the Enlightenment and progressive discourses by which they seemingly operate and the more subversive, emotionally charged meanings which disrupt this dominant grain. For Scott, however, eloquence is never only about meaning but is always fundamentally emotionally charged. Arguably the most emotional incident in *The Heart of Mid-Lothian* is the scene where Jeanie meets with the queen to plead for her sister's life. Again, drawing on what he has absorbed from Burns, it is the homely nature of Jeanie's appeal that wins the queen's sympathy, as she states:

> 'O, madam, if ever ye kenn'd what it was to sorrow for and with a sinning and a suffering creature, whose mind is sae tossed that she can be neither ca'd fit to live or die, have some compassion on our misery! – Save an honest house from dishonour, and an unhappy girl, not eighteen years of age, from an early and dreadful death!' (p. 340–1)

'This is eloquence,' responds the queen, and it is precisely that emotional effect which is implied by Scott's description of Burns's work by that term. 'Long life to thy fame and peace to thy soul, Rob Burns,' Scott writes in his *Journal* for 11 December, 1826. 'When I want to express a sentiment which I feel strongly, I find the phrase in Shakespeare or thee'.[33] If, as readers of Scott, we are alert to the fact that allusion to Burns signifies 'strong sentiment' we may well find that it frequently offers 'varied and discordant emotions' in his fiction, opening them up to new levels of emotional response on the part of the reader, new forms of affective capacity for those of us who engage with them today.[34]

CHAPTER ELEVEN

Burns and Virgil

Steven R. McKenna

Robert Burns was keenly aware of the relationships between poetry and a sense of nationalism. Yet it remains a curious fact about Burns that he has so very little to say about arguably the most nationalistic poet Western civilisation has ever produced – Rome's Virgil. One would think that a poet with an eye toward national poetry might have some extended reflections on the poet who set the European standard for the relationship of literature and land. Yet despite Virgil's influence in the 1,800 years separating him from Burns, the Scots Bard has relatively little to say about the Roman. In fact, Burns mentions Virgil rarely: most comprehensively to Mrs Dunlop (1730–1815) in May 1788 (*L* I, pp. 278–9), again in the little and oft neglected poem 'Sketch', and also in the Preface to his 'Kilmarnock' edition of *Poems, Chiefly in the Scottish Dialect*. Burns had ambivalent feelings for Virgil, and, as a poet rooted in a sense of the land, he ultimately preferred the Roman's *Georgics* to the *Aeneid*. The latter poem Burns found to be rather stiff and derivative. Because of its importance in revealing Burns's sparsely expressed feelings about Virgil, the letter to Mrs Dunlop deserves to be quoted at some length:

> Dryden's Virgil has delighted me. – I don't know whether the critics will agree with me, but the Georgics are to me by far the best of Virgil. – It is indeed a species of writing entirely new to me; and has filled my head with a thousand fancies of emulation: but alas! When I read the Georgics, and then survey my own powers, 'tis like the idea of a Shetland Pony drawn up by the side of a thoroughbred Hunter, to start for the Plate. –
>
> I own I am disappointed in the Eneid [sic]. – Faultless correctness may please, and does highly please the lettered Critic; but to that aweful [sic] character I have not the most distant pretentions. – I don't know whether I do not hazard my pretentions to be a Critic of any kind, when I say that I think Virgil, in many instances, a *servile* Copier of Homer. – If I had the Odyssey by me, I could parallel many passages where Virgil has evidently copied, but by no means improved Homer. – Nor can I think there is any thing of this [...] owing to the Translators; for, from every thing I have seen of Dryden, I think him, in genius

and fluency of language, Pope's master [. . .] I am conscious my criticism must be very inaccurate and imperfect, as *there* I have ever felt & lamented my want of Learning most. – (*L* I, pp. 278–9)

Burns claims such poetry as he found in the *Georgics* opened new vistas for him, to the point where he wishes to produce something similar to Virgil's piece. Burns in his simile of the pony realises his own powers of agricultural poetics would fall far short of Virgil's. Unfortunately, Burns leaves us precious little information about what exactly he finds so compelling in that work. In sum, Burns was deeply struck by what he saw as the originality and, for lack of a more precise term, greatness of the *Georgics*.

As for the *Aeneid*, Burns is a little more expansive in his opinion. The poem suffers from being too imitative of the Homeric model and too 'Faultless' (artificial? learned?) in its execution. Burns doesn't explain what his term 'Faultless' means, but it probably has something to do with Virgil's highly polished Latin (and Dryden's beautiful rendition of it) and the tight organisational structures of the story, even, as this was, left in unfinished condition.

This chapter suggests some possibilities about what in Virgil's poems Burns found attractive in the case of the *Georgics* and what he found less appealing in the *Aeneid* and in the *Eclogues*. Particularly, it will focus on Burns's thoughts about Virgil's originality and in a more speculative vein the poems' broad vision of society and history and how Virgil's treatment of these issues mesh and clash with Burns's. Beyond mere stylistics, the nominal imperialistic agenda at work in Virgil's epic ran counter to Burns's own socio-political philosophies, as a Scotsman the subject of an English imperialistic culture. As for the *Georgics*, in addition to being the poetry of an agrarian world, Virgil there displays a social philosophy and a world view that was far closer to Burns's than the epic and political view embodied in the Roman epic.

In his letter to Mrs Dunlop, Burns dismisses the 'lettered' critics, yet he also laments his own critical powers due to his felt deficiencies in education. As literary criticism, this letter proposes little in the way of analysis and creates no sustained argument. However, Burns's downplaying of his critical abilities is a bit disingenuous. Lettered or not, Burns appears to have a firm enough working knowledge of the *Aeneid*, via Dryden's translation, and Homer's *Odyssey*, via Pope's translation, to claim to be able to catalogue Virgil's copying of Homer. If Burns here is truly serious, as opposed to bragging, it would argue that for all his disappointment with the *Aeneid* he nevertheless read the epic carefully, closely, and with an eye toward situating the poem within the epic tradition (or at least the Odyssean tradition vis-à-vis the first six books of the *Aeneid*).

Since this letter to Mrs Dunlop, aside from the claim that Burns could cite many instances of borrowed passages in the *Aeneid*, offers us little else to go on, let us consider his short poem 'Sketch' (*K* 82). In this work, Burns develops a literary critical theory and applies it over a wide range of writers, one of whom is Virgil in the poem (Maro). Here, Burns offers a coherent and probing assessment of originality and imitation, language and realism. This poem opens a window onto Burns's thinking about and understanding of Virgil and his works.

In stanza one of the poem, Burns lauds 'Poesie' (l. 1) yet sees that the pursuit of her has sent 'crowds' (l. 2) of poets and aspiring poets off the path of 'Common Sense' (l. 3). In essence, Burns launches an attack on all the bad poets and their poetry produced in the attempt to chase this 'nymph reserv'd'(l. 1). In the second stanza, Burns first dismisses the epic poems (and presumably their composers as well): 'loud the trumps heroic clang' (l. 8). In other words, they are discordant as poetry. This line indicates that for Burns epics tend to be more noise than harmonious music, more flash and ostentation than true poetry.

The second genre, dramatic poetry, likewise draws a summary dismissal from Burns. Referring to the footwear of Classical comic and tragic actors, he writes that the 'Sock and buskin skelp along / To death or marriage' (ll. 9–10). Burns's use of the verb 'skelp' is telling, for it means 'to beat or thrash'. The verb can also mean 'to hurry'. In this sense, Burns observes that this sort of poetic output beats a hasty path to its last act – in this case, 'death or marriage'. Burns here criticises a formulaic type of literature that aims at clichéd, trite, or melodramatic conclusions.

Burns ends this stanza with a reference to pastoral poetry, and the later references in the poem to Theocritus and Virgil mean that here Burns has the entire tradition beginning with these poets' *Idylls* and *Eclogues* in mind when he thinks of this sort of poetry. To reduce stanza two to its basic question, then, Burns asks Poesie why in all her train of followers 'Scarce ane has tried the Shepherd-sang / But wi' miscarriage' (ll. 11–12). In his eyes, few poets who actually attempt to compose pastoral poetry actually succeed in producing anything of worth. The answer to his question is not immediately obvious in the poem, but the organisation of the stanza itself places the ultimate emphasis on the pastoral poetry. Epic and dramatic poetry have their poets, and the products might fail to satisfy Burns's tastes, but the real wonder for him is that attempts at pastoral poetry tend to be so botched when attempted. Epics and drama might generally be of poor quality, but he implies that they are at least somewhat successful at what they do and for what they are. In contrast, Burns in effect claims that most of the extant body of pastoral verse was and is less accomplished, as the notion of a 'miscarriage' would imply. This stanza indicates that the possibilities of pastoral verse are of no less importance than those of heroic epic or drama.

In the third stanza, Burns sharpens the argument's focus by paying homage to those whom he sees as masters of their genres and continuers of the poetics of Classical Antiquity: Milton vis-à-vis Homer, Shakespeare vis-à-vis Aeschylus, the thieving Pope vis-à-vis Horace and Anna Barbauld vis-à-vis Sappho. Burns sees that the Classical poets can and do have their rivals in the more recent periods, that the modern world can and did produce literature that matched the assumed greatness of the ancient masterpieces.

When Burns begins his next stanza with the word 'But' – 'But thee, Theocritus, wha matches?' (l. 19) – he again elevates pastoral poetry, in this case Theocritus (early 3rd century BCE) and his *Idylls*, to a supreme position in the hierarchy of poetry. The next line with its passing dismissal of Virgil's own attempts at imitating Theocritus (Virgil's ten eclogues) gives an indication of what exactly in Theocritus and the thirty Idylls concerns Burns so much and upon which he places so much importance as matters of great poetry. Burns summarily executes Virgil's *Eclogues* in a simple phrase: 'They're no' Herd's ballats, Maro's catches' (l. 20). Virgil's 'catches' fail to match the poetry and, we later discern, the realism of Theocritus in what Burns earlier referred to as 'Shepherd-sang'. As stanza four progresses, Burns dismisses Pope and his poetry as flashy work stitched together from 'Heathen tatters' (l. 22). Finally, in lumping together vast multitudes of poets, Burns effectively strikes at the core of his general dislike of Virgil (save for the *Georgics*): 'I pass by hunders, nameless wretches, / That ape their betters' (ll. 23–4). This is pretty strong stuff, and coming as it does at the conclusion of a dismissal of Virgil's *Eclogues* and a sharp jab at Pope, we can see that Burns has little or no use for poets and poetry that only 'ape' superior poets and works. This also distinctly echoes what Burns wrote to Mrs Dunlop. In sum, he sees Virgil (again, with the exception of the *Georgics*) as stale, imitative, derivative and missing the mark set by those whom Burns views as Virgil's masters – Theocritus in the case of the *Eclogues*, and Homer in the case of the *Aeneid*.

Before continuing the analysis of 'Sketch', it is helpful to consider the *Idylls* of Theocritus and Virgil's *Eclogues* in order to make some suggestions about what exactly Burns values so highly in the *Idylls* and what he finds lacking in Virgil's 'catches'. Theocritus is and has been universally regarded as the originator of what we know as Pastoral or Bucolic poetry. The thirty poems published under his name treat a variety of topics. His is a world of sunshine and the idealised Sicily of his youth, a world where shepherds and various other agricultural and peasant types work and play in the great outdoors. The most prominent struggles are to be found in the contests involving poetry and song. Love is a constant preoccupation. Through all the idealised landscapes and situations, Theocritus is able to maintain a sense of convincing human realism. For instance, in Idyll 4, Corydon and Battus, two herdsmen, discuss matters of love. Battus near the end of the poem complains that while in the hills with his flock he has got a thorn stuck in his foot. Instead of belabouring an obvious symbol of the love-struck herdsman, Theocritus merely has Corydon offer a piece of sound advice: 'Thou should'st put on thy shoes when thou goest into the hills'.[1] Another example, this from 'The Charities' (Idyll 16), concerns the deficiencies of a world obsessed with wealth, while the poet himself begs patronage from Hiero, future King of Syracuse. In lines that resemble Burns's own meditation in the second epistle to Lapraik on wealth, poverty and the place of the poet, Theocritus writes:

> Poor simple fools! What profits it a man that he have thousands of gold laid by? To the wise the enjoyment of riches is not that, but rather to give first somewhat to his own soul, and then something, methinks, to one of the poets [. . .] it is to bestow honour upon the holy interpreters of the Muses, that so you may rather be well spoken of even when you lie hid in death . . .[2]

In these, and in passages like them, Theocritus displays a colloquial touch, a language of everyday use, and the straightforward voice of the poet.

Virgil inherited the pastoral mode from Theocritus and other Greek intermediaries who followed in the tradition. As such, Virgil was not an originator. He was an imitator and a continuer. He desired to use the forms (dialogue, monologue, song) and the subjects (herding, love, landscape, the outdoor life of relative ease) found in the models. This, it would seem, is enough to make Burns pass over the imitations in favour of the originals. In dismissing Virgil's attempts at 'Herd's ballats' Burns seems to suggest that in some combination of form ('ballats') and content ('Herd's') Virgil's *Eclogues* fail to have the ring of truth about them that Theocritus displays in his *Idylls*.

In the fifth stanza, Burns continues to address the concern he voiced about pastoral poetry in the current world of letters as he viewed it. Picking up again on what he earlier called 'Shepherd-sang' and 'Herd's ballats', Burns now develops the question based on the metaphor of pastoral poetry as 'the Shepherd's whistle':

> In this braw age o' wit and lear,
> Will nane the Shepherd's whistle mair
> Blaw sweetly in his native air
>   And rural grace;
> And wi' the far-fam'd Grecian share
>   A rival place? (ll. 25–30)

There are a number of issues at work in this stanza. First, Burns turns his attention to his own day and age as one of wit and learning. Given the earlier scorn which he heaped upon poetic imitators, we can surmise that wit and learning result in little other than sterile imitation of past masters and prior models.

In a similar vein to this and the related point he makes in his letter to Mrs Dunlop, the first sentence of the Preface to *Poems, Chiefly in the Scottish Dialect* states:

> The following trifles are not the production of the Poet, who, with all the advantages of learned art, and perhaps amid the elegancies and idlenesses of upper life, looks down for a rural theme, with an eye to Theocritus or Virgil.[3]

Here again Burns treats the themes of 'learned art' and imitation. Since this sentence is the very first one of the 'Kilmarnock' edition's Preface, Burns emphatically rejects these linked concepts as his motive and method in the collection of poems. Moreover, he implies that the 'rural theme' of much contemporary verse is a form of condescension on the part of the upper class toward the lower. This further suggests that those who partake of the 'upper life' consider it superior to the rural life. As Burns makes clear in 'Sketch' also, such poetic condescension and imitation become merely a nod in the direction of a genre, an intellectual exercise rather than the product of a lived experience. Herein lies a basis for Burns's dismissal of Virgil's *Eclogues* as inferior to the *Idylls* of Theocritus.

The attraction to Virgil by those of the 'upper life' who could practise 'learned art' stemmed in part from the fact that Virgil had for centuries the reputation of being vastly learned in all the arts and sciences, and his poems thus were viewed as virtuoso displays of that learning. Virgil's multi-purpose poetry – that is, his employment of grammar, rhetoric, philosophy, religion, science, cosmology, history and so on – made of his work via its use in the schools an authority on and hence a model for just about everything. For Burns this Virgil of literary tradition was in fact the father of the 'wit and lear' that Burns saw as being so detrimental to the poetry of his own age. Burns's criticism of his contemporaries is exactly his criticism of Virgil. In the pastoral tradition, Theocritus was the originator. Virgil was the follower. In epic, Homer was the originator, Virgil the imitator. But in the arena of agricultural verse, Burns treats Virgil as the true originator with the *Georgics*. So we can see that for Burns the sense of beginnings looms large in his poetic theorising, for after originators more often than not there follows the band of imitators, usually with the inferior results Burns associates with imitation.

The remainder of the poem addresses the question of whether there is a successor to and rival of Theocritus in the present age, especially since Virgil is neither modern nor, in Burns's view, in the same league as 'the far-fam'd Grecian'. The answer is none other than Burns's predecessor in Scottish literature, Allan Ramsay (1684–1758). In the two millennia separating Theocritus from Burns, only one poet rises to the lofty poetic heights inhabited by the Greek, and it is not Virgil. It is that Edinburgh gentleman who was so instrumental in reviving Scots poetry and creating, according to Burns, pastoral poetry that was not for an age but for all time.

Burns in stanza seven praises Ramsay's poetry by saying, 'Thou paints auld Nature to the nines, / In thy sweet Caledonian lines' (ll. 37–8). We see here two important items that Burns earlier in the poem touched on, namely the pastoral world ('Nature' in l. 37) as a subject matter and the vehicle for it in a vernacular language (the 'Caledonian lines' of l. 38, what in l. 27 he called 'native air'). This matter of the native language, with its presumed powers to convey the essence of the pastoral world, contrasts sharply with the clangs of 'the trumps heroic' (l. 8) and the like that Burns dismissed earlier in the poem as being of little real value. Also, in contrast to Burns's view of the deficiencies of such ostentatious poetics, he tells Ramsay, 'Thou need na jouk behint the hallan' (l. 33), as though 'honest' Allan were in reality *bashful* Allan hiding himself and his talent behind a wall.

In the poem's last three stanzas Burns concentrates on Ramsay's beautiful evocations of the landscape and love, most likely with Ramsay's pastoral drama *The Gentle Shepherd* (1725) in mind. Indeed, Burns lavishes praise on Ramsay precisely for what his poetry *lacks*:

> Nae gowden stream thro' myrtles twines
>   Where Philomel,
> While nightly breezes sweep the vines,
>   Her griefs will tell! (ll. 39–42)

It is precisely the absence of such neoclassical artificiality as this that Burns finds so compelling in Ramsay's verse. Burns's praise for Allan Ramsay's pastoral poetics focuses mainly on what Burns sees as the inherent realism in subject and treatment of love and the other behaviours of the rustic folk. Virgil's agenda differs markedly from Ramsay's (and Theocritus's as well), and in the final analysis Burns views the straightforward poetry of Ramsay and Theocritus as being far superior to the technical sophistication and thematic complexity of Virgil's *Eclogues*.

Virgil's pastoral world in many ways doesn't measure up to the standards Burns sets up and which he thinks Ramsay fulfils. If we set aside the question of writing pastoral poetry in the native language (for Latin was Virgil's and his subjects' native tongue), we can look at some of what we might view as Virgil's disconnection from nature and the rustics who inhabit that world.

This evolving engagement on Virgil's part with humanity and civilisation achieves its second phase in his didactic farming poem, the *Georgics*. Unlike his attitude toward the *Eclogues*, Burns found the four books of the *Georgics* to be high and splendid poetry worthy of imitation, as he indicates in his letter to Mrs Dunlop quoted above.

Several aspects of the *Georgics* suggest possible reasons he favours this particular work over Virgil's others. In brief, they are, first, the lack of the Arcadian artifice in treating the natural world; second, the 'practical pastoral' element in the poem – that is, the didactic 'how to' of farming, viniculture, livestock management and bee-keeping; and third, a realistic treatment based on a realistic premise concerning the human being's relationship to the land, where humans are part of and integral to what can be broadly termed a hierarchical space, a world where everything from the lowest mineral and organism up through humanity to the gods themselves exists, or can exist, in a fundamental order and harmony.

The first of these elements, the lack of a typical Arcadian artifice, is rather easy to deal with. Burns, as we saw in his poem 'Sketch', rejected the clichés of pastoral verse that were so prevalent in his own day, and he saw in Virgil's *Eclogues* an imitative form of 'Herd's ballats' that he thought just rang falsely. In the *Georgics*, however, Virgil has in mind a treatise, not an eclogue. His agenda does not concern the impossible idealisation of farmer or farm land. Any worthwhile instructional manual must of necessity treat its subject realistically. As for the question of imitation and influence, that is a harder issue for the *Georgics* because the generally presumed models of didactic agricultural literature have largely vanished, existing mainly in scattered fragments. Two works, though, Lucretius's *De Rerum Natura* (unfinished at the time of the poet's death in c. 55 BCE) and Hesiod's *Works and Days* (c. 700 BCE) have long been known to have been important influences on Virgil and the *Georgics*.[4] Matters of this sort, however, seem not to enter Burns's thinking about the grandeur and originality he saw in the *Georgics*. And this brings me to the second point about the *Georgics* – their element of the practical pastoral. In the real world of farming, especially subsistence farming, pastoral poetry might offer a few examples of pleasant song and the vagaries of a love life, but it won't teach many survival skills. The *Georgics*, however, would provide farming information in addition to pleasant poetry. Indeed, many of the lessons Virgil packs into his treatise can be and are used in the modern world, especially by farmers who tend to practise what are often referred to as organic methods. A small sampling of Virgil will suffice to illustrate the point:

> Yet sprinkle sordid Ashes all around,
> And load with fat'ning Dung thy fallow Ground.[5]
>
> Be mindful when thou hast intomb'd the Shoot,
> With Store of Earth around to feed the Root;
> With Iron Teeth of Rakes and Prongs, to move
> The crusted Earth, and loosen it above. (BK 2, ll. 485–8)

Or when discussing the care of sheep, Virgil offers the following regarding wounds or ulcers:

>   searching all thy Store,
> The best is still at hand, to launch the Sore:
> And cut the Head; for till the Core be found,
> The secret Vice is fed, and gathers Ground:
> While making fruitless Moan, the Shepherd stands,
> And, when the launching knife requires his hands,
> Vain help, with idle Pray'rs, from Heav'n demands. (BK 3, ll. 690–6)

This practical element of the *Georgics* leads to the next point: its vision of a hierarchical space. The modern organic farmer, or even a farmer of Burns's age, would undoubtedly not see the hands of the Classical pantheon at work in the processes of nature, except in poetic flights of fancy unhinged from the realities of the agricultural world. Yet one thing that unites farmers and gardeners with their ancient and neoclassical forebears is what we might understand to be a spiritual connection with the land. Despite the rather non-mythological understandings of modern agricultural sciences, there is still something life-affirming and mysterious about working the soil, planting seeds, tending the crops and bringing forth food from the earth. This, in its Classical manifestation, is a theme that runs through Virgil's *Georgics* – the link between the earth, animals, human effort and the mysterious hands of the gods at work in and on the natural world. Surely, Farmer Burns had his own spiritual understandings of agriculture and the sacred.

Furthermore, Virgil in the *Georgics* develops an idea of human history that, in this poem at least, would have appealed to Burns the political man, even if it smacks of monarchy. Virgil's vision of salvation within historical time has its genesis in the *Eclogues* and *Georgics*, reaching its fruition in the *Aeneid*. In those two early works, we find the past, and in some cases even the present, corrupted by human failings and by urbanised life. In both works, salvation for the individual and society comes in the form of movement forward under the aegis of a saviour figure – the child in *Eclogue* 4, Augustus after the death of Julius Caesar (allegorised as the death of Daphnis in *Eclogue* 5), and in the figure of Aristaeus the bee-keeper in *Georgics* 4 (bees being here symbolic of human social organisation). In this section of the *Georgics*, Virgil presents the society of a bee-hive as an idealised and rational monarchic structure. Significantly, the ideal society here is linked to the divine mind:

>   Induc'd by such Examples, some have taught
>   That Bees have Portions of Etherial Thought:
>   Endu'd with Particles of Heavenly Fires:
>   For God the whole created Mass inspires . . . (BK 4, ll. 321–4)

For Virgil, this is no mere random collection of insects. The fact that apian 'society' can organise itself around a supreme 'monarch' with all members contributing to the harmony and well-being of the whole makes of bees an idealised image of what humanity should be. Virgil undoubtedly has in mind here contemporary Rome and the possibilities of a unified empire under Augustus, who two years prior to the completion of the *Georgics* defeated Antony and Cleopatra in the battle of Actium in 31 BCE and ended the civil wars.

But such processes and an understanding of the human place in the cosmic scheme, if such were attractions for Burns in the *Georgics*, failed to win his approval when he considers Virgil's epic, the *Aeneid*. Nominally, Burns faulted Virgil for being a second-rate imitator of the superior Homer. Recall that in his letter to Mrs Dunlop he wrote, 'I think Virgil, in many instances, a *servile* Copier of Homer' (*L* I, p. 279, Burns's emphasis). 'Servile' here becomes a dismissive term; 'Sketch', already discussed, shows just what Burns thinks about poetic copiers, servile or otherwise. If we take Burns at his word in the letter to Mrs Dunlop, he would be able to create a list of Homeric sources and analogues for the *Aeneid*. Fair enough. Though Burns doesn't in fact mention any of these imitations or borrowings, the critical literature on the poem catalogues them in great detail. Virgil modelled his *Aeneid* Books 1–6 on Homer's *Odyssey* and Books 7–12 on the *Iliad*, the first half being the wanderings of Aeneas in search of a destined homeland, and the second half being the battles to secure that land for the ancestors of the Romans. Within that broad outline, numerous scenes and passages, as Burns noted in his letter to Mrs Dunlop, are taken with a liberal hand from the Homeric models. A couple of these will serve to illustrate the point. In the *Odyssey* Book 11, Odysseus makes a journey to the land of the dead, interacts with the spirits, and gains a degree of prophetic wisdom just prior to his return to his homeland of Ithaka. Similarly, at roughly the *Aeneid*'s midpoint, Aeneas in Book 6 takes a journey to the underworld, interacts with the dead, and gains a degree of prophetic wisdom about his and his race's future, just prior to his arrival at his new homeland in Italy. Where Odysseus meets the shade of his mother, Aeneas meets that of his dead father. Another detail Virgil borrowed from Homer is the attempted embrace. When Odysseus sees his mother in the underworld:

> Thrice in my arms I strove her shade to bind,
> Thrice thro' my arms she slipt like empty wind,
> Or dreams, the vain illusions of the mind.[6]

Virgil takes this incident and superimposes it on Aeneas's meeting with his father, Anchises, in the underworld:

> Then thrice, around his Neck, his Arms he threw;
> And thrice the flitting Shadow slip'd away;
> Like Winds, or empty Dreams that fly the Day. (BK 6, ll. 950–2)

Virgil uses the same Homeric incident earlier in the poem as well. As Aeneas describes the fall of Troy to Dido, he details his escape from the burning city with his family. During the flight, his wife, Creusa, disappears and dies. When Aeneas goes searching for her, he finds her ghost and uses the exact same lines to describe the frustrated attempt to embrace her:

> And thrice about her Neck my Arms I flung;
> And thrice deceiv'd, on vain Embraces hung.
> Light as an empty Dream at break of Day,
> Or as a blast of Wind, she rush'd away. (BK 2, ll. 1077–80)

In general, Virgil as a continuator of the epic tradition and as a citizen of the emerging Roman Empire faced a novel situation – use the Homeric model for an age far removed in time and culture from Homer's own age of heroes. Virgil, as Brooks Otis has explored, had to revive the epic form from the artistic degeneracy to which it had fallen in the centuries between Homer and Augustan Rome.[7] The key to Virgil's success in the revived epic mode lies, as Otis notes, in the fact that Virgil was 'the first and only poet truly to recreate the heroic-age epic in an urban civilization'.[8] From Burns's point of view, the result was unsatisfactory. The sensibilities required for such an undertaking manifestly differed from those of Homer and his less urbanised culture. For Virgil, history and hence the urban Roman reality manifest themselves as largely human affairs with human autonomy a central and problematic concern. In this march of events there are winners and losers, the latter being part of the price that history exacts in its march toward fulfilment.

Given this, one major yet unspoken item of concern for Burns is Virgil's own sense of history that culminates within the story of Aeneas's wanderings and wars. The *Aeneid*'s concern with Roman politics demonstrates Virgil's belief that such politics can and do give discernible form to history and meaning to human life. As David Quint has argued, 'Virgil's poem attached political meaning to narrative form itself. To the victors belongs epic, with its linear teleology; to the losers belongs romance, with its random or circular wandering.'[9] The notion of teleological history entails a unity and an internal logic whereby Romans can fashion their own story and validate a particular view of historical events. Such a linearity in historical logic would make even the Roman civil wars something other than power politics. The historical narrative embedded in the sweep of the *Aeneid* makes of the wars' winners, chiefly Augustus, not creatures of chance but rather the embodiments of history's actual designs. As the image of Augustus, triumphant after Actium, on Aeneas's shield (BK 8, ll. 714–16) suggests also, the unitary aspect of the shield as the embodiment of Roman history culminates in the single figure of the emperor who has brought an end to the fractiousness of the civil strife and unified the state in such a way that empire was then possible. Such an image of imperialist triumph in turn argues for the triumph of the vision of history which culminates in the orderly unfolding of that very imperialist triumph. The linearity of the *Aeneid*'s view of history makes of all tangential material literal dead ends. Dido and Aeneas's delay in Carthage, the rivalry with Turnus, and quite literally the civil upheavals associated with Pompey and Antony – all must be viewed as closed and dead avenues of history. All these characters and events provide alternative voices and views of the linear trajectory of Roman history. Official history, therefore, must attempt to marginalise and foreclose these voices and views. So one of the lessons of the *Aeneid* is that history's losers have been effectively silenced (reinforced poignantly by Dido's mute reception of Aeneas in the underworld of Book 6).

This would suggest that myths of origin, such as embodied in the *Aeneid*, which in one way or another explain the present historical realities of culture serve to perpetuate those realities. This means that culture is constantly attempting to measure up to its own images of itself while producing new images that build upon the old in an endless loop of cultural production. The Trojan legend has as part of its appeal the fact that Troy itself can be seen as a prototype of Western urban culture – the city, prosperity, plentiful natural resources, livestock and the thriving agricultural infrastructure that will allow for the flourishing of all these conditions.[10] The legends of Troy therefore have embedded within them the model of culture that Rome and the West valorise and attempt to replicate. Burns himself appears to understand these matters of history, nations and individuals, and this awareness manifests itself in his attention to history and literature's victims.

Even the casual reader of Burns's poetry will immediately recognise the nationalistic zeal he displays towards Robert Bruce, William Wallace and matters Scots. When we turn to the letters, we can see some of these feelings fleshed out. For instance, in his letter of 15th November 1786 to Mrs Dunlop Burns mentions that two of his early favourite books were biographies of Hannibal and Wallace (*L* I, p. 62). Wallace is understandable. Curiously, though, Burns's choice of Hannibal relates directly to the figure of Wallace in that both men fought against the forces of a superior military power and lost. In the sweep of historical progress, both could be considered 'the enemy'; representatives of that which was subsumed into a dominant thread of history (Rome, England). Significantly, though, Burns finds them of great interest. Along these same lines, we see the numerous allusions to and mentions of Milton's Satan from *Paradise Lost*. Burns makes no bones about his admiration for this mythical figure, whom he referred to as, among other things, 'that great Personage' (*L* I, p. 123). Here again Burns sides with the loser. It is clearly within the realm of probability that one reason he finds the *Aeneid* less than satisfying is that its hero, Aeneas, is the founder and representative of such hegemonic imperial forces as embodied in Milton's heaven, England vis-à-vis Scotland, and quite literally in Rome vis-à-vis Hannibal and Carthage (a destructive relationship echoed in the Dido and Aeneas relationship, particularly in Book 4 of the *Aeneid*).[11] Burns knew at first hand what life was like on the side that lost, and his sympathies tended to lie there rather than with the winners.

We can see a facet of this thought in Burns's own erstwhile desire to be the composer of epic verse. In the letter of 15th November 1786, while reminiscing about his youthful attraction to William Wallace, he writes:

> [A]s I explored every den and dell where I could suppose my heroic Countryman to have sheltered, I recollect (for even then I was a Rhymer) that my heart glowed with a wish to be able to make a Song on him equal to his merits. – (*L* I, p. 62)

Even early in life, we see that Burns had the desire to write a national epic, and this desire again shows his attachment not to history's victors but to the representative of the struggle against those winners.

Burns's attitudes towards Virgil are by no means one-dimensional, simply seeing the Roman as largely a servile imitator of Greek models. Rather, and particularly in Burns's negative feelings towards Virgil, there exists a superstructure of potential political and philosophical conflict between the Scotsman and the Roman. Indeed, despite Burns's failure to produce a 'national epic' poem within his lifetime, his works and thoughts might be seen as existing in a dialogue with his Roman predecessor.

CHAPTER TWELVE

Burns and Transnational Culture

Leith Davis

In June 1786, Robert Burns wrote a number of letters informing his friends and acquaintances that he was preparing to depart his 'native soil' for a more promising situation 'among the mountains of Jamaica' (*L* I, p. 33). His letters link this decision to emigrate with his disappointment in love. As he wrote to the shoemaker David Brice, '[T]he Ship is on her way home that is to take me out to Jamaica; and then, farewell dear old Scotland, and farewell dear, ungrateful Jean, for never, never will I see you more!' (*L* I, p. 39).[1] In 'On a Scotch Bard Gone to the West Indies' (*K* 100) he projects this connection between love and leaving onto a third-person '*rhyme-composing billie* [lad]' (l. 55) as he rails against the circumstances that have prompted this poet to seek his fortune abroad:

> He saw Misfortune's cauld *Nor-west*
> Lang-mustering up a bitter blast;
> A Jillet [giddy wench] brak his heart at last,
>   Ill may she be!
> So, took a birth afore the mast,
>   An' owre the Sea! (ll. 31–6)

In fact, Burns's letters suggest that the rift with Jean Armour (1767–1834) – and the Kirk elders – has already rendered him an exile in his own country, as he describes himself wandering 'exil'd, abandoned, forlorn' (*L* 1, p. 44). The implication is that life will serve him, like his fictional poet, better in the New World.

The exact circumstances of Burns's proposed emigration are open to debate. But what is known is that at the same time as he was discussing his plans to leave Scotland, Burns published subscription bills for a book that would contain poems he had been circulating in manuscript around the parish. The resulting publication, *Poems, Chiefly in the Scottish Dialect*, was printed by John Wilson in Kilmarnock in September 1786. As Burns describes it in his autobiographical letter to John Moore (1729–1802), 'I had composed my last song I should ever measure in Caledonia . . . when a letter from Dr. [Thomas] Blacklock to a friend of mine overthrew all my schemes by rousing my poetic ambition' (L 1, p. 145). Blacklock (1721–91), a successful local poet himself, praised *Poems, Chiefly in the Scottish Dialect* and suggested that another printing would be met with great enthusiasm.[2] Accordingly, Burns decided to head not to 'the torrid zone' (L 1, p. 145) but to Edinburgh. This decision, however, launched him as much into the global marketplace as a move to one of Britain's sugar plantations ever could have, and it positioned him if not as an actual exile in his own country then at least as a virtual one. For as Richard Sher suggests, with the publication of the subscription proposals for the 'Edinburgh' edition of *Poems, Chiefly in the Scottish Dialect*, '[T]he Ayrshire poet was about to make the transition from a regional to a national – and international – poet.'[3]

It is that international dimension on which this chapter focuses, as it examines several of Burns's poems on global events as well as the works of critical reception that launched Burns and his work into the international marketplace. Many of Burns's early poems rework the relationship between England and Scotland, changing the nature of the conventional centre/margin binary. Other poems attempt to forge international connections that bypass the English centre in a spirit of what Françoise Lionnet and Shu-mei Shih call 'minor transnationalism', an attempt to make cross-border connections that avoid the centre/margin hierarchy altogether.[4] Burns's later work participates fully in the transnational circulation of radical ideas. The global packaging of Burns suggests quite a different story, however, as, tied to the biography of the poet as a tragic failure, his work became a marker of a Scottish identity that was overwhelmed by dominant forces even as it was proudly disseminated abroad.

Much of Burns's earlier work is concerned with questioning hierarchy. The first poem to appear in *Poems, Chiefly in the Scottish Dialect*, for example, 'The Twa Dogs', (*K* 71) brings this concern to the forefront, as it presents the reader with a not-so-subtle critique of class divisions. The poem is wrapped in the vague language of make-believe; it is 'A Tale' that describes a meeting that happened 'once upon a time' (l. 6) between two talking dogs, Caesar, a '*gentleman* an' *scholar* [. . .] o' high degree' (ll. 14–15) who belongs to a local laird, and Luath, a 'ploughman's collie' whose description as a 'rhyming, ranting, raving billie' (ll. 23–4) makes him an authorial analogue. Caesar opens the dialogue, inviting his companion to reflect on the difference between the life of the rich and that of 'poor bodies' (l. 49). His commentary delivers an insider's perspective on the corruption and excess that constitute 'the *gentry*'s life' (l. 49):

Our *Laird* gets in his racked rents,
His coals, his kane [payments in kind], an' a' his stents [dues]:
He rises when he likes himsel;
His flunkies answer at the bell;

> He ca's his coach; he ca's his horse;
> He draws a bonie, silken purse
> As lang's my *tail*, whare thro' the steeks, [stiches]
> The yellow, letter'd *Geordie* [guinea] keeks [peeps]. (ll. 51–8)

Despite being presented with the fact that the Laird's '*Whipper-in*' (l. 65) eats a better dinner than 'onie *Tenant-man*' (l. 67), Luath remains sanguine about the virtues of the poor: 'how it comes, I never kend [knew] yet, / They're maistly wonderfu' contented' (ll. 83–4). If anything it is Caesar who expresses indignation about the way that the labouring-class is treated:

> L—d man, our gentry care as little
> For *delvers* [labourers], *ditchers* [diggers], an' sic cattle;
> They gang as saucy by poor folk,
> As I wad by a stinkan brock [badger]. (ll. 89–92)

Luath acknowledges the fact that it does happen that 'decent, honest, fawsont [respectable] folk' (l. 142) are on occasion evicted, 'riven out [thrown out by force] baith root and branch' (l. 143), but he attributes this to the greed of a factor 'Wha thinks to knit himself the faster / In favor wi' some *gentle Master*' (ll. 145–6) while the '*Master*' is busy 'a *parliamentin*, / For *Britain's guid*' (ll. 146–8). Once more, it is Caesar who sets the record straight as he points out that a member of parliament is no more than a pawn of the 'PREMIERS', the party leaders, forced into a position of 'saying *aye* or *no*'s they bid him' (ll. 151–2). Moreover, he suggests that the main activities of government officials take place outside Westminster and even outside the nation's borders. The gentry amuse themselves 'At Operas an' Plays parading, / Mortaging, gambling, masquerading' (ll. 153–4) in London, with frequent trips across the English Channel 'To mak *a tour* an' tak a whirl, / To learn *bon ton*, an' see the worl' ' (ll. 157–8). It is this revelation that finally bursts Luath's optimistic bubble, as he exclaims, 'Hech man! dear sirs! is that the gate, [way] / They waste sae monie a braw estate!' (ll. 171–2). While he is content with his lot when he believes that the gentry are doing their job in governing the nation, the information that they are in fact wasting money arouses his political consciousness. From this point on, Luath is given more agency in the poem as he shifts from merely responding to Caesar's enquiries to questioning Caesar for more precise information about the '*great folk*' (l. 186) whom he has revered in his ignorance. 'The Twa Dogs' ends without resolution as the dogs run home at twilight. Their meeting 'some ither day' (l. 238), however, will presumably be on a different footing, as Luath now possesses new knowledge of his so-called betters.

In the friendship that it presents between the gentleman's dog and the ploughman's mutt, 'The Twa Dogs' embodies Robert Crawford's observation that Burns 'constantly impl[ies] that the manifestly little may stand confidently beside the mighty.'[5] According to Crawford, '[T]he effect of this technique is to upset established categories, raising questions about the way in which we casually assign cultural value.'[6] Part of this project involves questioning the way geographical value is assigned, too, as Burns promotes the values of rural Scotland over the fashionableness of metropolitan centres. In 'The Twa Dogs', the virtues of the poor in Kyle are juxtaposed to the vices of the rich in London and on the Continent. Luath delivers the moral of the poem in his observation that if the gentry would 'stay aback frae [away from] courts ... It wad for ev'ry ane be better, / The *Laird*, the *Tenant*, an' the *Cotter*!' (ll. 175–8). While this comment seems to advocate national over transnational activity, the poem itself complicates this perspective. Caesar, the initial voice of reason, is, after all, a transnational figure himself, brought to Scotland from the shores of Newfoundland. 'The Twa Dogs', like a number of other poems in *Poems, Chiefly in the Scottish Dialect*, is not so much concerned with promoting protectionism as with confounding the international hierarchy that places Scotland as 'remote' to England's cultural and political power.

In his unpublished poetry of this time, Burns indicates his objection to global hierarchies as well. 'When Guilford Good, or Ballad on the American War', (K 38), written around 1784, explores the fundamental effects on Britain of America's rejection of its subordinate role, beginning with the Boston Tea Party in 1773:[7]

When *Guilford* good our Pilot stood,
An' did our hellim thraw [turn], man,
Ae night, at tea, began a plea,
Within *America*, man (ll. 1–4)

Although 'When Guilford Good' does not champion the cause of the American Revolution per se, it subtly tips the balance in America's favour. The poem begins not with the actions of the Americans throwing tea in Boston Harbour, but with Lord North 'thrawing' the 'helm' of state; the preposition 'when' suggests that the actions of the Americans are precipitated by his piloting decisions.[8] The description of events at Boston is followed by three stanzas outlining the most important military engagements of the American War and concluding with Cornwallis's surrender at Yorktown. In this brief account, if anyone can be said to be praised, it is an American, or at least, an American of Scottish descent, as Burns devotes four lines of his brief poem to describing the brave death of Richard Montgomery who is said to fall 'Montgomery-like ... Wi' sword in hand, before his band' (ll. 14–15). The bulk of the poem, however, concentrates on the political chaos in Britain that follows the loss of America as one administration follows another, and unholy alliances such as that between Lord North (1732–92) and Charles James Fox (1749–1806) are formed:

> Then *R-ck-ngh-m* took up the game;
> Till Death did on him ca', man;
> When *Sh-b-rne* meek held up his cheek,
> Conform to Gospel law, man:
> Saint Stephen's boys [MP's], wi' jarring noise,
> They did his measures thraw, man;
> For *North* and *Fox* united stocks,
> An' bore him to the wa', man. (ll. 41–8)

The image of unity in America at the beginning of the poem as the 'full Congress' (l. 7) refuses 'our law, man' (l. 8) contrasts sharply with the dissolution of Britain into warring parliamentary factions at the end of the poem. The general election of 1784 which followed the defeat of the East India Bill is figured as a brawl, with the '*Suthron*' (l. 67) stripping off their clothes and the figure of '*Caledon*' (l. 69) throwing by the bagpipes and drawing her knife while swearing 'fu' rude, thro' dirt an' bluid, / To mak it guid in law, man' (ll. 71–2). The 'law' that the Americans initially refused is exposed at the end of the poem as nothing more than the law of the strongest.

The burden of 'When Guilford Good' is to demonstrate how with the margin gone, the centre cannot hold. At the same time, the poem also suggests the inter-relation between the various margins of Britain. While his focus is on America, Burns also alludes to other peripheries on the borders of the empire. Fox and North's coalition government falls because it tries to pass a bill pertaining to the governance of the East India Company:

> Then Clubs an' Hearts were *Charlie's* cartes,
> He swept the stakes awa', man,
> Till the Diamond's Ace, of *Indian* race,
> Led him a sair *faux pas*, man. (ll. 49–52)

A reference to 'Paddy *B-rke*' (l. 37) also raises the question of Ireland and the Catholic population who remained disenfranchised despite the recent passing of the Quebec Act (1774) which gave Catholics across the Atlantic the right to hold office. Moreover, the poem also suggests the inherent instability of the centre. The poem calls on the '*Suthron*' and the Caledonians to rally behind Pitt's opposition to the Fox and North government. However, it is clear that the deep divisions between 'the Saxon lads' (l. 53) and Scotland are still dangerously close to the surface, raising the question of whether the centre ever, in fact, held. The fact that Burns indicated that the song was to be sung to the tune of 'GILLICRANKIE' (or 'Killiecrankie'), a tune associated with the victory of John Graham of Claverhouse, who was fighting for King James II, over the forces of William of Orange, reinforces the poem's suggestion of the tenuousness of Britain's central unity.[9]

It was after Burns had completed the second edition of his poems in Edinburgh and had taken up the farm at Ellisland that another event occurred that would further influence his sense of the transnational connections: the French Revolution. Because the political climate in Britain was so volatile and because Burns was, after becoming an exciseman in 1789, a government employee, he was forced to keep his enthusiasm for the revolution and the reforming impulse it inspired in Britain in check. Nevertheless, his support for the revolutionary cause has been well documented. Liam McIlvanney points out the radical company that Burns kept: as well as Scottish reformists like Dugald Stewart (1753–1828), Lord Daer (1763–94) and James Maitland, Earl of Lauderdale (1759–1839), and the Erskine brothers, Henry (1746–1817), David (1742–1829) and Thomas (1750–1823) (the defender of Thomas Paine), 'Burns was also in correspondence with prominent English radicals like William Roscoe (1753–1831), Mary Wollstonecraft (1759–97), Helen Maria Williams (1762–1827) and Dr. Wolcot ("Peter Pindar") (1738–1819), and in contact with United Irish sympathisers like Samuel Thomson (1766–1816) and Luke Mullan.'[10] In his anonymously published works like 'Robert Bruce's Address to his Troops at Bannockburn' (K 425) and 'Is There for Honest Poverty' ('A Man's A Man'), for example, we see Burns aligning himself with the transnational circulation of radical ideas popularised by the Friends of the People and late eighteenth-century corresponding societies.

'Robert Bruce's Address to his Troops at Bannockburn' was printed anonymously in *The Morning Chronicle* on 8th May 1794. With its pitting of Scottish 'LIBERTY' (l. 23) against 'proud EDWARD'S power,' (l. 7) the song is conventionally read as an anthem for Scottish nationalism. But in his letter to George Thomson regarding this piece, Burns sketches out the complicated story of its genesis, a process which follows a chain of Humean associations. The letter begins with Burns's suggestion of a dichotomy between learned 'Art' and 'untaught & untutored' 'Nature' in musical appreciation, with his own preferences on the side of 'many little melodies, which the learned Musician despises as silly & insipid' (*L* II, p. 235). From the beginning, then, the song is associated with the democratic impulses of the 'simple lug [ear]' rather than the educated tastes of 'Conoisseurs' (*L* II, p. 235). From here Burns proceeds to comment on the effect that the tune 'Hey Tutti Taitie' has on him: 'it has often filled my eyes with tears' (*L* II, p. 235), not only because of its simple appeal, it would seem, but also because of its patriotic associations: 'There is a tradition . . . that it was Robert Bruce's March at the battle of Bannock-burn' (*L* II, p. 235). Thinking about this, he notes, 'warmed me to a pitch of enthusiasm on the theme of Liberty & Independence, which I threw into a kind of Scots Ode, fitted to the Air' (*L* II, p. 235). Burns notes that it is Bruce's 'glorious struggle for Freedom, associated with the glowing ideas of some other struggles of the same nature, *not quite so ancient*' that 'roused my rhyming Mania' (*L* II, p. 236). The date of the letter, about 30 August 1793, suggests the basis of these other '*not quite so ancient*' struggles, as the last two days of the month had seen the trial of Thomas Muir (1765–99), the first of the so-called 'Scottish Martyrs'. Muir was tried for sedition before Lord Justice Clerk Braxfield (1722–99), four other judges and a jury composed of members of the Goldsmith's Hall Association, an anti-Jacobin group.[11] He was found guilty and sentenced to fourteen years' transportation to Botany Bay, which had become the dumping ground for British criminals since the loss of the American colonies. The sentence caused moral outrage among reformers at the time, with Charles James Fox, Charles Grey (2nd Earl Grey), and Richard Sheridan arguing against it in parliament, and Lord Lauderdale proclaiming, that 'not one case in the whole history of Scottish criminal law stood upon record, either to justify, or even to countenance, the proceedings.'[12] It is small wonder that Burns should be thinking about 'Liberty & Independence' at this time.

Burns performs an interesting sleight of hand in 'Robert Bruce's Address', folding Scottish national identity into larger concerns regarding the proper relationship between those who rule and those whom they govern. The poem begins with an interpellation of 'Scots' in the historical moment of the Wars of Independence:

> SCOTS, wha hae wi' WALLACE bled,
> Scots, wham Bruce has aften led,
> Welcome to your gory bed,–
> Or to victorie. (ll. 1–4)

The references to blood ('bled', 'gory') conjure up images of national identity based on consanguinity. But instead of figuring England or the English as the opponents of a Scots army united by blood, the poem concentrates on the 'power' of 'Proud EDWARD' which is described in terms of a metaphor ('Chains') and its tenor (Slaverie)' (l. 8). Moreover, the song suggests that the condition of slavery is a choice made by the individual:

> Wha will be a traitor-knave?
> Wha can fill a coward's grave?
> Wha sae base as be a Slave?
>   Let him turn, and flie. (ll. 9–12)

By the end of the poem, this element of choice has shifted the terms of engagement from a clash between nations to a conflict between tyranny and 'LIBERTY' (l. 23). In this new figuration, Scottishness becomes, not a symbol of blood-ties, but a metaphor for freedom, while 'Scotland's king and law' (l. 13) are reconfigured in a new covenant linking 'FREE-MAN' with 'FREE-MAN' (l. 15) in the right to bear arms. 'Robert Bruce's Address' contains interesting echoes of the words of Muir before his sentence:

> 'Were I to be led this moment from the bar to the scaffold, I should feel the same calmness and serenity which I do now [. . .] *I have engaged in a* GOOD, *a* JUST, *and a* GLORIOUS *cause* – A CAUSE WHICH, SOONER OR LATER, MUST AND WILL PREVAIL, AND, BY TIMELY REFORM, SAVE THIS COUNTRY FROM DESTRUCTION.[13]

'Robert Bruce's Address', like other works such as 'A Man's a Man' (published in the *Glasgow Magazine*, August 1795), suggest Burns's participation in what Nigel Leask calls the 'cosmopolitan energy lying at the heart of Scottish radicalism in the 1790s'.[14]

But this transnational aspect of Burns, such an important component of his later work, was discounted and suppressed by commentary which appeared after his death. The first influential biography of the poet, Robert Heron's *A Memoir of the Life of the Late Robert Burns*, initially issued in two parts in the *Monthly Magazine* then republished separately in 1797, positions Burns uncomfortably between his local rural community and the more worldly society of Edinburgh, an articulation which is presented as ultimately causing the poet's demise. Heron revises the myth of Burns's natural genius that Henry Mackenzie (1745–1831) had originated in *The Lounger* (December 1786), representing him as only one example among many of Scotland's foresight in educating its poor:

> The establishment of PARISH-SCHOOLS; but for which, perhaps, the infant energies of this young genius might never have received that first impulse by which alone they were to be excited into action; is one of the most beneficial that have been ever instituted in any country; and one that, I believe, is no where so firmly fixed, or extended so completely throughout a whole kingdom, as in Scotland. (p. 4)

According to Heron, Burns's genius was nurtured by the annual shift he experienced between the particulars of 'labour' and the universal values of 'learning': 'From the *spring* labours of a plough-boy, from the *summer* employment of a shepherd, the peasant-youth often returns, for a few months, eager to receive new instruction in the parish-school' (pp. 4–5). Through such a process, Burns had his literary sensibilities honed until he no longer looked upon the world as a simple ploughman would: 'his mind's eye opened to perceive affecting beauty and sublimity, where, by the mere gross peasant, there was nought to be seen, but water, earth, and sky, but animals, plants, and soil' (p. 5). But there are negative effects involved in this process. Burns, like Elisha, to whom Heron compares him, began to perceive himself as chosen, set apart from others like him. He read the poetry of Ramsay, Fergusson, Thomson, Blair, Gray, Milton, Macpherson's Ossian and James Beattie, and soon began

> to regard with sullen disdain and aversion, all that was sordid in the pursuits and interests of the peasants among whom he was placed. He became discontented with the humble labours to which he saw himself confined, and with the poor subsistence that was all he could earn by them. (pp. 10–11)

Moreover,

> He was excited to look upon the rich and great, whom he saw around him, with an emotion between envy and contempt; as if something had still whispered to his heart, that there was injustice in the exterior inequality between his fate and theirs. (p. 11)

For Heron, a contributor to the *Anti-Jacobin Review*, the seeds of Burns's later dissolution are discernible in his democratic impulses at this early stage.

Although Burns is able to use the 'native rectitude of his understanding, and the excellent principles in which his infancy had been educated' to withstand the temptations of a profligate life while he is in Ayrshire, Heron laments that 'Alas! it was not always so' (p. 12). In particular, when Burns goes to Edinburgh to oversee the second edition, he loses his 'native' powers of discernment, becoming the companion of those 'to whom he was recommended by licentious wit, and with whom he could not long associate without sharing in the excesses of their debauchery' (p. 26). What is most pertinent for the purposes of this argument is the way that Heron figures Burns's dissolution, as he compares Burns to Omai, the Tahitian native who was brought to England in 1774:

> BURNS [. . .] led a life differing from that of his original condition in Ayrshire, almost as widely as differed the scenes and amusements of London, to which OMIAH was introduced, under the patronage of the Earl of SANDWICH, from those to which he had been familiar in the Friendly Isles. (p. 23)

The move to Edinburgh is represented, then, not as just a geographical relocation but also a temporal one. Although there was some debate about whether Otaheite was indeed the 'Gay Eden of the south' that Anna Seward refers to in her 'Elegy on Captain Cook', the people were considered less advanced than the British, according to the stadial theories advanced by Burns's fellow countrymen, Adam Smith and Adam Ferguson.[15] Ayrshire, by analogy, becomes representative of an earlier stage in history. Omai's return to his native land in 1776 was fraught with difficulties. An image in the *Journal of Captain Cook's Last Voyage to the Pacific Ocean on Discovery* (1781) shows him mounted on a horse wearing heavy armour and firing a gun while the thinly robed natives recoil in dismay; according to the illustration, Omai has adopted ways of living in London that alienate him from his original society.[16] Heron outlines similar difficulties in Burns's attempt to reintegrate into rural Scotland, noting that both Burns and his patrons were deluded if they thought that 'it was still possible for him to return in cheerful content, to the homely joys and simple toils of undissipated rural life' (p. 33). On the contrary, according to Heron, Burns's situation worsens as he continues to live his loose Edinburgh lifestyle, but is forced to associate with less sophisticated companions: '[A]lmost every drunken fellow, who was willing to spend his money lavishly in the ale-house, could easily command the company of BURNS' (p. 39). Behind Heron's relation of Burns's tragedy is a narrative of an individual steeped in a traditional way of life who is ruined by being dragged into modernity – with all its attendant indulgences – without having been given the opportunity to develop organically the necessary qualities of discernment that would have ensured his success in the situation. Burns becomes in Heron's hands a victim – albeit a willing one – of uneven development.

The next major biography of Burns, James Currie's *The Works of Robert Burns; with an Account of his Life and a Criticism on his Writings* (1800) reconceives Heron's narrative, so that although Burns's personal life is still represented as a failure, he becomes emblematic not of Scotland's backwardness, but of its global influence. Like Heron, Currie suggests that Burns's downfall was partly due to the fact that his education had given him aspirations well above his station and partly due to his own weakness in resisting temptations: '[T]o the thousands who share the original condition of Burns, and who are doomed to pass their lives in the station in which they were born, delicacy of taste . . . would, if not a positive evil, be at least a doubtful blessing.'[17] Given what Currie describes as the 'extraordinary sensibility' of Burns's mind (1, p. 234), the cultivation of 'delicacy of taste' proves disadvantageous. Currie, a medical doctor, notes the changes in his physical as well as his poetic tastes after his move to the capital:

> The sudden alteration in his habits of life, operated on him physically as well as morally. The humble fare of an Ayrshire peasant he had exchanged for the luxuries of the Scottish metropolis, and the effects of this change on his ardent constitution could not be inconsiderable. (1, p. 150)[18]

Like Heron, Currie suggests that Burns was ruined by being exposed to the 'luxuries' of Edinburgh which he then imported back into provincial society with disastrous effects. In the *Works of Robert Burns*, Burns becomes a somatic site in which the flows of the modern 'metropolis' make incursions into the less developed provinces, as Currie sums up the poet's demise with a cryptic statement about the foreign substances that Burns allows into his body: 'He who suffers the pollution of inebriation, how shall he escape other pollutions?' (1, p. 219).

The details of Burns's personal history are folded in Currie's account, however, into a larger narrative of the flows of Scotland itself in the global arena. Currie prefaces his work with *Some Observations on the Character and Condition of the Scottish Peasantry* in which he attempts to 'form a more correct notion of the advantages with which [Burns] started, and of the obstacles which he surmounted'. Burns, it seems, is not the only Scottish peasant to stand out because of his superior intellect: 'A slight acquaintance with the peasantry of Scotland, will serve to convince an unprejudiced observer that they possess a degree of intelligence not generally found among the same class of men in the other countries of Europe.' In particular, Currie notes that everyone, even those 'in the very humblest condition' (1, p. 3) can read, and discusses the statute passed in 1696 that made literacy law. Heron is ambivalent about the effects of literacy on Burns and on labourers in general; it can give them democratic ideas and make them discontented with their lot. Currie, too, as we have seen in his discussion of Burns, ponders the effects of education on the Scottish peasantry: 'Delicacy of taste may make necessary labours irksome or disgusting, and should it render the cultivator of the soil unhappy in his situation, it presents no means by which that situation may be improved' (1, p. 109). In the end, however, he is more positive than Heron. Although he admits that there are 'doubtless [. . .] some individual exceptions', including, by implication, Burns, education 'is on the whole favorable to industry and morals' (1, p. 6). If education makes the peasantry discontented with their life, it also gives them the motivation to alter that life by leaving. Education, Currie pronounces, is 'the cause of that spirit of emigration and of adventure so prevalent among the Scotch' (1, p. 6). Currie suggests that this penchant for emigration started at the time of the Union, when the 'greater degree of instruction' that the peasantry enjoyed and the removal of the trade barriers between Scotland and England persuaded many Scots to head south. But the 'adventurous natives of the north' did not just target 'the fertile plains of England'; their 'knowledge and poverty' poured 'more especially, over the colonies which she had settled in the east and in the west' (1, p. 7). Currie suggests that 'Knowledge has, by Lord Verulam, been denominated power; by others it has, with less propriety, been denominated virtue or happiness: we may with confidence consider it as motion' (1, p. 6). In Currie's account, motion is a power practiced by Scots especially.

Currie also points out another striking feature of Scots in general, and of Burns in particular. Despite their tendency to wander, Scots are extremely patriotic, more so Currie implies than other nations. 'An attachment to the land of their birth, is indeed common to all men,' he comments, however, it, like other 'affections of the mind', is strengthened 'where the comforts, and even necessaries of life, must be purchased by patient toil' (1, p. 28). In harsh climates, where men are forced to bond together 'for mutual defence, as well as for the supply of common wants', their 'mutual goodwill' increases. Currie describes a process of transference, as 'social affections' extend this 'goodwill' from 'the men with whom we live, to the soil on which we tread' (1, p. 29). Such a feeling unites humans with the geographic space which they inhabit. If this highly developed sense of patriotism is found among ordinary Scots, how much more must it be seen in a character like Burns, who had such extraordinary powers of sensibility, suggests Currie:

> If this reasoning be just, it will explain to us why, among the natives of Scotland, even of cultivated minds, we so generally find a partial attachment to the land of their birth, and why this is so strongly discoverable in the writings of Burns, who joined to the higher powers of the understanding, the most ardent affection. (1, p. 31)

Moreover, this patriotic feeling as Curries describes it proves remarkably durable:

> [T]he images of infancy, strongly associating with the generous affections, resist the influence of time, and of new impressions; they often survive in countries far distant, and amidst far different scenes, to the latest periods of life, to sooth the heart with the pleasures of memory, when those of hope die away. (1, p. 31)

While the Scots distinguish themselves by travelling around the globe, they maintain a little corner of their hearts which is forever Scotland.

Burns not only exemplifies the 'partial attachment to the land of their birth' that Scots feel. He also becomes an object of that attachment through the same kind of transference that makes people regard the 'soil on which we tread' as a link in the chain of sociability. Burns's poetry, suggests Currie, 'displays, as it were embalms, the peculiar manners of his country; and it may be considered as a monument not to his own name only, but to the expiring genius of an ancient and once independent nation' (1, pp. 31–2). Scotland is associated here not only with an earlier stage of individual history – 'images of infancy' – but with an earlier stage of national history – it is a 'once independent' nation. Currie is unwavering in his support of the Union. But he also uses Burns to assert the difference of Scotland within a united Britain that is expanding its empire. Appropriately, Currie's *Works of Burns* is dedicated to a wandering Scot, Captain Graham Moore of the Royal Navy, who first recommended the poems of Burns to him. In the dedication, Currie presents the volumes to Moore in a gesture of friendship:

> When you were stationed on our coast, about twelve years ago, you first recommended to my particular notice the poems of the Ayrshire ploughman, whose works . . . I now present to you. In a distant region of the world, whither the service of your country has carried you, you will, I know, receive with kindness this proof of my regard. (1, p. v)

Burns's poetry becomes an object of negotiation between two expatriate Scots, one who applied for a post in Jamaica but settled for a living in Liverpool and one who commanded a frigate in the war with Napoleon. Currie notes the peculiar role that Burns's work occupies in the life of a Scot abroad:

> Homer, and Shakspeare, and Ossian, cannot always occupy your leisure. These volumes may sometimes engage your attention, while the steady breezes of the tropics swell your sails, and in another quarter of the earth, charm you with the strains of nature, or awake in your memory the scenes of your early days. (1, p. v)

Burns is positioned here as a lesser poet. At the same time, however, he plays an important part as he provides a transnational link between the images of nature to the native soil (which are connected to 'the images of infancy' in the emigrant's memory) and experiences in an unfamiliar 'quarter of the earth'. Burns may not be as potent as Homer, Shakespeare and Macpherson, but he is more portable.

Although Burns himself did not travel to 'anither shore' ('On a Scotch Bard Gone to the West Indies,' [K 100, l. 17]) his poetry did. Nigel Leask has suggested that Burns's poetry proved a symbolic focus for Scottish identity in the colonial diaspora, an identity that often proved more durable than 'Britishness'.[19] In fact, Currie's *Works of Burns* provided a template through which Burns's poetry could be appreciated not just by Scots but by all people touched by the forces of modernity, including the metropolitanisation of the periphery and the increasing migrations of peoples around the globe. Currie suggests that,

> Though the dialect in which many of the happiest effusions of Robert Burns are composed, be peculiar to Scotland, yet his reputation has extended itself beyond the limits of that country, and his poetry has been admired as the offspring of original genius, by persons of taste in every part of the sister islands. (1, p. 1)

It is, arguably, not only his association with the traditional, rooted society of Scotland and its dialect but also his representation as a casualty of the forces of modernity that has made that 'reputation' appealing to readers not only in 'every part of the sister islands', but those 'owre the Sea' ('On a Scotch Bard Gone to the West Indies,' l. 18), as time and time again he is interpreted as an icon of passionate but ill-fated resistance to dominant forces.[20]

Burns's reputation in the academy has suffered from the fact that his poetry is so often read through his biography, a practice instantiated by Currie, and one which has served to marginalise him as a Scottish poet in a British canon. Joining other efforts to recuperate Burns, this essay has aimed to reposition his work during his lifetime in the context of what Felicity Nussbaum calls 'the connective tissues of resistance' operating in 'the global eighteenth century'[21] and to advance our understanding of the uses made of Burns after his death. It has attempted to read Burns not as the national bard of Scotland, but as a transnational poet who subsequently became an object of cultural exchange in a global system.

Endnotes

Introduction – Carruthers

1. I am grateful to Dr Zasheem Ahmed of the Nazrul-Burns Centre, Glasgow, for informing me of this development.
2. James Mackay, *Burns: A Biography of Robert Burns* (Mainstream: Edinburgh, 1992), p. 688.
3. I am grateful to Murray Pittock whose work for the Advanced Humanities Research Council funded 'Global Responses to Burns' network has made me and many others aware of this situation in much particular detail.
4. On 6 and 7 October 2008, many of the British broadsheet and popular newspapers covered Bob Dylan's statements on his admiration for Burns, most especially the song, 'A Red, Red Rose'. Burns has also been attractive to jazz musicians, such as the superb arrangements recorded in 2000 by The Jim Mullen Quartet.
5. For an illuminating essay on the use of Burns by various political and religious ideologies in Scotland through the nineteenth and first part of the twentieth centuries, see Richard J. Finlay, 'The Burns Cult and Scottish Identity' in Kenneth Simpson, *Love and Liberty: Robert Burns, A Bicentenary Celebration* (Tuckwell Press: East Linton, 1997), pp. 69–78. See also the beginnings of the fascinating ongoing work by David Goldie on the use of Burns in the recruiting campaigning of World War one in his 'The British Invention of Scottish Culture', *Review of Scottish Culture* 18 (2006), pp. 128–48.
6. See Mary Ellen Brown, *William Motherwell's Cultural Politics* (The University Press of Kentucky: Lexington, 2001).
7. See the highly interesting analysis in Andrew Nash, 'The Cotter's Kailyard' in Robert Crawford (ed.), *Robert Burns & Cultural Authority* (Edinburgh: Edinburgh University Press, 1997), pp. 180–97.
8. J. De Lancey Ferguson, 'They Censored Burns', *Scotland's Magazine* (January, 1955), pp. 38–40.
9. *The Canongate Burns* ed. by Andrew Noble and Patrick Hogg (Edinburgh: Canongate, 2001), see p. 458 and p. 474 for the missing attributions, and

p. 495 for the insertion of 'R.B' in footnotes where these do not exist at source; for further details, see Gerard Carruthers, 'The Canongate Burns: Misreading Robert Burns and the Periodical Press of the 1790s', *Review of Scottish Culture* 18 (2006), pp. 41–50; 'The New Bardolatry', *Burns Chronicle* (winter, 2002), pp. 9–15 and 'The Problem of Pseudonyms in the Burns "Lost Poems"', *Studies in Scottish Literature* XXXIII–XXXIV (2004a), pp. 97–106. Re the 'Airdrie' poet, see Ian Reid, 'In Search of William Yates of Airdrie, Contemporary of Burns', *Scottish Studies Review* 9 (1) (2008), pp. 27–48.

10. Work has begun during 2009 on the new multi-volume edition of the *Works of Robert Burns*, of which the general editor is Gerard Carruthers (Oxford University Press). By the end of 2009, major scholarly conferences will have been held in Columbia (South Carolina), Edinburgh, Glasgow, Oxford, Prague and Vancouver among other places. Numerous exhibitions and publications in this year also show the popular interest to be as great as ever and the scholarly attention to be increasing. The year has also been marked by a commemorative stamp and coin.
11. *The Poems and Songs of Robert Burns*, ed. James Kinsley, 3 vols (Oxford: Clarendon Press, 1968), vol. 3, p. 971.
12. Ibid., vol. 3, p. 977.
13. Reprinted in Donald Low (ed.), *Robert Burns: The Critical Heritage*(London and Boston: Routledge and Kegan Paul, 1974), pp. 67–71.

Chapter 1 – Carruthers

1. Gerard Carruthers, *Robert Burns* (Tavistock: Northcote House, 2006).
2. Robert Burnss, *Robert Burns's Commonplace Book, 1783–1785*, intro. by David Daiches (Fontwell and London: Centaur 1965).
3. The stanza derives its name in Scotland from its use in the seventeenth-century poem, 'The Life and Death of the Piper of Kilbarchan' (about the musician, Habbie Simson) and is renamed the 'standart habby' by Allan Ramsay in the early eighteenth century.
4. See John Wain's Introduction in Hogg, *The Private Memoirs and Confessions of a Justified Sinner* (Harmondsworth: Penguin, 1983), pp. 14–15.
5. See, for useful background, James Mackay, *Burns: A Biography of Robert Burns* (Edinburgh: Mainstream, 1992), pp. 160–6. The notes to 'Holy Willie's Prayer' provided in Carol McGuirk (ed.), [Robert Burns,] *Selected Poems* (London: Penguin, 1993), pp. 200–2 are particularly helpful.
6. For a useful reprinting of Irving's comments, see Donald Low (ed.), *Robert Burns: The Critical Heritage* (London and Boston: Routledge & Kegan Paul, 1974), p. 166.
7. Reprinted in ibid., p. 198.
8. Ibid., p. 81.
9. Ibid., p. 94.

10. Ibid., p. 69.
11. Ibid., p. 77.
12. Ibid., p. 105.
13. Ibid., pp. 187–8, 303, 326.
14. Ibid., p. 343.
15. Thomas Crawford, *Burns: A Study of the Poems and Songs*, TC Mercat Press: Edinburgh, [1960] 1978) p. 174.
16. Hans Hecht, *Archiv* cxxx (1913), pp. 65–72.
17. Donald Low (ed.), *Robert Burns*, p. 82.
18. See Pauline Gray, 'Prudes, Pirates and Bills of Suspension: The Correspondence of Burns and Clarinda', in *Burns Chronicle* (autumn 2007), pp. 10–11.
19. Quotations are from the facsimile version of *The Merry Muses of Caledonia* introduced by G. Ross Roy (Columbia: University of South Carolina Press for the Thomas Cooper Library, 1999).
20. See Smith's annotation to *The Merry Muses of Caledonia* ed. James Barke and Sydney Goodsir Smith (Edinburgh: The Auk Society, 1959), p. 112.
21. Liam McIlvanney, *Burns the Radical: Poetry and Politics in Late Eighteenth-Century Scotland* (East Linton: Tuckwell Press, 2002), p. 75.

Chapter 2 – Dunnigan

1. J. De Lancey Ferguson, *Pride and Passion. Robert Burns 1759–1796* (New York: Oxford University Press, 1939), p. 144.
2. Catherine Carswell, *The Life of Robert Burns*, intro. Tom Crawford (Edinburgh: Canongate, 1990 [1930]), p. 312.
3. A. L. Kennedy, 'Love Composition; the Solitary Vice', in Robert Crawford (ed.), *Robert Burns and Cultural Authority* (Edinburgh: Edinburgh University Press, 1997), p. 28.
4. *Ae Fond Kiss. The Love Letters of Robert Burns and Clarinda*, ed. Donny O' Rourke (Edinburgh: Mercat Press, 2000), p. xxvi. Subsequent page references within the text are to this edition.
5. A. L. Kennedy, 'Love Composition', p. 39.
6. It was first published in the *Dumfries Weekly Journal* in 1796.
7. Ian McIntyre, *Dirt & Deity: A Life of Robert Burns* (London: Harper Collins, 1995).
8. Cited in Carol McGuirk, *Robert Burns and the Sentimental Era* (Athens: University of Georgia Press, 1985), p. 103.
9. Their correspondence was first fully published in 1898 by William Wallace as *Robert Burns and Mrs Dunlop*.
10. J. De Lancey Ferguson, *Pride and Passion*, pp. 148–9.
11. Gavin Sprott, *Robert Burns: Pride and Passion* (Edinburgh: Mercat, 1996), pp. 152–5.
12. C. Carswell, *The Life*, p. 170.

13. Simone de Beauvoir, *The Second Sex*, trans. and ed. H. M. Parsley (London: Picador, 1988 [1949]), p. 213.
14. D. O'Rourke (ed.), *Ae Fond Kiss*, p. 7. All subsequent references are to this edition.
15. C. Carswell, *The Life*, p. 243.
16. Ibid., p. 248.
17. Chapter headings taken from *Burns' Clarinda: Select Papers concerning the Poet's Renowned Correspondent Compiled from Various Sources* by John D. Ross (John Grant, 1897).
18. D. O' Rourke (ed.), *Ae Fond Kiss*, p. ix.
19. Cited in Michèle Crampe-Casnabet, 'A Sampling of Eighteenth-Century Philosophy', in Georges Duby and Michelle Perrot (eds), *A History of Women in the West*, 5 vols (Cambridge: The Belknap Press of Harvard University Press, 1992–4), vol. 3, *Renaissance and Enlightenment Paradoxes*, ed. Natalie Zemon Davis and Arlette Farge, p. 328. See further Mary Catherine Moran, 'Between the Savage and the Civil: Dr John Gregory's Natural History of Femininity', in Sarah Knott and Barbara Taylor (eds), *Women, Gender, and Enlightenment, 1650–1850* (Basingstoke: Palgrave Macmillan, 2005), pp. 8–30.
20. Letter to Frances Dunlop, cited in C. McGuirk *Robert Burns*, p. 128.
21. Ibid., p. 129.
22. Quotations are drawn from G. Ross Roy's facsimile edition (Columbia: University of South Carolina Press, 1999).
23. But see Gerard Carruthers, *Robert Burns* (Tavistock: Northcote House, 2006), pp. 65–7. Pauline Gray is currently working on *The Merry Muses* as part of her doctoral dissertation at the University of Glasgow.
24. Gerard Carruthers, *Robert Burns*, p. 65; Robert Crawford, 'Robert Fegusson's Robert Burns', in Robert Crawford (ed.), *Robert Burns and Cultural Authority*, p. 13.
25. Lynn Hunt, 'Obscenity and the Origins of Modernity, 1500–1800', in Lynn Hunt (ed.), *The Invention of Pornography. Obscenity and the Origins of Modernity, 1500–1800* (New York: Zone Books, 1996), p. 10.
26. Ibid., pp. 10 and 11.
27. C. McGuirk, *Robert Burns*, pp. 77–8.
28. For example, Mrs Dunlop expressed anxiety about Burns's revolutionary sympathies.
29. See further G. J. Barker Benfield, *The Culture of Sensibility. Sex and Society in Eighteenth-Century Britain* (Chicago: University of Chicago Press, 1992); George E. Haggerty, *Men in Love. Masculinity and Sexuality in the Eighteenth Century* (New York: Columbia University Press, 1999).
30. On this subject in general, see further Sarah Knott and Barbara Taylor (eds).
31. Robert Crawford, 'Robert Fergusson's Robert Burns', p. 14.
32. Gerard Carruthers, *Robert Burns*, p. 75.

33. Barbara Taylor, 'Feminists versus Gallants: Manners and Morals in Enlightenment Britain', in *Representations* 87 (2004), pp. 126, 127.
34. See, for example, Pamela Norris, *The Story of Eve* (London: Picador, 1998).
35. Gerard Carruthers, *Robert Burns*, p. 68.
36. A. L. Kennedy, 'Love Composition', p. 3; see also Sarah M. Dunnigan and Gerard Carruthers, 'Two Tales of Tam o' Shanter', *Southfields* 6 (2) (2000), pp. 36–43.
37. Robert Crawford, 'Robert Fergusson's Robert Burns', p. 19.
38. Christopher Whyte, 'Defamiliarising "Tam o' Shanter"', *Scottish Literary Journal* 20 (1993), pp. 5–18.
39. Simone de Beauvoir, *The Second Sex*, p. 180.

Chapter 3 – Simpson

1. Aristotle, *Rhetoric*, I, 1, in Jonathan Barnes (ed.), *The Complete Works of Aristotle*, 2 vols (Princeton: Princeton University Press, 1984, vol. 2, p. 2152.
2. R. D. S. Jack, 'Burns as Sassenach Poet', in Kenneth Simpson (ed.), *Burns Now* (Edinburgh: Canongate Academic, 1994), [pp. 150–166] p. 158.
3. *The Life and Works of Robert Burns*, ed. Robert Chambers, revd. William Wallace, 4 vols (Edinburgh and London: W and R Chambers, 1896), vol. 1, p. 48.
4. Ibid., pp. 68–9.
5. Cited James Mackay, *Burns: A Biography of Robert Burns* (Edinburgh: Mainstream, 1992), p. 76.
6. Henry Mackenzie, *Lounger* 97 (9 Dec. 1786); reprinted in Donald Low (ed.), *Robert Burns: The Critical Heritage* (London and Boston: Routledge and Kegan Paul, 1974), [pp. 67–71], p. 70.
7. R. D. S. Jack, 'Burns as Sassenach Poet', p. 156.
8. Cited in F. H. Colson (ed.), *Institutio Oratoria* (Cambridge, MA: University of Harvard Press, 1924), p. xxviii.
9. See further John D. O'Banion, 'Narration and Argumentation: Quintilian on *Narratio* as the Heart of Rhetorical Thinking', *Rhetorica* 5 (4) (1987), pp. 325–51.
10. Burns had read Pope's translation of Homer and Dryden's Virgil (see *L* I, pp. 278–9).
11. Unpublished paper, 'A Humanist Poetics: Sixteenth-Century Scots Poetry', delivered to the Glasgow-Strathclyde School of Scottish Studies. I am indebted to Theo van Heijnsbergen for this introduction to the tradition of 'sle' poetry, and for sight of his paper.
12. Ian S. Ross, '"Proloug" and "Buke" in the *Eneados* of Gavin Douglas', in Dietrich Strauss and Horst W. Drescher (eds), *Scottish Language and Literature, Medieval and Renaissance: Fourth International Conference, 1984 – Proceedings*, (Frankfurt: Peter Lang, 1986), p. 393.

13. Cf. *Eneados*, Prologue 1, l. 41: 'Alsweill. Na, na, impossibill war, per de!'; also Prologue 7, l. 156: 'Full laith to leif our wark swa in the myre'.
14. Gerard Carruthers, '"Tongues Turn'd Inside Out": The Reception of "Tam o' Shanter"' *Studies in Scottish Literature* 35 (6) (2007), [pp. 455–63], p. 461.
15. *The Poems and Songs of Robert Burns*, ed. James Kinsley, 3 vols (Oxford: Clarendon Press, 1968), vol 3, p. 1362.
16. Robert L. Kindrick, *Henryson and the Medieval Arts of Rhetoric* (New York and London: Garland Publishing, 1993), p. 23.
17. Unpublished paper, 'A Humanist Poetics: Sixteenth-Century Scots Poetry'.

Chapter 4 – Leask

1. 'Robert Burns and British Poetry', The Chatterton Lecture on Poetry, *Proceedings of the British Academy* 121 (British Academy, 2003), p. 191.
2. See Andrew Lindsay's intelligent *Illustrious Exile: A Novel*, that fictionalises Burns's aborted Caribbean career, in the process giving him the benefit of the doubt (Leeds: Peepal Tree, 2006).
3. In a letter of 27 August 1789, Burns uses the term in an entirely apolitical and metaphorical manner to describe indolence, when 'the soul with all her powers is laden with weary fetters of ever-increasing weight; a Slavery which involves the mind in dreary darkness and almost a total eclipse of every ray of God's image' (*L* I, p. 436). Here it is 'God's image' rather than 'Nature's Law' that is violated by slavery, even if the metaphorical referent is rather facetious.
4. Thomas Crawford, 'Political and Protest Songs in Eighteenth-Century Scotland I: Jacobite and Anti-Jacobite', *Scottish Studies* 14 (1970), p. 21. Like the song's unrepentant Jacobite turning the tables on the 'rebel Whig', at line 2 Burns' 'honest man' refuses to 'hang his head' before the 'birkie, ca'd a lord'. He is urged to disdain the corrupt Hanoverian patronage system and its social hierarchy: in a line later in the song 'When Geordie mun fling by the Crown, / His Hat and Wig, and a' that', the king's trappings of authority are deftly reworked by Burns as the lord's 'ribband, star, and a' that'.
5. Murray Pittock, *Poetry and Jacobite Politics and Poetry in Eighteenth-Century Great Britain and Ireland* (Cambridge: Cambridge University Press, 1990), p. 217.
6. I borrow the term from Markman Ellis, who thus employs it in *The Politics of Sensibility: Race, Gender and Commerce in the Sentimental Novel* (Cambridge: Cambridge Univerity Press, 1996), p. 55.
7. For the difficulties involved in dating composition, see Thomas Crawford, *Boswell, Burns and the French Revolution* (Edinburgh: Saltire Society, 1990), pp. 61–3. For the song's complicated publishing history, in addition to Kinsley, see also the editors' commentary in *The Poetry of Robert Burns*, ed. W. E. Henley and T. F. Henderson, Centenary Edition, 4 vols (London:

Blackwood, 1896), vol. 3, pp. 489–91; and *The Canongate Burns*, ed. Andrew Noble and Patrick Scott Hogg (Edinburgh: Canongate), pp. 512–16.

8. *The Glasgow Magazine*'s anonymous text was reprinted by the radical Belfast *Northern Star* for 19–22 October 1795. More worryingly for Burns as excise employee, the song appeared again the following year in the Tory London *Oracle* on 2 June 1796, and was reprinted in the London *Star* the following day, but this time bearing the poet's name. It appeared again under Burns's name in the oppositional *Morning Chronicle* in late 1796. None of these versions included the first stanza. See Lucyle Werkmeister, 'Robert Burns and the London Newspapers', *Bulletin of the New York Public Library* 65 (1961), pp. 502–3.

9. D. Duncan Rice, 'Controversies over Slavery in Eighteenth- and Nineteenth-Century Scotland', in Lewis Perry and Michael Fellman (eds), *Antislavery Reconsidered: New Perspectives on the Abolitionists* (Baton Rouge and London: Louisiana State University Press, 1979), pp. 24–48; Iain Whyte, *Scotland and the Abolition of Black Slavery, 1756–1838* (Edinburgh: Edinburgh University Press, 2006); Colin Kidd, *The Forging of the Races: Race and Scripture in the Protestant Atlantic World, 1600–2000* (Cambridge: Cambridge University Press, 2006). Thanks to Karina Williamson for alerting me to the work of Duncan Rice, and for sending me a draft of part of her important work in progress on Scottish abolitionist poetry 'The Antislavery Poetry of John Marjoribanks'.

10. Imports to Scotland from the West Indies (mainly sugar, rum and cotton, all produced by slave labour) rose from £164,848 in 1783 to £288,121 in 1785, and to £371,656 in 1790. In 1785 Caribbean imports represented 21 per cent of Scotland's total imports and 12 per cent of her exports. Henry Hamilton, *An Economic History of Scotland in the Eighteenth Century* (Oxford: Clarendon Press, 1963), p. 279.

11. Iain Whyte, *Scotland and the Abolition of Black Slavery*, p. 74.

12. Wylie Sypher, *Guinea's Captive Kings: British Anti-Slavery Literature in the Eighteenth Century* (New York: Octagon Books, 1969 [1942]), p. 17.

13. Moira Ferguson, *Subject to Others: British Women Writers and Colonial Slavery, 1670–1834* (New York and London: Routledge, 1992), p. 147.

14. See James G. Basker, *Amazing Grace: An Anthology of Poems about Slavery, 1660–1810* (New Haven & London: Yale University Press, 2002).

15. Iain Whyte, *Scotland and Abolition*, p. 73.

16. Henley and Henderson trace the song to a seventeenth-century broadside *The Trepann'd Maiden*. In the original, the subject is a white English female, not an African slave: *The Poetry of Robert Burns*, ed. W. E. Henley and T. F. Henderson, vol. 3, p. 393. Thanks to Valentina Bold for her helpful unpublished commentary on the song.

17. Gerard Carruthers, *Robert Burns* (Tavistock: Northcote Publisher House, 2006), p. 60; see also Carruthers's essay 'Robert Burns and Slavery', *The Drouth* 26 (winter, 2008), pp. 21–6.

18. My text for the poem is that published in Andrew Ashfield (ed.), *Romantic*

Women Poets, 1788–1848 (Manchester: Manchester University Press, 1998), vol. 2, pp. 12–19.
19. See my essay 'Salons, Alps and Cordilleras: Helen Maria Williams, Alexander von Humboldt, and the Discourse of Romantic Travel', in E. Eger et al. (eds), *Women, Writing and the Public Sphere 1700–1830* (Cambridge: Cambridge University Press, 2001), pp. 217–38.
20. Deborah Kennedy, *Helen Maria Williams and the Age of Revolutions* (Lewisburg and London: Bucknell University Press, 2002), p. 39.
21. Ibid., p. 38.
22. Ibid., p. 42.
23. Wylie Sypher, *Guinea's Captive Kings*, p. 198.
24. An ECCO search does, however, reveal that the phrase 'honest poverty' appeared in a large number of eighteenth-century texts, including Dryden's *All for Love*, L'Estrange's translation of Aesop's *Fables* and *The Spectator*.
25. Another source familiar to Burns which employed the metaphor of the king's stamp was his friend John Goldie's *Essays on Various Important Subjects, Moral and Divine: Being an Attempt to Distinguish True from False Religion* (Glasgow, 1779, p. 8): '[T]here is nothing depends so much upon the king's stamp as bar or counterfeit metal.' Burns referred to the theological furore caused by 'Goudie's Bible' in his 'Epistle to John Goldie' (K 63).
26. John Stedman, *Narrative of a Five Years's Expedition, against the Revolted Negroes of Surinam, in Guinea . . . from the Year 1772 to 1777*, 2 vols (London, 1796), vol. 1, p. 206.
27. 'Visions of the Daughters of Albion', in Mary L. Johnson and John E. Grant (eds), *Blake's Poetry and Designs* (New York and London: Norton, 1979), p. 72. Bromian here also subscribes to the creed of the 'coward slave'.
28. One additional connection between the poem and the song might be noted. In his letter to Williams, Burns wrote that the line '"to dare to feel", is an idea that I do not altogether like' (*L* I, pp. 428–9). This didn't prevent him, in the fourth line of 'Honest Poverty', from writing the line 'we dare be poor for a' that'.
29. Andrew Ashfield (ed.), *Romantic Women*, vol. 2, p. 13, ll. 69–70.
30. J. Wordsworth, M. H. Abrams and S. Gill (eds), *The Prelude, 1799, 1800, 1805, 1850* (New York and London: Norton, 1979), pp. 368–9.
31. William Campbell, 'To the People of Scotland' in a manuscript volume entitled *Poems*, n. d., Mitchell Library MS. 73, pp. 3–4. The fact that the poems that make up the remaining eighty pages or so of this manuscript book (following the unequivocally radical 'People of Scotland') are uniformly written in support of the government cause suggests that Campbell may have accepted a pension from Henry Dundas. It is significant that Campbell's abolitionist poem 'The Negroes Complaint' was written after this compromise.
32. Marcus Wood, *Slavery, Empathy, and Pornography* (Oxford: Oxford University Press, 2002), pp. 178 and 170.

33. Andrew Ashfield, *Romantic Women*, vol. 2, p. 21, ll. 19–26.
34. For the contemporary sensitivities under the law with regard to the monarch, see John Barrell, *Imagining the King's Death: Figurative Treason, Fantasies of Regicide 1793–1796* (Oxford: Oxford University Press, 2000).
35. I'd like to thank Valentina Bold, Brycchan Carey, Gerry Carruthers, Colin Kidd, Peter Kitson, Kirsteen McCue, Jon Mee, Alan Rice, James Robertson, Karina Williamson and Marcus Wood, all of whom have been generous with their expertise in helping me research this essay.

Chapter 5 – Kidd

1. Richard J. Finlay, 'Myths, Heroes and Anniversaries in Modern Scotland', *Scottish Affairs* 18 (1997), pp. 108–26; Finlay, 'The Burns Cult and Scottish Identity in the Nineteenth and Twentieth Centuries', in Kenneth Simpson (ed.), *Love and Liberty: Robert Burns, a Bicentenary Celebration* (East Linton: Tuckwell, 1997), pp. 69–78.
2. 'Introduction' in Andrew Noble and Patrick Hogg (eds), *The Canongate Burns* (Edinburgh: Canongate, 2001), esp. p. xxiii.
3. David Daiches, 'Robert Burns and Jacobite song', in Donald A. Low (ed.), *Critical Essays on Robert Burns* (London and Boston: Routledge and Regan Paul, 1975), p. 141. See also William Donaldson, *The Jacobite Song: Political Myth and National Identity* (Aberdeen: Aberdeen University Press, 1988), pp. 72–89.
4. Maurice Lindsay, *The Burns Encyclopedia* (London: Robert Hale, 1980), pp. 287–90; Thomas Crawford, *Burns: A Study of the Poems and Songs* (Edinburgh: Canongate Academic, 1994), esp. pp. 202–3, 236–56, who also draws attention to the role of agrarian crisis in the radicalising of Burns; William Donaldson, 'The Glencairn Connection: Robert Burns and Scottish Politics, 1786–1796', *Studies in Scottish Literature* 16 (1981), pp. 61–79.
5. Thomas Crawford, *Burns*, p. 254.
6. William Donaldson, 'Glencairn Connection', p. 68.
7. Liam McIlvanney, *Burns the Radical: Poetry and Politics in Late Eighteenth-Century Scotland* (East Linton: Tuckwell, 2002); McIlvanney, 'Robert Burns and the Calvinist Radical Tradition', *History Workshop Journal* 40 (1995), pp. 133–49; McIlvanney, 'Sacred Freedom: Presbyterian Radicalism and the Politics of Robert Burns', in Kenneth Simpson (ed.), *Love and Liberty*, pp. 168–82.
8. William Donaldson, *Jacobite Song*, p. 73.
9. Burns to Dr John Moore, 2 August 1787 (*L* I, p. 134) and Burns to Lady Winifred Maxwell Constable, 16 December 1789 (*L* I, p. 461).
10. Quoted in Daiches, 'Burns and Jacobite Song', pp. 137–8.
11. Linda Colley, *In Defiance of Oligarchy: The Tory Party 1714–60* (Cambridge: Cambridge University Press, 1982).
12. See the different interpretations and chronologies – though, from our perspective, the same overall conclusion – of John Brewer, *Party Ideology and*

Popular Politics at the Accession of George III (Cambridge: Cambridge University Press, 1976); J. C. D. Clark, 'The Decline of Party, 1740–1760', *English Historical Review* 93 (1978), pp. 499–527; Clark, *The Dynamics of Change: The Crisis of the 1750s and English Party Systems* (Cambridge: Cambridge University Press, 1982).

13. Ian R. Christie, 'Party in Politics in the Age of Lord North's Administration', *Parliamentary History* 6 (1987), p. 60.
14. Ian Christie, 'Was There a New Toryism in the Earlier Part of George III's Reign?', in *Myth and Reality in Late Eighteenth-Century British Politics* (London: Macmillan, 1970).
15. For the clearest statement of this interpretation of eighteenth-century British politics, see J. C. D. Clark, 'A General Theory of Party, Opposition and Government, 1688–1832', *Historical Journal* 23 (1980), pp. 295–325. The only serious modern-day exception to this picture is B. W. Hill, *British Parliamentary Parties 1742–1832* (London: Macmillan, 1985), which argues for the long-term continuity of the two-party system. However, the Hill thesis has been effectively criticised by Christie, 'Party in Politics'.
16. 'Introductory survey', in Lewis Namier and John Brooke (eds), *The House of Commons 1754–90: History of Parliament* (London: HMSO, 1964), vol. 1, pp. 42 and 171.
17. Leslie J. Mitchell, *Charles James Fox and the Disintegration of the Whig Party, 1782–94* (Oxford and London: Oxford University Press, 1971).
18. John Cannon, *The Fox-North Coalition* (Cambridge and London: Cambridge University Press, 1970).
19. Donald Ginter (ed.), *Whig Organization in the General Election of 1790; Selections from the Blair Adam Papers* (Berkeley: California University Press, 1967), p. lv. See also I. R. Christie, 'The Anatomy of the Opposition in the Parliament of 1784', *Parliamentary History* 9 (1990), pp. 50–77.
20. For the ideological context of Dundas's rise, particularly contemporary anxieties in Scotland about nabobery which are far removed from conventional expectations about the supposed agenda of 'Whigs' or 'Tories', see John Dwyer and Alexander Murdoch, 'Paradigms and Politics: Manners, Morals and the Rise of Henry Dundas, 1770–1784', in J. Dwyer, Roger A. Mason and Alexander Murdoch (eds), *New Perspectives on the Politics and Culture of Early Modern Scotland* (Edinburgh: John Donald, 1982), pp. 210–48.
21. Jennifer Mori, 'The Political Theory of William Pitt the Younger', *History* 83 (1998), p. 235.
22. Michael Fry, *The Dundas Despotism* (Edinburgh: Edinburgh University Press, 1992), pp. 173 and 245. See also David J. Brown, 'The Government of Scotland under Henry Dundas and William Pitt', *History* 83 (1998), pp. 265–79.
23. See, for example, Robert Blake, *The Conservative Party from Peel to Churchill* (London: Methuen, 1970), pp. 1–9; Eric J. Evans, *The Forging of the Modern*

State: Early Industrial Britain 1783–1870 (Harlow: Longman, 1983), p. 56. Cf. Frank O'Gorman, 'Pitt and the "Tory" Reaction to the French Revolution 1789–1815', in H. T. Dickinson (ed.), *Britain and the French Revolution 1789–1815* (Houndmills: Macmillam, 1989).

24. See R. Pares, *King George III and the Politicians* (Oxford: Clarendon Press, 1967), p. 194: 'The Portland whigs, rather than Pitt's circle of professional administrators, were the real nucleus of the Tory party.' However, see also D. Wilkinson, 'The Pitt–Portland Coalition of 1794 and the Origins of the "Tory" Party', *History* 83 (1998), pp. 249–64.
25. John Ehrman, *The Younger Pitt* 3 vols (London: Constable, 1969–96, esp. vol. 1, pp. 223–8; vol. 2, pp. 81–3; vol. 3, pp. 506–7; Jennifer Mori, 'Political Theory', p. 236; Michael Fry, *Dundas Despotism*, pp. 71, 235–8.
26. See, for example, J. J. Sack, *From Jacobite to Conservative: Reaction and Orthodoxy in Britain, c. 1760–1832* (Cambridge: Cambridge University Press, 1993).
27. Leslie G. Mitchell, *Charles James Fox* (Oxford: Oxford University Press, 1992), pp. 1–3.
28. The standard authority remains William Ferguson, 'Electoral Law and Procedure in Eighteenth- and Early Nineteenth-Century Scotland' (Glasgow University PhD, 1957).
29. Lewis Namier and John Brooke, 'Introductory Survey', vol. 1, p. 172.
30. Ibid., vol. 2, p. 686.
31. R. L. Thorne (ed.), *The Commons 1790–1820*, 5 vols (London: History of Parliament Trust, 1986), vol. 2, pp. 552–4; vol. 4, p.187; vol. 5, p. 269.
32. Dundas to Earl of Galloway, 31 March 1796, National Archives of Scotland [NAS], Melville Castle Muniments, GD 51/1/198/14/9.
33. See, for example, Maurice Lindsay, *Burns Encyclopedia*, p. 164; Thomas Crawford, *Burns*, p. 253; William Donaldson, 'Glencairn Connection', p. 66. The only scholar to question this identification is Norman R. Paton, *Song O'Liberty: The Politics of Robert Burns* (Fareham: Sea-Green Ribbon, 1994), p. 120.
34. R. L. Thorne (ed.), *The Commons*, vol. 4, p. 187.
35. Earl of Galloway to John Bushby, 18 December 1794, NAS Broughton and Cally Muniments, GD 10/1421/361; Galloway to James Murray, 10 March 1796, NAS GD 10/1421/364; Galloway to Dundas, 30 March 1796, NAS GD 51/1/198/14/9.
36. Christopher Whatley, 'Burns and the Union of 1707', in K. Simpson (ed.), *Love and Liberty*, pp. 190–5.
37. John Brims, 'The Scottish "Jacobins", Scottish Nationalism and the British Union', in Roger A. Mason (ed.), *Scotland and England 1286–1815* (Edinburgh: John Donald, 1987), pp. 247–65.
38. Kenneth Simpson, *The Protean Scot: The Crisis of Identity in Eighteenth-Century Scottish Literature* (Aberdeen: Aberdeen University Press, 1988).

39. For the influence of the *Spectator* on the Scottish Enlightenment, see Nicholas Phillipson, 'The Scottish Enlightenment', in Roy Porter and M. Teich (eds), *The Enlightenment in National Context* (Cambridge: Cambridge University Press, 1981), pp. 19–40.
40. Colin Kidd, 'Macpherson, Burns and the Politics of Sentiment', *Scotlands* 4 (1997), pp. 36–8.
41. Hew Scott (ed.), *Fasti Ecclesiae Scoticanae*, 7 vols (Edinburgh: Paterson, 1915–28, vol. 2, pp.226 and 273.
42. Duncan Forbes, *Hume's Philosophical Politics* (Cambridge: Cambridge University Press, 1975); Colin Kidd, *Subverting Scotland's Past: Scottish Whig Historians and the Creation of an Anglo-British Identity, 1689-c.1830* (Cambridge: Cambridge University Press, 1993).
43. Adam Smith, *The Theory of Moral Sentiments* (Oxford: Clarendon Press [1771], 1976).
44. Henry Mackenzie, *The Man of Feeling* (Oxford: Oxford University Press [1771], 1967).
45. Cf. Carol McGuirk, *Robert Burns and the Sentimental Era* (Athens: University of Georgia Press, 1985).
46. Thomas Crawford, *Burns*, pp. 240–1.
47. For the political and social dimensions of the sentimental, see John Mullan, *Sentiment and Sociability: The Language of Feeling in the Eighteenth Century* (Oxford: Oxford University Press, 1988); Markman Ellis, *The Politics of Sensibility: Race, Gender and Commerce in the Sentimental Novel* (Cambridge: Cambridge University Press, 1996).
48. Patrick Hogg, *Robert Burns: The Lost Poems* (Glasgow: Clydeside Press, 1997); 'Introduction', in *The Canongate Burns* (Edinburgh: Canongate), pp. ix–xcii. But see Gerard Carruthers, 'Alexander Geddes and the Burns "Lost Poems" Controversy', *Studies in Scottish Literature* 31 (1999), pp. 81–5; Carruthers, 'The Problem of Pseudonyms in the Burns "Lost Poems"', *Studies in Scottish Literature* 33–4 (2004), pp. 97–106; and Carruthers, '*The Canongate Burns*: Misreading Robert Burns and the Periodical Press of the 1790s', in *Review of Scottish Culture* 18 (2006), pp. 41–50.
49. Paul H. Scott, 'Robert Burns, Patriot', in Kenneth Simpson (ed.), *Love and Liberty*, p. 272.
50. See, for example, Richard B. Sher, '1688 and 1788: William Robertson on Revolution in Britain and France', in Paul Dukes and John Dunkley (eds), *Culture and Revolution* (London: Pinter, 1990), pp. 100–2.
51. Colin Kidd, 'The Rehabilitation of Scottish Jacobitism', *Scottish Historical Review* 77 (1998), pp. 58–76.
52. See, for example, H. T. Dickinson, 'The Eighteenth-Century Debate on the Glorious Revolution', *History* 61 (1976), pp. 28–45; Kathleen Wilson, 'Inventing Revolution: 1688 and Eighteenth-Century Popular Politics', *Journal of British Studies* 28 (1989), pp. 349–86.

Chapter 6 – McCue

1. Thomas Carlyle, review of J. G. Lockhart's *The Life of Robert Burns* published in 1828 in the *Edinburgh Review* xcvi (December, 1828). This quotation appears on p. 286 of the *Review*.
2. Robert Louis Stevenson, 'Some Aspects of Robert Burns', *Familiar Studies of Men & Books* (London: Heinemann [1882], 1925, p. 53.
3. Fred Freeman directed the 1990s project *The Complete Songs of Robert Burns* released by Linn Records. See: http://www.linnrecords.com/artist-robert-burns-series.aspx
4. The three key editions of Burns's songs are: *The Songs of Robert Burns*, ed. James C. Dick (London: Henry Frowde, 1903); *The Poems and Songs of Robert Burns*, ed. James Kinsley (Oxford: Clarendon Press, 1968); and *The Songs of Robert Burns*, ed. Donald A. Low (Aldershot: Routledge, 1993). Articles on songs appear throughout the *Burns Chronicle* and there are notable essays by Cedric Thorpe Davie and David Daiches in Donald A. Low (ed.), *Critical Essays on Robert Burns* (London and Boston: Routledge, 1975). See also relevant essays in Kenneth Simpson (ed.), *Burns Now!* (Edinburgh: Canongate Academic, 1994); and Kenneth Simpson (ed.), *Love and Liberty: A Bicentenary Celebration* (East Linton: Tuckwell, 1997). See also Hans Hecht's song chapter in *Robert Burns*, (London: William Hodge [1936], 1950).
5. Thomas Crawford, *Burns: A Study of the Poems and Songs* (Edinburgh: Canongate Academic [1960], 1994. By far the most important secondary source of eighteenth-century Scottish song is Crawford's *Society and the Lyric: A study of the Song Culture of eighteenth-century Scotland* (Edinburgh: Scottish Academic Press, 1979).
6. The only other key study is that by Catarina Ericson-Roos, 'The Songs of Robert Burns: A Study of the Unity of Poetry and Music', doctoral dissertation from the University of Uppsala (1977).
7. Robert Burns's, *Robert Burns's Commonplace Book 1783–1785* ed. David Daiches (Fontwell and London: Centaur Press, 1965), pp. 3–5.
8. William Stenhouse, *Illustrations of the Lyric Poetry and Music of Scotland* (Edinburgh: Blackwood, 1853), provides detailed notes to the 600 songs in James Johnson's *Scots Musical Museum*; and John Glen, *Early Scottish Melodies* (Edinburgh: J. and R. Glen, 1900), focuses more specifically on older Scottish melodies and has one section (Chap. 6) on the *Scots Musical Museum*.
9. Emily Lyle, '"Thus With Me Began Love and Poesy": Burns's First Song and "I Am a Man Unmarried"', in Kenneth Simpson (ed.), *Love and Liberty*, pp. 334–40.
10. Emily Lyle, 'Thus With Me . . .', p. 335.
11. 'The Roving Bachelor', or a version of it, appears in a Kilmarnock-printed chapbook around 1800 which also includes the Irish song 'Paddy Carey' and Burns's 'The Lass of Ballochmyle'.

12. See Robert Burns, *Poems Chiefly in the Scottish Dialect* (Edinburgh: William Creech, 1787), p. xlviii. Burns's first ten songs were: A Fragment, 'When Guildford Good our Pilot Stood'; Song, 'It was Upon a Lammas Night'; Song, 'Now Westlin Winds and Slaughtering Guns'; Song, 'Behind yon Hills where Stinchar Flows'; A Fragment, 'Green Grow the Rashes'; Song, 'Again Rejoicing Nature Sees'; Song, 'The Gloomy Night is Gath'ring Fast'; Song, 'From Thee, Eliza, I Must Go'; 'The Farewell'. To the Brethren of St James's Lodge, Tarbolton; Song, 'No Churchman am I for to Rail and to Write'. I don't list 'John Barleycorn' here, though it also appeared in this collection and was apparently 'partly composed on the plan of an old song known by the same name', however there is no melody given. See K 23.
13. 'Behind yon Hill' was amended by Burns to 'Behind yon Hill where Lugar Flows' by October 1792 – see *L* II, pp. 153–4. Here Burns notes his respect for Thomas Percy's ballad to the same tune.
14. This collection may well have been John Aikin's *Essays on Song-Writing: With a Collection of such English Songs as are Most Eminent for Poetical Merit, to which are Added, Some Original Pieces* (London: Joseph Johnson, 1772). A second edition was published in Warrington in 1774. Ritson's collection didn't appear until 1783. Hecht believes the 'vade mecum' to have been *The Lark* of 1765: Hans Hecht, *Robert Burns*, p. 196.
15. See John Purser, '"The Wee Apollo": Burns and Oswald', in Kenneth Simpson (ed.), *Love and Liberty*, pp. 326–33.
16. *Burns's Commonplace Book*, ed. Daiches, p. 37.
17. See Hamish Mathison, 'Robert Burns and National Song', in David Duff and Catherine Jones (eds), *Scotland, Ireland and the Romantic Aesthetic* (Lewisburg: Bucknell University Press, 2007), pp. 77–92. This chapter accounts for Burns's own knowledge and comments on this practice.
18. See Leith Davis, 'At "Sang About": Scottish Song and the Challenge to British Culture', in Leith Davis, Ian Duncan and Janet Sorenson (eds), *Scotland and the Borders of Romanticism* (Cambridge: Cambridge University Press, 2006), pp. 188–203. Davis notes that the title was *The Tea Table Miscellany: A Collection of Choice Songs Scots and English*. This title was, it appears, only from its tenth edition in 1740. Prior to this the title was *The Tea Table Miscellany: Or, Allan Ramsay's Collection of Scots Sangs*.
19. The bibliography of Ramsay's *TTM* is highly complex as noted by Burns Martin in *Allan Ramsay: A Study of his Life and Works* (Cambridge: Harvard University Press, 1931); and Martin's *A Bibliography of the Writings of Allan Ramsay*, in *Records of the Glasgow Bibliographical Society* (Glasgow: Jackson, Wylie and Co., 1931 (vol. 10)). My thanks to G. Ross Roy for his generosity in imparting his own experience here, having compiled the entry for Ramsay in George Watson (ed.), *The New Cambridge Bibliography of English Literature, 1600–1800* (Cambridge: Cambridge University Press, 1971 (vol. 2)). I was

able to benefit from discussions with Professor Roy as the Ormiston Roy Fellow at the University of South Carolina in 2006, and I gratefully acknowledge the award of the fellowship.
20. There is no evidence as to which edition of Ramsay's 'works' or his songs Burns had access. Possibly this came through Robert Riddell's library at Friar's Carse, yet to be established.
21. Ramsay's chagrin over this act of piracy is clearly noted in his Introduction to the *TTM*.
22. Burns's letter to Mr John M'Auley of 4 June 1789.
23. See *Notes on Scottish Songs by Robert Burns*, ed. James C. Dick (London: Henry Frowde, 1908).
24. See Kirsteen McCue, '"An Individual Flowering on a Common Stem": Melody, Performance and National Song', in Philip Connell and Nigel Leask (eds), *Romanticism and Popular Culture in Britain and Ireland* (Cambridge: Cambridge University Press, forthcoming 2009).
25. See Thomas Crawford, *Society and the Lyric*, p. 92.
26. Carol McGuirk, *Robert Burns and the Sentimental Era* (East Linton: Tuckwell Press, 1997), pp. 121–4.
27. *Songs*, ed. James C. Dick, p. xiii.
28. *The Scots Musical Museum*, ed. Donald A. Low (Aldershot: Scolar Press, 1991), p. 2. Facsimile reprint of the *Museum* in two volumes with an appendix of Burns's contributions and his 'Notes on Scottish Song'.
29. Murray Pittock, *Scottish and Irish Romanticism* (Oxford: Oxford University Press, 2007), p. 163.
30. See James A. McKay, *A Biography of Robert Burns* (Edinburgh: Mainstream, 1992), pp. 432–3; see also *L* II, p. 92.
31. Nigel Leask's work on *Burns and Pastoral* (Oxford: Oxford University Press, forthcoming 2010) presents a new perspective on Burns as songwriter and collector. My thanks to him for sharing his work so generously.
32. *Scots Musical Museum*, ed. Donald A. Low, vol. 2, pp. 693–9.
33. See Kirsteen McCue, 'George Thomson (1757–1851): His Collections of National Airs in their Scottish Cultural Context', unpublished DPhil thesis, Oxford, 1993.
34. See R. D. S. Jack and P. A. T. Rozendaal (eds), *The Mercat Anthology of Early Scottish Literature 1375–1707* (Edinburgh: Mercat Press, 1997), pp. 520–1. Here they list extracts of the song from the Bannatyne MS through the seventeenth century to Robert Burns.

Chapter 7 – Brown

1. Robert Crawford, 'Introduction' in *'Heaven-Taught Fergusson': Robert Burns's Favourite Scottish Poet* (East Linton: Tuckwell, 2003), p. 2.
2. Ibid., p. 1.

3. *The Poems of Robert Fergusson*, ed. Matthew P. McDiarmid, 2 vols (Edinburgh and London: Blackwood, 1954–6, vol. 1, pp. 178–81.
4. Ibid., p. 178.
5. Carol McGuirk, 'The "Rhyming Trade": Fergusson, Burns and the Marketplace', in Robert Crawford (ed.), *'Heaven-Taught Fergusson'*, p. 135.
6. See also Burns's letter to the Honourable Bailies of the Canongate, Edinburgh, 6 February 1787 (*L* I, p. 90) and to Peter Hill, 5 February 1792 (*L* II, p. 133).
7. *Robert Burns: Selected Poems* ed. Carol McGuirk (London: Penguin, 1993), p. 227.
8. 'Mutual Complaint of Plainstanes and Causey, in their Mother Tongue' in McDiarmid (ed.), *The Poems of Robert Fergusson*, vol. 2, pp. 122–6.
9. Ibid., 'A Drink Eclogue', vol. 2, pp. 210–14.
10. Ibid., 'The Ghaists: A Kirkyard Eclogue', vol. 2, pp. 141–5.
11. Thomas Crawford, *Burns: A Study of the Poems and Songs* (Edinburgh: Mercat Press), 1978, p. 194.
12. Ibid., p. 197.
13. Ibid., p. 196.
14. 'Hallow-Fair', in *The Poems of Robert Fergusson*, vol. 2, pp. 89–93.
15. F. W. Freeman, 'Robert Fergusson: Pastoral and Politics at Mid-Century', in Andrew Hook (ed.), *History of Scottish Literature: 1660–1800* (Aberdeen: Aberdeen University Press, 1987), vol. 2, pp. 147–8.
16. Carol McGuirk, 'The "Rhyming Trade"', p. 151.
17. 'Leith Races', in *The Poems of Robert Fergusson*, vol. 2, pp. 160–7.
18. Ibid., 'Caller Water', pp. 106–8.
19. Ibid., 'Caller Oysters', pp. 66–9.
20. Ibid., 'Good Eating', pp. 99–103. For further discussion of the comparison of 'Good Eating' and 'To a Haggis', see Carol McGuirk, 'The "Rhyming Trade"'.
21. 'The Author's Life', in *The Poems of Robert Fergusson*, vol. 2, p. 224.
22. *The Poems of Robert Fergusson*, vol. 1, p. 182.

Chapter 8 – Stafford

1. Jane Austen, 'Sanditon', in R. W. Chapman (ed.) B. C. Southam (rev.), *Minor Works* (London: Oxford University Press, 1988), p. 397–8.
2. Francis Jeffrey, review of R. H. Cromek, *Reliques of Robert Burns*, *Edinburgh Review* 13 (1809), in Donald Low (ed.), *Robert Burns: The Critical Heritage*, (London: Routledge and Kegan Paul, 1974), p. 189.
3. Lamb to Coleridge, 28 July 1800, in Donald Low (ed.), *Robert Burns*, p. 112.
4. *The Letters of Samuel Taylor Coleridge*, ed. E. L. Griggs, 6 vols (Oxford: Clarendon, 1956–71), vol. 1, p. 607.
5. William Wordsworth, *A Letter to a Friend of Robert Burns*, in Stephen Gill (ed.), *The Major Works* (Oxford: Oxford University Press, 2000), p. 665.

6. William Wordsworth, *The Major Works*, pp. 261–2. See G. Dekker, *Coleridge and the Literature of Sensibility* (London: Vision, 1978), pp. 68–74.
7. *The Letters of John Keats*, ed. H. E. Rollins, 2 vols (Cambridge: Harvard University Press, 1958), vol. 1, p. 320. Subsequent page references within the text are to this edition.
8. Alexander Peterkin, *A Review of the Life of Robert Burns*, in Donald Low (ed.), *Robert Burns*, p. 268.
9. Donald Low (ed.), *Robert Burns*, p. 255.
10. Ibid. (ed.), p. 172.
11. Jane Austen, 'Sanditon', p. 397.
12. *A Defence of Poetry, Shelley's Poetry and Prose*, ed. D. Reiman and S. Powers (New York: Norton, 1977), p. 506.
13. William Wordsworth, *A Letter*, p. 665.
14. William Wordsworth, *The Major Works*, p. 668; Lord Byron, *Don Juan*, ed. T. G. Steffan, E. Steffan and W. W. Pratt (London: Penguin, 1996), vol. 3, p. 92.
15. *The Poems and Songs of Robert Burns*, ed. J. Kinsley, 3 vols (Oxford: Clarendon, 1968), vol. 3, p. 978.
16. Donald Low (ed.), *Robert Burns*, pp. 91–9.
17. *The Letters of Mary Wollstonecraft Shelley*, ed. Betty T. Bennett, 3 vols (Baltimore: Johns Hopkins Press, 1980–8), vol. 2, p. 333.
18. *Lectures on the English Poets, The Complete Works of William Hazlitt*, ed. P. P. Howe, 21 vols (London: Dent, 1930–4), vol. 5, p. 127.
19. Samuel Taylor Coleridge, *Biographia Literaria*, ed. J. Engell and W. J. Bate, 2 vols (Princeton: Princeton University Press, 1983), vol. 1, p. 81.
20. M. H. Abrams, *The Mirror and the Lamp* (London: Oxford University Press, 1953), p. 22.
21. *The Letters of William and Dorothy Wordsworth, The Early Years, 1787–1805*, ed. C. L. Shaver, 2nd edn (Oxford: Clarendon, 1967), vol. 1, p. 256.
22. Ibid., p. 597.
23. *Letters of Coleridge*, vol. 1, p. 607. See also D. S. Roberts, 'Literature, Medical Science and Politics, 1795–1800: *Lyrical Ballads* and Currie's *Works of Robert Burns*', in C. C. Barfoot (ed.), '*A Natural Delineation of the Passions*': *The Historic Moment of the Lyrical Ballads* (Amsterdam: Rodopi, 2003), pp. 115–28.
24. William Wordsworth, *The Major Works*, p. 80.
25. Seamus Heaney, 'Burns's Art Speech', in *Finders Keepers* (London: Faber, 2002), p. 357.
26. William Wordsworth, *The Major Works*, p. 53.
27. Ibid., p. 603.
28. Robert Anderson, 'Epistle I. To Robert Burns', in *Poems on Various Subjects* (Carlisle, 1798), p. 73.
29. Gillian Hughes (ed.), 'Memoir of the Author's Life', in *Altrive Tales* (Edinburgh: Edinburgh University Press, 2003), p. 18.

30. John Lockhart, 'Cockney School of Poetry. No IV', *Blackwood's Edinburgh Magazine* 3 (August 1818), p. 519.
31. *Letters of Keats*, vol. 1, p. 323.
32. *Letters of Mary Shelley*, vol. 3, p. 407.

Chapter 9 – Andrews

1. J. D. Ross (ed.), *Early Critical Reviews on Robert Burns* (New York: AMS Press [1900], 1973), p. 3.
2. Ibid., p. 6.
3. Carol McGuirk, *Robert Burns and the Sentimental Era* (Athens: University of Georgia Press, 1985), p. 76.
4. Robert Burns, *Robert Burns' Commonplace Book*, ed. R. L. Brown (East Ardsley: S.R. Publishers, 1969), p. 1. Subsequent page references within the text are to this edition.
5. G. Ross Roy, 'Robert Burns: A Self-Portrait', in Donald Low (ed.), *Critical Essays on Robert Burns* (London: Routledge and Kegan Paul, 1975), p. 15.
6. *Robert Burns' Commonplace Book*, p. 21.
7. David Daiches, *Robert Burns* (New York: Macmillan, 1966), p. 86.
8. Ibid., p. 86.
9. Ibid., p. 86.
10. *Robert Burns' Commonplace Book*, p. 52.
11. Kenneth Simpson, *The Protean Scot: The Crisis of Identity in Eighteenth-Century Scottish Literature* (Aberdeen: Aberdeen University Press, 1985), p. 219.
12. Jeffrey Skoblow, *Dooble Tongue: Scots, Burns, Contradiction* (Newark: University of Delaware Press, 2001), p. 116.
13. Kenneth Simpson, *The Protean Scot*, p. 195.
14. Thomas Crawford, *Burns: A Study of the Poems and Songs* (Stanford: Stanford University Press, 1960), p. 261.
15. Robert Burns, *Notes on Scottish Song*, ed. J. C. Dick (London: Henry Frowde, 1908), pp. 1–2. Subsequent page references within the text are to this edition.
16. Carol McGuirk, 'Loose Canons: Milton and Burns, Artsong and Folksong', in Kenneth Simpson (ed.), *Love and Liberty* (East Linton: Tuckwell Press, 1997), p. 322.

Chapter 10 – Lumsden

1. J. G. Lockhart, *Memoirs of the Life of Sir Walter Scott, Bart*, 7 vols (Edinburgh: Robert Cadell, 1837–8), vol. 1, p. 137.
2. Ibid., 1 p. 138.
3. The papers given at this conference were subsequently published as *Scott in Carnival: Selected Papers from the Fourth International Scott Conference,*

Edinburgh, 1991, ed. J. H. Alexander and David Hewitt (Aberdeen: Association for Scottish Literary Studies, 1993).
4. Ainsley McIntosh, *Approaching Influence: A Study of Paratextuality in Two Novels by Walter Scott*, unpublished MA dissertation (University of Aberdeen, 2003), p. 28.
5. Sheena Sutherland, 'Scott's Voices: An Analysis of Discourse Competition in the Waverley Novels', unpublished PhD thesis (University of Aberdeen, 1997), p. 174.
6. Walter Scott, *Chronicles of the Canongate*, Edinburgh Edition of the Waverley Novels, ed. Claire Lamont (Edinburgh: Edinburgh University Press, 2000), p. 9.
7. Claire Lamont, 'Historical Note to "The Highland Widow"', in *Chronicles*, p. 413.
8. Christopher Worth, 'Scott, Story-telling and Subversion: Dialogism in *Woodstock*', in *Scott in Carnival*, p. 383.
9. *The Journal of Sir Walter Scott*, ed. W. E. K. Anderson (Oxford: Oxford University Press, 1972).
10. This review was originally published in the *Quarterly Review* for 1809 and reprinted in *The Prose Works of Sir Walter Scott*, Bart., 28 vols (Edinburgh: Robert Cadell, 1834–6), vol. 17, pp. 242–66.
11. Ibid., pp. 250–1.
12. Ibid., p. 251.
13. This unsigned review of *Childe Harold's Pilgrimage* originally appeared in the *Quarterly Review* (February 1817) and is reprinted in *Byron: The Critical Heritage*, ed. Andrew Rutherford (London: Routledge and Kegan Paul, 1970), p. 96.
14. *Journal*, p. 82.
15. *The Prose Works of Sir Walter Scott*, p. 255.
16. Walter Scott, *The Heart of Mid-Lothian*, Edinburgh Edition of the Waverley Novels, ed. David Hewitt and Alison Lumsden (Edinburgh: Edinburgh University Press, 2004), p. 6. Subsequent page references within the text are to this edition.
17. This alludes to both Deuteronomy 28:5 and to 'Holy Willie's Prayer' (written 1785; first published 1799 (chapbook) and 1801), (K 53, l. 77).
18. *The Prose Works of Sir Walter Scott*, p. 262.
19. Ibid., p. 243.
20. Ibid.
21. Ibid.
22. Ibid., p. 244.
23. Walter Scott, *Redgauntlet*, Edinburgh Edition of the Waverley Novels, ed. G. A. M. Wood and David Hewitt (Edinburgh: Edinburgh University Press, 1997), p. 81.
24. For a description of Willie and his wife see *Redgauntlet*, pp. 79–80.

25. *The Prose Works of Sir Walter Scott*, p. 247.
26. Ibid.
27. 'Explanatory Notes', Note to 200.23–4 in *Redgauntlet*, p. 497.
28. Tony Inglis, '. . .And an Intertextual Heart: Rewriting Origins in *The Heart of Mid-Lothian*', in *Scott in Carnival*, p. 221.
29. David Hewitt and Alison Lumsden, 'Historical Note', in *The Heart of Mid-Lothian*, p. 593.
30. For a full discussion of this argument, see David Hewitt and Alison Lumsden, 'Historical Note', in *The Heart of Mid-Lothian*, pp. 596–8.
31. Walter Scott, *The Pirate*, Edinburgh Edition of the Waverley Novels, ed. Mark Weinstein and Alison Lumsden (Edinburgh: Edinburgh University Press, 2001), p. 12. Subsequent page references within the text are to this edition.
32. *Journal*, p. 39.
33. Ibid., p. 252.
34. The statistics in this chapter are based on the work of the EENN editorial team to whom I extend my grateful thanks.

Chapter 11 – McKenna

1. 4.56; p. 59. The citations from Theocritus refer to the original Greek lines and the corresponding translations from 'The Poems of Theocintus' ([The 'Idylls'] in *Greek Bucolic Poets* ed. and trans. Jeffrey Henderson (Cambridge, MA: Harvard University Press, 2001), pp. 8–361.
2. Ibid., 16.22–33; p. 201.
3. *The Poems and Songs of Robert Burns* James Kinsley (ed.) (Oxford: Oxford University Press, 1968), vol. 3, p. 971.
4. See Philip Hardie, *Virgil's Aeneid: Cosmos and Imperium* (Oxford: Clarendon Press, 1986), pp. 157–67 on sources for the *Georgics*. See also the prefatory 'An Essay on the Georgics' by Joseph Addison in Dryden's *Works of Virgil*, ed. William Frost and Vinton Dearing (Berkeley: University of California Press, 1987), vol. 5, pp. 145–53.
5. John Dryden (trans.), *The Works of Virgil in English 1697*, in William Frost and Vinton Dearing (eds), *The Works of John Dryden*, ed. William Frost and Vinton Dearing vols 5 and 6 (Berkeley: University of California Press, 1987), BK 1, ll. 118–19. Subsequent page references within the text are to this edition.
6. Alexander Pope (trans.), in Maynard Mack (ed.), *The Poems of Alexander Pope*, vols 9 and 10 (New Haven: Yale University Press, 1967), BK 11, ll. 248–50.
7. Brooks Otis, *Virgil: A Study in Civilized Poetry* (Oxford: Clarendon Press, 1963), pp. 5–40.
8. Ibid., p. 2.

9. David Quint, *Epic and Empire: Politics and Generic Form from Virgil to Milton* (Princeton: Princeton University Press, 1993), p. 9.
10. See Richard Waswo, *The Founding Legend of Western Civilization from Virgil to Vietnam* (Hanover: University Press of New England, 1997), p. 18.
11. When Dido realises that Aeneas will depart Carthage and that there is nothing she can do to prevent this event, she pronounces a curse on the nation he will found: 'Perpetual Hate, and mortal Wars proclaim, / Against the Prince, the People, and the Name' (BK 4, ll. 895–6). In terms of a *translatio imperii*, one item of note should be that England's own self-definition from the Arthurian legends and historian Geoffrey of Monmouth (early twelfth century) to the Renaissance posits a Trojan origin for the British monarchy.

Chapter 12 – Davis

1. He continues, 'You will have heard that I going [sic] to commence Poet in print; and tomorrow, my works go to the press. – I expect it will be a Volume of about two hundred pages. – It [is ju]st the last foolish action I intend to do; and then turn a wise man as fast as possible' (*L* 1, p. 39).
2. Robert Heron, *A Memoir of the Life of the Late Robert Burns* (Edinburgh: printed for T. Brown, 1797), p. 17. Subsequent page references within the text are to this edition.
3. Richard Sher, *The Enlightenment and the Book: Scottish Authors and their Publishers in Eighteenth-Century Britain, Ireland and America* (Chicago: University of Chicago Press, 2006), p. 231.
4. Françoise Lionnet and Shu-mei Shih (eds), *Minor Transnationalism* (Durham: Duke University Press, 2005).
5. Robert Crawford, *Devolving English Literature* (Oxford: Clarendon Press, 1992), p. 89.
6. Ibid., p. 89.
7. Burns did not publish 'When Guilford Good' in the 'Kilmarnock' edition, but, upon obtaining the approval of Lord Glencairn and Henry Erskine, he did include it in the second edition of his poems under the title, 'A Fragment'.
8. In fact, North had been conciliatory toward America, repealing four of the five Townshend Duties, but his government had also passed the Tea Act in 1773 which precipitated the resistance at Boston.
9. There seem to be two different versions of this song, one Jacobite and one Williamite. It may be that this very ambiguity had its appeal to Burns.
10. Liam McIlvanney, *Burns the Radical: Poetry and Politics in Late Eighteenth-Century* Scotland (East Linton: Tuckwell, 2002), p. 197.
11. See 'Memoirs and Trials of the Political Martyrs of Scotland; Persecuted during the Years 1793–4–5', *Tait's Edinburgh Magazine* (January 1837), pp. 1–20; Marjorie Masson and J. F. Jameson Source, 'The Odyssey of Thomas

Muir,' *The American Historical Review* 29(1) (1923), pp. 49–72; and Nigel Leask, 'Thomas Muir and The Telegraph: Radical Cosmopolitanism in 1790s Scotland', *History Workshop Journal* 63(1) (2007), pp. 48–69.
12. Quoted in Marjorie Masson and J. F. Jameson, 'The Odyssey' Source, p. 50.
13. *Tait's Edinburgh Magazine* (January 1837), p. 13. The Trial of Muir was published numerous times, including in an account by the Goldsmith's Hall group.
14. Nigel Leask, 'Thomas Muir', p. 66.
15. Anna Seward, *Elegy on Captain Cook. To which is Added, an Ode to the Sun* (London: J. Dodsley, 1780), p. 15. For an illuminating discussion of the relationship between Britain and the South Seas, see Kathleen Wilson, *The Island Race: Englishness, Empire and Gender in the Eighteenth Century* (London: Routledge, 2003), Chapter 2.
16. John Rickman, *Journal of Captain Cook's Last Voyage to the Pacific Ocean on Discovery: Performed in the Years 1776, 1777, 1778, 1779, Illustrated with Cuts, and a Chart, Shewing the Tracts of the Ships Employed in this Expedition. Faithfully Narrated from the Original MS* (London: Printed for E. Newbery, 1781). See 'Cook & Omai: The Cult of the South Seas,' <http://www.nla.gov.au/exhibitions/omai/section3/nk5094.html>
17. James Currie, *The Works of Robert Burns with an Account of his Life and a Criticism on his Writings to which are Prefixed Some Observations on the Character and Condition of the Scottish Peasantry*, 4 vols (London: T. Cadell and W. Davies, 1820); 8th edn, vol. 1, p. 109. Subsequent references are to this edition.
18. Currie later remarks, 'He was liable, from a very early period of life, to that interruption in the process of digestion, which arises from deep and anxious thought, and which is sometimes the effect, and sometimes the cause of depression of spirits' (1, p. 218).
19. Nigel Leask, 'Scotland's Literature of Empire and Emigration', in Ian Brown, Thomas Owen Clancy, Susan Manning and Murray Pittock (eds), *The Edinburgh History of Scottish Literature: Enlightenment, Britain and Empire*, vol. 2 (Edinburgh: Edinburgh University Press, 2007), p. 157.
20. In the United States, the conflict between tradition and modernity that characterised Burns's representation was interpreted chiefly in terms of class struggle. Emerson, for example, pronounced that 'Robert Burns, the poet of the middle class, re-presents in the mind of men to-day that great uprising of the middle class against the armed and privileged minorities' ('Robert Burns Speech Delivered at the Celebration of the Burns Centenary, Boston, January 25, 1859', in Edward Waldo Emerson (ed.), *The Complete Works of Ralph Waldo Emerson: Miscellanies* [Boston and New York: Houghton, Mifflin, 1903–4), vol. 11, p. 440. In Germany, thanks to the commentary of Goethe, he was recognised as a remnant of a folk culture that was thriving in the late eighteenth century despite vast social changes.
21. Felicity Nussbaum, 'Introduction' in *The Global Eighteenth Century* (Baltimore: Johns Hopkins University Press, 2003), p. 10.

Further Reading

Primary Materials

Brown, R. L. (ed.), *Robert Burns'* Commonplace Book (East Ardsley: S. R. Publishers, 1969).
— (ed.), *Robert Burns, Tour of the Borders* (Totowa: Rowman and Littlefield, 1972).
— (ed.), *Robert Burns, Tour of the Highlands and Stirlingshire* (Ipswich: The Boydell Press, 1973).
Daiches, David (ed.), *Robert Burns's Commonplace Book, 1783–1785* (Fontwell and London: Centaur, 1965).
Dick, J. C. (ed.), *The Songs of Robert Burns* (London: Henry Frowde, 1903).
— *Notes on Scottish Songs by Robert Burns* (London: Henry Frowde, 1908).
Kinsley, James (ed.), *The Poems and Songs of Robert Burns*, 3 vols (Oxford: Clarendon Press, 1968).
Low, Donald (ed.), *The Kilmarnock Poems* (London: J.M. Dent, 1985).
—, *The Songs of Robert Burns* (Aldershot: Routledge, 1993).
McGuirk, Carol (ed.), *Robert Burns, Selected Poems* (London: Penguin, 1993).
The Merry Muses of Caledonia, introduced by G. Ross Roy (Columbia: University of South Carolina Press for the Thomas Cooper Library, 1999).
O' Rourke, Donny (ed.), *Ae Fond Kiss. The Love Letters of Robert Burns and Clarinda* (Edinburgh: Mercat Press, 2000).
Roy, G. Ross and J. De Lancey Ferguson (eds), *The Letters of Robert Burns*, 2 vols Oxford: Oxford University Press, rev'd edn, 1985).

Recordings

There are many recordings of Burns's songs (and also his poetry and prose). A few among many are performers such as David Arditti, Pamela Campbell, Dick Gaughan, Bill McCue, Kenneth McKellar, Karine Polwart, Eddi Reader, Jean Redpath, Shosana Shay, Stramash and Sheena Wellington. An excellent starting point is to listen to *The Complete Songs of Robert Burns* (Linn Records, 1995–2002), twelve compact disks whose recordings have been produced by Dr Fred Freeman;

and also Jean Redpath, *The Complete Songs of Robert Burns* (Philo Recordings, 1996), six CDs; and *Robert Burns 1759–1796* performed by Scottish Early Music Consort (Chandos, 1988) one disc, compilation of songs from *The Scots Musical Museum*, tunes by Niel Gow, and songs from George Thomson's *Select Collection*.

(See Thomas Keith, 'A Discography of Robert Burns, 1948–2002, in *Studies in Scottish Literature* 33–4 (2004), pp. 387–412.)

Secondary Materials

Reference

Egerer, J. W., *A Bibliography of Robert Burns* (Edinburgh: Oliver and Boyd, 1964).
Lindsay, Maurice, *The Burns Encyclopedia*, 3rd edn (London: Robert Hale, 1980).
Low, Donald (ed.), *Robert Burns: The Critical Heritage* (London and Boston: Routledge and Kegan Paul, 1974).
McQueen, Colin Hunter and Douglas Hunter, *Hunter's Illustrated History of the Family, Friends and Contemporaries of Robert Burns* (Glasgoe: Messrs Hunter McQueen and Hunter, 2008).
Ross, J. D. (ed.), *Early Critical Reviews on Robert Burns* (New York: AMS Press [1900], 1973).

See also the *Burns Chronicle*, organ of the World Burns Federation, from 1892 to the present for many articles on the life and works of Burns. For some older essays on Burns not listed below, see the *Scottish Literary Journal* and *Studies in Scottish Literature* among other Scottish periodicals.

Biography

Carswell, Catherine, *The Life of Robert Burns*, Tom Crawford (Edinburgh: Canongate Publishing Limited, [1930] 1990).
Crawford, Robert, *The Bard: Robert Burns, A Biography* (London: Jonathan Cape, 2009).
Douglas, Hugh, *Robert Burns: The Tinder Heart* (Stroud: Sutto, 1996).
Ferguson, J. De Lancey, *Pride and Passion. Robert Burns 1759–1796* (New York: Oxford University Press, 1939).
Hecht, Hans, *Robert Burns: The Man and his Work* (London: Hodge [1936], 1950).
McIntyre, Ian, *Dirt & Deity: A Life of Robert Burns* (London: HarperCollins, 1995).
MacKay, James, *Burns: A Biography of Robert Burns* (Edinburgh: Mainstream, 1992).
McQueen, Colin Hunter, *Rantin, Rovin Robin*, Illustrated life (Irvine: Irvine Burns Club, 1999).

Paton, Norman R., *Scotland's Bard: A Concise Biography* (Fareham: Sea-Green Ribbon Publications, 1998).
Sprott, Gavin, *Robert Burns: Pride and Passion* (Edinburgh: Mercat, 1996).

Criticism

Monographs

Bentman, Raymond, *Robert Burns* (Boston: Twayne, 1987).
Brown, Mary Ellen, *Burns and Tradition* (London: Macmillan, 1984).
Carnie, Robert Hay, *Burns Illustrated: A Short Study of Selected Illustrations (1795–1925) of the Poems and Songs of Robert Burns* (Calgary: Calgary Burns Club, 2000).
Carruthers, Gerard, *Robert Burns* (Tavistock: Northcote House, 2006).
Crawford, Thomas, *Burns: A Study of the Poems and Songs* (Edinburgh: Mercat Press, 1978).
—, *Society and the Lyric: A study of the Song Culture of Eighteenth-Century Scotland* (Edinburgh: Scottish Academic Press, 1979).
—, *Boswell, Burns and the French Revolution* (Edinburgh: Saltire Society, 1990).
—, *Burns: A Study of the Poems and Songs* (Edinburgh: Canongate Academic, 1994).
Daiches, David, *Robert Burns* (London: G. Bell and Sons, 1952).
—, *Robert Burns* (New York: Macmillan, [1950] (1966).
Ericsson-Roos, Catarina, 'The Songs of Robert Burns: A Study of the Unity of Poetry and Music', unpublished doctoral dissertation from the University of Uppsala (1977).
Grant, Raymond J. S., *The Laughter of Love: A Study of Robert Burns* (Calgary: Detselig Enterprises, 1986).
Keith, Christina, *The Russet Coat: A Critical Study of Burns' Poetry and of its Background* (London: Robert Hale, 1956).
Low, Donald, *Burns* (Edinburgh: Scottish Academic Press, 1986).
McGinty, J. Walter, *Robert Burns & Religion* (Aldershot: Ashgate, 2003).
McGuirk, Carol, *Robert Burns and the Sentimental Era* (East Linton: Tuckwell Press, [1985] (1997).
McIlvanney, Liam, *Burns the Radical: Poetry and Politics in Late Eighteenth-Century Scotland* (East Linton: Tuckwell Press, 2002).
Paton, Norman R., *Song o' Liberty: The Politics of Robert Burns* (Fareham: Sea-Green Ribbon Publications, 1994).
Pittock, Murray, *Robert Burns and British Poetry*, The Chatterton Lecture on Poetry, *Proceedings of the British Academy* 121 (London: British Academy, 2003).
Simpson, Kenneth G., *Robert Burns* (Aberdeen: Association for Scottish Literary Studies, 1994).

Skoblow, Jeffrey, *Dooble Tongue: Scots, Burns, Contradiction* (Newark: University of Delaware Press, 2001).
Snyder, Franklyn Bliss, *Robert Burns: His Personality, His Reputation and His Art* (Washington: Kennikat Press, 1936).
Thornton, Robert D., *James Currie: The Entire Stranger and Robert Burns* (Edinburgh and London: Oliver and Boyd, 1963).

Collections of Critical Essays

Crawford, Robert (ed.), *Robert Burns and Cultural Authority* (Edinburgh: Edinburgh University Press, 1997).
Jack, R. D. S. and Andrew Noble (eds), *The Art of Robert Burns* (London: Vision, 1982).
Low, Donald (ed.), *Critical Essays on Robert Burns* (London and Boston: Routledge and Kegan Paul, 1975).
McGuirk, Carol (ed.), *Critical Essays on Robert Burns* (New York: G.K. Hall, 1998).
Rodger, Johnny and Gerard Carruthers (eds), *Fickle Man: Robert Burns in the 21st Century* (Dingwall: Sandstone Press, 2009).
Roy, G. Ross (ed.), *Studies in Scottish Literature* 30 (1998), special Burns issue.
Simpson, Kenneth (ed.), *Burns Now* (Edinburgh: Canongate Academic, 1994).
—, *Love and Liberty: Robert Burns, A Bicentenary Celebration* (East Linton: Tuckwell Press, 1997).

Essays in Journals and Chapters in Books

Andrews, Corey, *Literary Nationalism in Eighteenth-Century Scottish Club Poetry* [Burns is a substantial presence in different parts] (Lewiston: Edwin Mellen Press, 2004).
Bittenbender, J. C., 'Bakhtinian Carnival in the Poetry of Robert Burns', *Scottish Literary Journal* 21(2) (1994), pp. 23–38.
Brown, Stephen, 'William Smellie and the Reconciliation of Maria Riddell with Robert Burns', *Studies in Scottish Literature* 35–6, (2007), pp. 331–8.
Carruthers, Gerard, '*The Canongate Burns*: Misreading Robert Burns and the Periodical Press of the 1790s', *Review of Scottish Culture* 18 (2006), pp. 41–50.
—, 'The New Bardolatry', *Burns Chronicle* (winter, 2002), pp. 9–15.
—, 'The Problem of Pseudonyms in the Burns "Lost Poems"', *Studies in Scottish Literature* 33–4 (2004a), pp. 97–106.
—, 'The Procedure of Life: Carswell's Biography of Burns', in Carol Anderson (ed.), *Opening the Doors: The Achievement of Catherine Carswell* (Edinburgh: Ramsay Head, 2001), pp. 165–78.
—, 'Remaking Romantic Scotland: Lockhart's Biographies of Burns and Scott'

in Arthur Bradley and Alan Rawes (eds), *Romantic Biography* (Aldershot: Ashgate, 2003), pp. 93–108.
—, Robert Burns's Epigram on Edmund Burke published in *Politics for the People*, October 1794, *Studies in Scottish Literature* 33–4 (2004b), pp. 469–71.
—, '"Tongues Turn'd Inside Out": The Reception of "Tam o' Shanter"', in *Studies in Scottish Literature* 35–6 (2007), pp. 455–63.
Davis, Leith, 'At "Sang About": Scottish Song and the Challenge to British Culture', in Leith Davis, Ian Duncan and Janet Sorenson (eds), *Scotland and the Borders of Romanticism* (Cambridge: Cambridge University Press, 2006), pp. 188–203.
—, 'The Poetry of Nature and the Nature of Poetry: Robert Burns and William Wordsworth', in *Acts of Union: Scotland and the Literary Negotiation of the British Nation 1707–1830* (Stanford: Stanford University Press, 1998, pp. 107–43.
Dunnigan, Sarah M. and Gerard Carruthers, 'Two Tales of Tam o' Shanter', *Southfields* 6(2) (2000), pp. 36–43.
Ferguson, J. De Lancey, 'They Censored Burns', *Scotland's Magazine* (January 1955), pp. 38–40.
Fielding, Penny, 'Burns's Topographies', in Leith Davis, Ian Duncan and Janet Sorenson (eds), *Scotland and the Borders of Romanticism* (Cambridge: Cambridge University Press, 2006), pp. 170–87.
Fulton, Henry L., 'Robert Burns, John Moore, and the Limits of Writing Letters', *Studies in Scottish Literature* 35–6, (2007), pp. 526–50.
Gray, John, 'Burns and his Visitors from Ulster: From Adulation to Disaccord', *Studies in Scottish Literature* 33–4 (2004), pp. 320–34.
Gray, Pauline, 'Prudes, Pirates and Bills of Suspension: The Correspondence of Burns and Clarinda', *Burns Chronicle* (autumn 2007), pp. 10–11.
Husemann, Mary M., 'The Uncensored Burns: Two Editions of *The Merry Muses of Caledonia*', *Studies in Scottish Literature* 33–4 (2004), pp. 454–68.
Leask, Nigel, 'Burns, Wordsworth and the Politics of Vernacular Poetry', in Peter de Bolla, Nigel Leask and David Simpson (eds), *Land, Nation and Culture, 1740–1840* (Basingstoke: Palgrave Macmillan, 2005), pp. 202–22.
McCulloch, Margery Palmer, 'Volksdichter und Künstler: German Responses to Robert Burns', *Studies in Scottish Literature* 33–4 (2004), pp. 1–41.
McGuirk, Carol, 'Scottish Hero, Scottish Victim: Myths of Robert Burns', in Andrew Hook (ed.), *The History of Scottish Literature, 1660–1800* (Aberdeen: Aberdeen University Press, 1987), pp. 219–38.
—, 'The Crone, the Prince, and the Exiled Heart: Burns's Highlands and Burns's Scotland', *Studies in Scottish Literature* 35–6 (2007), pp. 184–201.
—, 'Writing Scotland: Robert Burns', in Susan Manning (ed.), *The Edinburgh History of Scottish Literature: Enlightenment, Britain and Empire (1707–1918)* (Edinburgh: Edinburgh University Press, 2007), pp. 169–77.
McIlvanney, Liam, 'Robert Burns and the Calvinist Radical Tradition', *History Workshop Journal* 40 (1995), pp. 133–49.

McKenna, Steven R., 'Take Your Flag and Shove It! Nationalistic Humour in Fergusson and Burns', *Studies in Scottish Literature* 33–4 (2004), pp. 209–22.

Mathison, Hamish, 'Robert Burns and National Song', in David Duff and Catherine Jones (eds), *Scotland, Ireland and the Romantic Aesthetic* (Lewisburg: Bucknell University Press, 2007), pp. 77–92.

Pittock, Murray, 'Robert Burns, "Tam o' Shanter"', in Christine Gerrard (ed.), *A Companion to Eighteenth-Century Poetry* (Oxford: Blackwell, 2006), pp. 329–37.

—, 'Robert Burns', in *Scottish and Irish Romanticism* (Oxford: Oxford University Press, 2008), pp. 144–65.

Purdie, David, '"Never Met – and Never Parted": The Curious Case of Burns and Boswell', *Studies in Scottish Literature* 33–4 (2004), pp. 169–76.

Rawes, Alan, '"The Very First of his Art": Reading Burns through Byron', *Studies in Scottish Literature* 33–4 (2004), pp. 138–49.

Sharp, N. C. Craig, 'Robert Burns's Missing Weekend, Hogmanay, 1986', *Studies in Scottish Literature* 33–4 (2004), pp. 413–20.

Simpson, Kenneth, 'The Many Voices: The Poetry of Burns', in *The Protean Scot* (Aberdeen: Aberdeen University Press, 1988), pp. 185–218.

—, 'A Highly Textual Affair: The Sylvander–Clarinda Correspondence', *Studies in Scottish Literature* 35–6 (2007), pp. 258–69.

Stafford, Fiona, 'Scottish Bards and English Epigraphs: Robert Burns's "A Winter Night"', in *Starting Lines in Scottish, Irish and English Poetry from Burns to Heaney* (Oxford: Oxford University Press, 2000), pp. 43–90.

Stauffer, Andrew M., 'Burns's Other Poem for Jean The "Blue-Eyed Lassie"', *Studies in Scottish Literature* 33–4 (2004), pp. 366–71.

Thornton, Robert D., 'Editing the Correspondence of Robert Burns', *Studies in Scottish Literature* 35–6 (2007), pp. 403–18.

Werkmeister, Lucyle, 'Robert Burns and the London Newspapers', *Bulletin of the New York Public Library* 65 (1961), pp. 483–504.

White, Kenneth, '"Tam o' Shanter": An Interpretation', *Scottish Literary Journal* 17(2) (1990), pp. 5–15.

Whyte, Christopher, 'Defamiliarising "Tam o' Shanter"', *Scottish Literary Journal* 20 (1993), pp. 5–18.

—, 'Competing Idylls: Fergusson and Burns', *Scottish Studies Review* 1 (2000), pp. 47–62.

Notes on Contributors

Corey E. Andrews is an assistant professor of English at Youngstown State University. His book *Literary Nationalism in Eighteenth-Century Scottish Club Poetry* was published in 2004. His current book project is entitled *Scots in English: Cross-Cultural Poetics in Eighteenth-Century Scotland*.

Rhona Brown is a lecturer in the Department of Scottish Literature at the University of Glasgow. She specialises in eighteenth-century Scottish literature, and is currently preparing a monograph on the works of Robert Burns's biggest poetic influence, Robert Fergusson.

Gerard Carruthers is head of the Department of Scottish Literature at the University of Glasgow, where he is also director of the Centre for Robert Burns Studies and general editor of the Oxford University Press edition of the works of Robert Burns.

Leith Davis is a professor of English and the director of the Centre for Scottish Studies at Simon Fraser University in Canada. She is the author of *Acts of Union: Scotland and the Literary Negotiation of the British Nation, 1707–1832* (1998) and *Music, Postcolonialism and Gender: The Construction of Irish National Identity, 1724–1874* (2005) as well as co-editor (with Ian Duncan and Janet Sorensen) of *Scotland and the Borders of Romanticism* (2004).

Sarah Dunnigan is a senior lecturer in English Literature at Edinburgh University. She has published on medieval, Renaissance and twentieth-century Scottish literature, and is completing a book on Scottish literary fairy tales.

Colin Kidd is Professor of Modern History at the University of Glasgow. He was editor of the *Scottish Historical Review* between 1999 and 2004. His most recent book is *Union and Unionisms: Political Thought in Scotland 1500–2000* (2008).

Nigel Leask is Regius Professor of English Language and Literature at the University of Glasgow. He has published widely on eighteenth-century and Romantic literature and culture and is currently completing a study of 'Robert Burns and Pastoral'. He is a co-editor of the new Oxford Collected Works of Robert Burns and is responsible for the first volume 'Miscellaneous Prose'.

Alison Lumsden is a senior lecturer in English and Scottish Literature at the University of Aberdeen. She is a general editor of the Edinburgh Edition of the Waverley Novels and co-director of the Walter Scott Research Centre. She has published on many aspects of Scottish literature and edited several volumes of Scott's fiction.

Kirsteen McCue is lecturer in the Department of Scottish Literature at the University of Glasgow where she is also associate director of the Centre for Robert Burns Studies. She has published on Scottish song culture of the eighteenth and nineteenth centuries and is currently editing two volumes of songs for the Stirling/South Carolina Research edition of the Collected Works of James Hogg. She will be the editor of Burns's songs for George Thomson as part of the forthcoming Oxford University Press edition of the Collected Works of Robert Burns.

Steven R. McKenna has taught in several colleges and universities in the USA. Presently, he teaches at Graceland University. In addition to articles on Burns, he has also published in other areas of Scots literature.

Kenneth Simpson was founding director of the Centre for Cultural Studies at the University of Strathclyde and co-organiser of the annual Burns International Conference, 1990–2008. He is currently Honorary Professor of Burns Studies at the University of Glasgow and his publications include *The Protean Scot* (1988), *Burns Now* (1994) and *Love and Liberty: Robert Burns – A Bicentenary Celebration* (1997).

Fiona Stafford is a professor of English Language and Literature at the University of Oxford and tutorial fellow in English at Somerville College. She has published widely on Scottish poetry and the literature of the four nations. Her books include *Starting Lines in Scottish, English, and Irish Poetry: From Burns to Heaney* (2000).

Index

Aiken, Robert, 10
American Revolution, 3, 78, 153–4
Anderson, Robert, 106
Aristotle, 34–5
   Poetics, 35
Armour, Jean, 15–16, 20, 22, 23, 51, 150
Austen, Jane, *Sanditon*, 97–9
Autobiographical letter, 8, 36, 51, 54, 116, 150

Ballantine, John, 18–19
Blair, Hugh, 12, 16, 50
Blake, William, 56, 105
Breadalbane, John, Earl of, 19
Broun, Agnes, 62
Bruce, Robert, 148, 155–7
Brydges, Sir Egerton, 99
Burnes, William, 62
Burns Clubs, 1, 2, 20
Burns, Gilbert, 10, 17, 19
Burns, Robert
   and Fergusson *see* Fergusson, Robert
   and global/international identity, 1, 5, 61, 150–63
   and narrative, 34–46
   and politics, 2–5, 17–19, 23, 61–73
   and publishing, 6–19
   and religion, 9–10, 11–15, 38, 95–6
   and romantic movement, 23, 25, 74–5, 97–109
   and slavery, 3, 47–60, 156
   and songwriting/collecting, 74–85, 115
   and sensibility, 6–7, 24–35, 70, 159, 161
   and women, 20–33, 104; *see also* individual titles of Poems and Songs
   as critic, 110–24, 76, 137–46
   as 'heaven-taught ploughman', 4, 53–4, 100–1, 105, 110, 111, 115
   POEMS AND SONGS
   'A Bard's Epitaph', 96
   'Address of Beelzebub', 19
   'A Dream', 18, 104
   'A Fragment – On Glenriddell's Fox breaking his chain', 66
   'A Poet's Welcome to his love-begotten Daughter', 21
   'Auld Lang syne', 1, 74, 84–5, 131, 136
   'The Author's Earnest Cry and Prayer', 18, 65
   'Awa Whigs Awa', 3
   'Behind yon Hill where Stinchar Flows', 78, 177n
   'The Bonie Lad that's Far Awa', 26
   'The Brigs of Ayr', 91–4
   'Ca the Yowes', 26
   'Comin' Thro' the Rye', 17

INDEX

'The Cotter's Saturday Night', 13–14, 26–7, 54, 96, 104, 131
'Death and Doctor Hornbook', 39–40
'The Death and Dying Words of Poor Mailie', 7, 37–8, 105
'Epistle to J. Lapraik, An Old Scotch Bard', 7–8, 20, 86–7, 111–12
'Second Epistle To John Lapraik', 21, 106, 108, 141
'Epistle to Robert Graham Esq. of Fintry on the Election for the Dumfries String of Boroughs, anno 1790', 68
'Fête Champêtre', 19
'The Five Carlins', 67–8
'The Fornicator', 27
'Green Grow the Rashes', 17, 30, 113
'Halloween', 94–5, 132
'Here's a Health to Them That's Awa'', 66–7
'Highland Mary', 23, 97
'The Highland Widow's Lament', 127
'The Holy Fair', 8–9, 11–12, 13, 14, 95–6, 132, 134
'Holy Willie's Prayer', 8–11, 12, 14–15, 38, 131, 132–3
'I Look to the North', 26
'Is there for honest poverty', 2, 47–9, 55–8, 59–60, 105, 131, 155
'It Was Upon a Lammas Night', 79–82
'Lament for Mary Queen of Scots', 23
'Libel Summons', 15–16
'Love and Liberty a Cantata', 10, 11, 16, 105, 129–30, 132
'Man was Made to Mourn, A Dirge', 48, 103–4
'My Father was a Farmer', 113
'My Nanie O', 113
'My Tochers the Jewel', 26
'Now Westlin' Winds', 78–9
'Ode [for General Washington's Birthday]', 19
'Ode to the Departed Regency Bill', 19, 65–6
'On a Celebrated Ruling Elder', 7
'On a Scotch Bard Gone to the West Indies', 51, 150
'On Cessnock Banks a Lassie Dwells', 24–5
'On Fergusson I', 87–8
'On Fergusson II', 88
'O Once I Lov'd' ('Handsome Nell'), 6, 7, 75–7, 112
'The Ordination', 12, 13, 132, 133–4
'The Posie', 25
'The Rights of Women', 30
'Robert Bruce's Address to his Troops at Bannockburn', 155–7
'Robert Bruce's March to Bannockburn', 2, 156
'Scotch Drink', 96, 99
'Sketch' 137, 138–42, 144
'The Slaves Lament', 51–2
'Song' ('My Girl She's Airy'), 7
'Song. On Miss W.A.', 25
'Such a Parcel of Rogues in a Nation', 48, 69–70
'Tam o'Shanter. A Tale', 14, 31–3, 36, 39, 40–5, 99, 106, 107, 129, 132, 134–5
'The Twa Dogs', 4, 18, 37, 88–92, 104, 151–3
'The Vision', 21
'To A Louse', 4, 7, 31, 38, 101
'To Robert Graham of Fintry', 110

Burns, Robert (*cont.*)
  POEMS AND SONGS (*cont.*)
    'To the Weaver's Gin Ye Go', 123
    'To W. Simson, Ochiltree', 86–7
    'What Can a Young Lassie Do wi' an Auld Man', 26
    'When Guilford Good', 18–19, 153–5, 184n
    'Why Shouldna Poor Folk Mowe', 17–18
Burns Night, 1, 20, 31
Burns Supper, 1, 61, 65
Byron, George Gordon, Lord, 14, 99–100, 101, 105, 128
  Don Juan, 99–100

Campbell, Margaret, 22–3; *see also* Highland Mary
Campbell, William, 'To the People of Scotland', 58–9
Carlyle, Thomas, 74, 101
Carruthers, Gerard, 30, 31, 43, 52
Carswell, Catherine, *The Life of Robert Burns*, 15, 23
Catholicism, 8, 64, 154
Christ's Kirk stanza form, 11, 13, 94, 95
Coleridge, Samuel Taylor, 14, 59, 98, 101–3
Commonplace Book *see First Commonplace Book*
Covenanting Movement, 62, 133
Crawford, Robert, 30, 86, 152–3
Crawford, Thomas, 14, 48, 62, 71, 75, 81, 91, 122
Crochallan Fencibles, 17, 27
Cunningham, James, 11
Currie, James, 86, 103
  The Works of Robert Burns, 10, 11, 16–17, 19, 98–9, 103, 129, 132, 159–63, 185n

Daiches, David, 61, 115
Dick, James C., 75, 76–7, 78, 82
Donaldson, William, 62
Douglas, Gavin, 40–1, 46
  Eneados, 32, 40–1
Dryden, John, *Works of Virgil*, 137–8, 171n
Dunbar, William, 1, 36
Dundas, Henry, 3, 50, 62, 64, 68–9, 171n, 173n
Dunlop, Frances, 11, 19, 22, 35, 52, 84, 104–5, 116, 117, 123, 137, 142, 143, 146, 148, 167n

Enlightenment, 30–1, 33, 73, 91–2, 134, 135, 136
Erskine, Henry, 19, 117, 184n

Ferguson, J. De Lancey, 3, 36
Fergusson, Robert, 4, 8, 11, 86–96
  'The Author's Life', 96
  'The Farmer's Ingle', 13, 96
  'The Ghaists: A Kirkyard Eclogue', 89–90, 91, 92
  'Hallow-Fair', 94–5
  'Leith Races' 95
  'Mutual Complaint', 89, 91, 93
  'The Sow of Feeling', 7
First Commonplace Book, 6–8, 76–9, 112–15
Fox, Charles James, 63–72
Fox-North coalition *see* Fox, Charles James and Guilford, Lord North
French Revolution, 3, 50–1, 52, 59, 61, 62, 63, 67, 71, 72–3, 105, 155

Guildford, Lord North, 64–5, 153–4, 184n

Habbie Simson stanza form, 8, 13, 24, 165n

Hamilton, Gavin, 10
Hannibal, 148–9
Hazlitt, William, 14, 101–2, 107
Heaney, Seamus, 105
Henryson, Robert, 1, 36, 37, 41, 45, 46, 169
Herd, David
  Ancient and Modern Scots Songs, 77
  'Herd's ballats', 140–4
The Heron Ballads, 3, 19, 68
Heron, Patrick, 68–9, 72
Heron, Robert, *A Memoir of the Life of the Late Robert Burns*, 157–60
Highland Mary, 10; see also Margaret Campbell
Hill, Peter, 56, 116, 118–19
Hogg, James, 9, 106
Homer, 137–8, 140, 142, 146–7, 162
  Odyssey, 137, 138, 146
Hume, David, 71

Jack, R. D. S., 34, 36
Johnson, James, *The Scots Musical Museum*, 77–9, 82–3, 84, 127
Johnstone, James, 68, 69

Kailyard fiction, 2
Keats, John, 98, 101, 107–9
  'Lines written in the Highlands after a Visit to Burns's Country', 108–9
Kennedy, A. L., 31
Kilpatrick, Nelly, 22, 75–7
Kinsley, James, 15, 51–2, 56, 58, 75, 77
Kirkpatrick, Rev. Joseph, 70–1

Lamb, Charles, 98, 101
Lamont, Claire, 126–7
Leask, Nigel, 83, 157, 162
Lockhart, John Gibson, 14, 107, 125
The Lounger see Mackenzie, Henry
Lyle, Emily, 77

MacDiarmid, Hugh, 1, 2
McDiarmid, Matthew P., 86, 96
McGuirk, Carol, 26, 29, 82, 87, 88, 95, 112, 124
McIlvanney, Liam, 18, 62, 105, 155
Mackenzie, Henry, 46, 50, 71
  The Man of Feeling, 35, 46, 71, 87
  review in *The Lounger*, 13, 54, 100, 110, 157
Maclaren, Ian, 2
  Beside the Bonnie Brier Bush, 2
McLehose, Agnes, 16, 20, 21, 23–4, 33; see also 'Sylvander and Clarinda Correspondence'
McNaught, Duncan, 18
Mary Queen of Scots, 23
Maxwell, James, 12–13
  'On the Ayr-shire Ploughman Poet, or Poetaster, R.B.', 12–13
The Merry Muses of Caledonia, 17–18, 27–9
Milton, John, 105, 148–9
  Paradise Lost, 105, 148
Moore, Captain Graham, 162
Moore, Dr John, 36, 38, 52, 54, 116, 117; see also Autobiographical letter
More, Hannah, *Slavery, a Poem*, 59
Motherwell, William, 2
Muir, Thomas, 49, 156, 157
Murdoch, John, 34, 35

Omai, 158–9
Oswald, James, *Caledonian Pocket Companion*, 78

Paine, Thomas, *The Rights of Man*, 30
Pitt, William, 50, 53, 57, 64–5, 67, 68, 69, 72, 73, 154
Pittock, Murray, 47, 49, 82–3
Poems, Chiefly in the Scots Dialect
  Edinburgh edition, 3–4, 11, 13, 77, 100–1, 151, 153

Poems, Chiefly in the Scots Dialect (*cont.*)
  Kilmarnock edition, 3, 10, 11, 13, 77, 100–1, 137, 142, 150–1, 153
Pope, Alexander, 4, 35, 116, 138, 140

Ramsay, Allan, 4, 5, 8, 9, 11, 78, 84, 91, 93, 123, 142–3, 165n, 178n
  'Lucky Spence's Last Advice', 37
  'My Patie is a Lover Gay', 79–82
  Tea Table Miscellany, 79, 177n
  The Gentle Shepherd, 79, 81, 143
Reliques of Robert Burns, 10–11, 19
  and review by Walter Scott, 127–30, 131, 133, 134
Riddell, Captain Robert, 11, 66, 83
Riddell, Maria, 14, 20, 29
Rodger, Hugh, 34
Ross, Ian S., 41

Scott, Sir Walter, 5, 10, 15, 125–36
  The Waverley Novels, 125–36
Shelley, Mary, 101, 109
Shelley, P., 99–100, 101, 105
Sillar, David, 34, 35
Simpson, K., 116, 121
Smith, Adam, 4, 31, 71, 158
Smollett, Tobias, 36, 119
  The Expedition of Humphry Clinker, 46
Stedman, John, 56
Sterne, Laurence, 35, 36, 70, 105
Stewart, Thomas, 10–11, 16
  Letters Addressed to Clarinda, 16–17
  Poems Ascribed to Robert Burns, 10

'Sylvander and Clarinda Correspondence', 16, 17, 21, 23–4, 29–30, 35, 36

Theocritus, *Idylls*, 139–43
Thomson, George, 121, 123, 155
  Select Collection of Scottish Airs, 77, 79, 82–4, 121–3, 132
Thomson, James, 35
  The Seasons, 118, 120
Thomson, William, *Orpheus Caledonius*, 79
Tytler, Alexander Fraser, 44

Union of 1707, 48, 69–70, 72–3, 160, 161

Van Heijnsbergen, Theo, 41, 46
Virgil, 40–1, 137–49
  The Aeneid, 40, 43, 137–8, 145–9
  Eclogues, 140–5
  Georgics, 137–46

Wallace, William, 148–9
Whyte, Christopher, 31
Williams, Helen Maria, 51–5, 58, 119, 121, 155
Wollstonecraft, Mary, 155
  A Vindication of the Rights of Woman, 30
Wood, Marcus, 59
Wordsworth, William, 98, 99, 100, 101, 102–4, 106, 107, 109
  Prelude, 58
  'Resolution and Independence', 98
World Burns Federation, 1, 18

EU representative:
Easy Access System Europe
Mustamäe tee 50, 10621 Tallinn, Estonia
Gpsr.requests@easproject.com

www.ingramcontent.com/pod-product-compliance
Lightning Source LLC
Chambersburg PA
CBHW051059230426
43667CB00013B/2367